# SPINOZA'S *ETHICS*

Spinoza's *Ethics* is one of the most remarkable, important, and difficult books in the history of philosophy: a treatise simultaneously on metaphysics, knowledge, philosophical psychology, moral philosophy, and political philosophy. It presents, in Spinoza's famous "geometric method," his radical views on God, Nature, the human being, and happiness. In this wide-ranging introduction to the work, Steven Nadler examines the philosophical background to Spinoza's thought and the dialogues in which Spinoza was engaged – with his contemporaries (including Descartes and Hobbes), with ancient thinkers (especially the Stoics), and with his Jewish rationalist forebears. He explains the doctrines and arguments of the *Ethics*, and shows why Spinoza's endlessly fascinating ideas may have been so troubling to his contemporaries, as well as why they are still so relevant today. His book is written for the student reader but will also be of interest to specialists in early modern philosophy.

STEVEN NADLER is Professor of Philosophy at the University of Wisconsin-Madison. His books include *Spinoza: A Life* (1999) and *Spinoza's Heresy* (2002), as well as *The Cambridge Companion to Malebranche* (2000). In 2004 he was a finalist for the Pulitzer Prize for general non-fiction.

# CAMBRIDGE INTRODUCTIONS TO
## KEY PHILOSOPHICAL TEXTS

This new series offers introductory textbooks on what are considered to be the most important texts of Western philosophy. Each book guides the reader through the main themes and arguments of the work in question, while also paying attention to its historical context and its philosophical legacy. No philosophical background knowledge is assumed, and the books will be well suited to introductory university-level courses.

Titles published in the series:

DESCARTES'S 'MEDITATIONS' by Catherine Wilson

WITTGENSTEIN'S 'PHILOSOPHICAL INVESTIGATIONS' by David G. Stern

WITTGENSTEIN'S 'TRACTATUS' by Alfred Nordmann

ARISTOTLE'S 'NICOMACHEAN ETHICS' by Michael Pakaluk

KANT'S 'CRITIQUE OF PURE REASON' by Jill Vance Buroker

SPINOZA'S 'ETHICS' by Steven Nadler

# SPINOZA'S *ETHICS*

## *An Introduction*

STEVEN NADLER

*University of Wisconsin-Madison*

CAMBRIDGE
UNIVERSITY PRESS

CAMBRIDGE UNIVERSITY PRESS
Cambridge, New York, Melbourne, Madrid, Cape Town,
Singapore, São Paulo, Delhi, Mexico City

Cambridge University Press
The Edinburgh Building, Cambridge CB2 8RU, UK

Published in the United States of America by Cambridge University Press, New York

www.cambridge.org
Information on this title: www.cambridge.org/9780521836203

First published 2006
Third printing 2009

*A catalogue record for this publication is available from the British Library*

*Library of Congress Cataloguing in Publication Data*
Nadler, Steven M., 1958–
Spinoza's ethics : an introduction / Steven Nadler. – 1st edn
p. cm. – (Cambridge introductions to key philosophical texts)
Includes bibliographical references and index.
ISBN-13: 978-0-521-83620-3 (hardback)
ISBN-10: 0-521-83620-4 (hardback)
ISBN-13: 978-0-521-54479-5 (paperback)
ISBN-10: 0-521-54479-3 (paperback)
1. Spinoza, Benedictus de, 1632–1677. Ethica. 2. Ethics. I. Title. II. Series.
B3974.N28 2006

ISBN 978-0-521-83620-3 Hardback
ISBN 978-0-521-54479-5 Paperback

*For Arch Nadler, z"l*

In loving memory

# Contents

# *Preface*

Philosophy, it has often been said, begins with wonder. For the first thinkers in the Western philosophical tradition, Thales and his early Greek colleagues, it was wonder about the world. It moved them to inquire into the origin and nature of things around them and to offer, instead of mytho-poetic accounts of phenomena that appealed to gods and mystifying powers, natural explanations drawn from experience. At a certain point, however – and this is true whether what is at issue is the historical development of philosophy as a discipline or the intellectual development of an individual philosopher – wonder turns inward and philosophy becomes a very personal affair. Questions about the heavens and the earth, about objects and forces in nature, both visible and hidden, give way to questions about the self and about the life one is leading. It was Socrates, we are told, who first turned philosophy from a search for nature's causes and ultimate constituents to an inquiry into how to be good and achieve well-being.

> He did not discuss that topic so favored by other talkers, "the nature of the Universe," and avoided speculation on the so-called "Cosmos" of the professors, how it works, and on the laws that govern the phenomena of the heavens. Indeed, he would argue that to trouble one's mind with such problems is sheer folly . . . Rather, his own conversation was always about human things. (Xenophon, *Memorabilia* I.i. 11–16)

To Socrates, the most important questions were those not of science or metaphysics, but of ethics. What mattered was not understanding nature, but knowing how best to live one's life. More than a search for knowledge about the world, philosophy, for Socrates, was a quest for true happiness and human flourishing.

The inward turn is usually inspired by a kind of disenchantment. A person, perhaps highly successful in mundane endeavors, may still, in the light of some lingering disappointment or lack of fulfillment, begin to question the value of the ends he or she has been pursuing. What initially seemed to be good and worthwhile goals – wealth, perhaps, or power or honor – have in fact left one feeling empty, either because their possession was uncertain or because the benefits they conferred were short-lived or unsatisfying. In a sufficiently reflective and self-critical person – someone given to what Socrates called "the examined life" – the result of this kind of realization could be a reordering of one's priorities and a realignment of the direction of one's life.

It was just this kind of disenchantment with the transitory goods of the world and with the values that had informed his life that led a young, intellectually gifted Dutch-Jewish merchant in the middle of the seventeenth century to make a radical break with his past and turn to philosophy as his vocation. Endowed with a deep sense of the *vanitas* of ordinary pursuits, he opted to divest himself of the materialistic commitments that had occupied him to that point and devote himself to the search for truth – not just scientific truths about nature but, more important, an understanding of the proper goods of a human life and the means to true happiness. As the fruit of his reflective labors, he would end up composing one of the greatest and boldest works of philosophy of all time.

Spinoza's *Ethics* is a wide-ranging treatise that touches on almost every major area of philosophy: metaphysics, theory of knowledge, philosophy of mind, philosophical psychology, moral philosophy, political philosophy, and the philosophy of religion. There seem to be few philosophical problems of any importance that do not find some treatment within its five parts. In the *Ethics*, Spinoza discusses the existence and nature of God, the relationship of mind and body in a human being, freedom and determinism, truth, teleology, the laws of nature, passions, virtue and happiness, the grounds of political obligation, the status of good and evil, personal identity, eternity, immortality and – as if that were not enough – the meaning of life. I would venture to argue that the only other work in the history of philosophy that can match the *Ethics* in terms of sheer thematic scope and systematic presentation is Plato's *Republic*.

The *Ethics*, then, is a highly ambitious and multifaceted work. Furthermore, it is bold to the point of audacity. Spinoza attacks some of the most basic philosophical assumptions – about God, the human being, and the universe – that had long been defended by thinkers and taken for granted by laypersons, and offers nothing less than a systematic and unforgiving critique of the moral and theological beliefs grounded thereupon.

The *Ethics* is also an extraordinarily difficult book. While the issues that Spinoza addresses are perennial philosophical ones, and thus familiar to anyone who has done some elementary study in philosophy, the book may appear, on first approach, highly forbidding. (And I am sorry to report that, like most great works of philosophy, it only gets harder on each subsequent reading.) To the modern reader, its mode of presentation will seem opaque, its vocabulary strange, and its themes extremely complicated, even impenetrable. My aim in this volume is to dispel some of that opacity and impenetrability and provide an accessible introduction to the philosophy in the *Ethics* – to its theses, arguments, methods, and more generally to its broad philosophical project.

Here, to begin with, is a brief synopsis of the work.

Spinoza's ultimate goal in the *Ethics* is to demonstrate the way to human happiness in a deterministic world filled with obstacles to our well-being, obstacles to which we are naturally prone to react in not entirely beneficial ways. Before he attempts to answer that ethical question, though, it is necessary for Spinoza to reveal the nature of the world itself, as well as the nature of ourselves as human beings and our place as knowers and agents in that world. Thus, before it enters the terrain of moral philosophy (in Parts Four and Five), the *Ethics* begins with metaphysics (Part One), a philosophical anthropology and a theory of human knowledge (Part Two), and a philosophical psychology (Part Three).

Part One, "On God," argues that the universe is a single, infinite, eternal, necessarily existing substance. This is "God or Nature." Everything else that is, is a part of Nature. All things within Nature – that is, everything – are invariably and necessarily determined by

Nature. There is nothing that escapes Nature's laws; there are no exceptions to Nature's ways. Whatever is follows with an absolute necessity from Nature's necessary universal principles. There are thus no purposes for Nature or within Nature. Nothing happens for any ultimate reason or to serve any goal or overarching plan. Whatever takes place does so only because it is brought about by the ordinary causal order of Nature. And because God is identical with the universal, active causal principles of Nature – the substance of it all – it follows that all of the anthropomorphic conceptions of God that characterize sectarian religions are nothing but superstitious fictions.

In Part Two, "On the Nature and Origin of the Mind," Spinoza turns to the nature of the human being and his place in Nature. Nature has an infinite number of attributes or essences, each constituting a kind of universal nature of things. We know of only two of these attributes: Thought (or thinking essence) and Extension (material essence). The course of Nature is one, since Nature is one substance, a unity. But it proceeds under each attribute in parallel coordination with its unfolding in every other attribute. Any individual thing or event is only a "mode" of Nature, manifesting itself under the different attributes. One and the same thing or event, then, manifests itself in Thought (as a mental or spiritual thing or event), in Extension (as a material thing or event), and so on through the other attributes. Thus, the human mind and the human body are one and the same thing in Nature, manifesting itself under Thought and Extension, respectively. Their union in a human being and the correlation of their states is a function of their ultimate metaphysical identity in Nature. The human being is therefore as much a part of Nature as any other thing, and is subject to the same causal determinism that governs all of Nature.

Now many readers never get past the first two parts of the *Ethics* – it is not uncommon for students in college courses on early modern philosophy to be asked to read only those propositions touching on metaphysics and epistemology, since it makes for a tidy pedagogical package with Descartes and Leibniz ("The Rationalists") – and are thus left wondering why the work has the title that it does. But historically and philosophically important as the opening parts are, they also lay the foundations for the moral conclusions that follow in the subsequent propositions.

Part Three, "On the Origin and Nature of the Affects," demonstrates the various ways in which the human being is affected by the world around him, and investigates the striving to persevere in existence in the face of these external forces that characterizes his (and any being's) essence. The human psychological life is made up of various passions and actions. The former are our affective responses to the ways in which objects causally impinge upon us; the latter derive from our own inner resources. Both represent ways in which our powers are increased or decreased by the causal nexuses within which we exist. The picture of human life that emerges from Spinoza's catalogue of the passions is a tormented one, where a person is emotionally tossed about and at the mercy of things and forces beyond his control.

In Part Four, "On Human Bondage, or the Power of the Affects," Spinoza continues his investigation of the life governed by the passions, but also seeks its remedy in virtue, that is, in knowledge and understanding. The human being can never be entirely free from the passions, since he is necessarily a part of Nature and subject to external influences. He can, however, achieve some degree of autonomy and freedom from their turmoil to the extent that he is active and guided by reason. The ideal of the free individual provides a model for a virtuous human life and a guide for seeking what is good and avoiding what is evil. In this way, the power of the passive affects is diminished.

"The Power of the Intellect, or On Human Freedom" is the title of Part Five. Spinoza here turns to the ultimate benefits of the highest form of knowledge. This is a thorough understanding of Nature and its ways and an intellectual intuition of how the essence of anything follows from Nature's most universal elements – or, since God and Nature are one and the same, how the essence of anything relates to God. In this final part of the work, Spinoza takes on the issue of immortality, and demonstrates how the true rewards of virtue lie not in some otherworldly recompense but in the happiness, well-being, and blessedness that understanding confers upon us in this life.

There is much more to be said, of course. Untangling the ideas of the *Ethics* and drawing them out of the formal structure of propositions, demonstrations, corollaries, scholia, and appendices that make up the book will require a good deal of slow, careful work.

It will also demand some attention to Spinoza's various intellectual sources. Despite a dearth of explicit references to past thinkers, the *Ethics* exhibits enormous erudition, and quite a few philosophical traditions converge in its pages. Spinoza's knowledge of ancient, medieval, Renaissance, and modern authors – pagan, Christian, and Jewish – is quietly evident throughout. His most important philosophical mentor was, without question, Descartes. But Plato, Aristotle, and the ancient (and modern) Stoics all belong to the intellectual background of the work. It is also clear that he was impressed by his reading of contemporary political thinkers, especially the Englishman Thomas Hobbes, but also Dutch and French theorists; and by recent scientific developments (including those of Bacon, Galileo, and Boyle). And many of the central elements of the *Ethics* derive from Spinoza's study of medieval Jewish thought, particularly Maimonides and Gersonides.

None of this, however, should distract us from the sheer originality of the *Ethics*. It is a singular work in the history of philosophy. It is also, as I hope to show throughout this study, as relevant today as it was three and a half centuries ago.

This book has been written primarily for the reader who is approaching the *Ethics* for the first time and who desires a guide through its intimidating maze of propositions, demonstrations, scholia, and other elements. It does not provide an account of Spinoza's philosophy as a whole. His political philosophy and his account of the origins and interpretation of the Bible, as well as (to a lesser degree) his theory of religion, as important as these are, do not receive detailed and adequate treatment here; they are discussed only insofar as they are a part of the context of the *Ethics* and relevant to an understanding of its metaphysical, epistemological, psychological, and moral ideas. Nor am I concerned with Spinoza's intellectual development and the changes in his thought from his earliest writings through his mature treatises. Rather, my goal is simply to walk the reader slowly through the doctrines of the *Ethics* and to show how one can make sense of them. To this end, I pay a good deal of attention to the order and manner in which Spinoza himself addresses various topics. Instead of offering a breezy summary and paraphrase of Spinoza's ideas, I want to take the reader on a systematically ordered tour of Spinoza's theses and arguments. I therefore follow the lead of the propositions themselves and hew closely to the text, allowing the reader to trace Spinoza's own progress from the metaphysics of God to the conclusions about human happiness.

While aimed at the beginner, I hope that this study will also be of use and interest to more advanced students of Spinoza, including seasoned scholars, insofar as I address issues and questions that seem to be of perennial dispute. I have not devoted much space in these pages to discussions of secondary literature; but the experienced reader will often easily recognize, from the text and especially from the notes, the positions being taken on particularly thorny and controversial problems of interpretation and assessment. Nor have I pursued many important and complex exegetical and philosophical questions as deeply as they could be (and need to be) pursued. This would not have served well my primary audience. Indeed, it would have proven a distraction from the immediate project at hand: a basic understanding of what Spinoza is saying in one of the most important works of Western philosophy.

# *Acknowledgements*

I am very grateful to a number of people who kindly provided their help during my writing of this book. I profited from discussions with Michael Della Rocca, Don Garrett, and Larry Shapiro, who were willing to go through various tangled issues with me. And I am indebted to Yitzhak Melamed and an anonymous reader for the Press for reading through the entire manuscript and offering useful comments and suggestions. I would especially like to acknowledge the members of my Spinoza seminar at the University of Chicago, where I was a visiting professor in the spring of 2005. It was a wonderful class, and I found our conversations immensely fruitful and stimulating. Finally, my thanks to Hilary Gaskin for the invitation to write such a volume, and the staff at Cambridge University Press for their work on its production.

I dedicate this book to the memory of my father, Arch (Aaron) Nadler, who passed away just as it neared completion. A son with a father whom he loves is fortunate; but a son with a father whom he also admires is truly blessed.

# *Abbreviations*

References to the five-part *Ethics* are by the standard format of part and proposition; specific page numbers are provided only when necessary for ease in finding a passage in the text. The following abbreviations are used in citations:

| | |
|---|---|
| A | Axiom |
| D | Definition |
| L | Lemma |
| Post. | Postulate |
| P | Proposition |
| c | corollary |
| d | demonstration |
| s | scholium |

Thus, IIIP32s is Part 3, proposition 32, scholium.

The following abbreviations are used in citations of Spinoza's texts:

| | |
|---|---|
| CM | "Metaphysical Thoughts" |
| E | *Ethics* |
| KV | *Short Treatise on God, Man and His Well-Being* |
| PPC | *Parts One and Two of the Principles of Philosophy of René Descartes Demonstrated According to the Geometric Method* |
| TIE | *Treatise on the Emendation of the Intellect* |
| TTP | *Theological-Political Treatise* |

The following abbreviations are used for editions and translations of Spinoza's writings:

C Edwin Curley (trans.), *The Collected Works of Spinoza*, 2 volumes (Princeton: Princeton University Press, vol. I: 1984; vol. II, in preparation)

G Carl Gebhardt (ed.), *Spinoza Opera*, 5 vol. (Heidelberg: Carl Winters Verlag, 1972 [1925])

NS *Nagelate Schriften* (1677)

OP *Opera Posthuma* (1677)

S Samuel Shirley (trans.), *Theological-Political Treatise*, 2nd edition (Indianapolis: Hackett Publishing, 1998)

SL Samuel Shirley (trans.), *Spinoza: The Letters* (Indianapolis: Hackett Publishing, 1995)

The following abbreviations are used in citations of works by Descartes:

AT *Oeuvres de Descartes*, ed. Charles Adam and Paul Tannery, 11 vols. (Paris: J. Vrin, 1964–75)

CSM *The Philosophical Writings of Descartes* (vols. I and II), trans. John Cottingham, Robert Stoothoff, and Dugald Murdoch (Cambridge: Cambridge University Press, 1985)

CSMK *The Philosophical Writings of Descartes* (vol. III, Correspondence), trans. John Cottingham, Robert Stoothoff, Dugald Murdoch, and Anthony Kenny (Cambridge: Cambridge University Press, 1991)

# CHAPTER I

# Spinoza's life and works

## A JEWISH MERCHANT OF AMSTERDAM

Bento de Spinoza was born in Amsterdam on November 24, 1632, to a prominent merchant family of that city's Portuguese-Jewish community.[1] He was the second of three sons, and one of five children of Michael de Spinoza and his wife, Hannah Deborah Senior, recent immigrants to the Netherlands from Portugal.[2]

New Christians – the descendants of Jews who had been forcibly converted to Christianity in Spain and Portugal at the end of the fifteenth century – had been living in the Low Countries, still under Spanish dominion, throughout most of the sixteenth century. Many of them resided in Antwerp, where they were able to pursue their business affairs at a relatively safe remove from the heart of the Inquisition. With the beginning of the armed revolt of the seven northern provinces, now called the United Provinces of the Netherlands, in the 1570s, and the consequent eclipse of Antwerp by Amsterdam as a major center for trade, many of these families moved up to that more liberal and cosmopolitan city on the Amstel River. In Amsterdam, with its generally tolerant environment and greater concern for economic prosperity than for religious uniformity, the Portuguese New Christians, or "conversos," were able to

---

[1] This chapter is drawn from the more extensive biography in Nadler 1999.
[2] It is actually unclear whether Spinoza's older brother, Isaac, is Hannah's son or the child of Michael's first wife, Rachel, who died in 1627; and likewise whether Spinoza's younger sister Rebecca is Hannah's child or the daughter of Esther, Michael's third wife (whom he married after Hannah died in 1639). There was also a brother, Gabriel (Abraham), and a sister, Miriam, who certainly are Michael and Hannah's children, and thus Spinoza's full siblings. My suspicion (but it is certainly no more than that) is that all were the offspring of Michael and Hannah.

return to the religion of their ancestors and reestablish themselves in Jewish life.

By the middle of the second decade of the seventeenth century, Amsterdam was home to three congregations of Iberian, or Sephardic, Jews. While formal approval by the city's leaders of public Jewish worship was still a few years away, the Jews enjoyed de facto recognition and were able to meet and follow their traditions in relative peace. There were always conservative sectors of Dutch society clamoring for their expulsion, but the more liberal regents of the city, not to mention the more enlightened elements in Dutch society at large, were unwilling to make the same mistake that Spain had made a century earlier by expelling a part of its population whose economic productivity would make a substantial contribution to the flourishing of the Dutch Golden Age.

The Spinoza family was not among the wealthiest of the city's Sephardim – whose wealth was, in turn, dwarfed by the fortunes of the wealthiest Dutch – but they were comfortably well-off. They lived on the Houtgracht, one of the main boulevards of the neighborhood where Jews tended to reside in Amsterdam. (This quarter, called "Vlooienburg," was favored by artists and art dealers as well, and the Spinoza home was one block away from the house in which Rembrandt lived from 1639 to 1658.) Michael's business was importing dried fruit and nuts, mainly from Spanish and Portuguese colonies. To judge both by his accounts and by the respect he earned from his peers, he seems for a time to have been a fairly successful merchant.

The family belonged to the Beth Ya'acov congregation, the first one established in the city. Michael served in various leadership capacities both in his synagogue and in the community, including a stint as a member of the Senhores Quinze, the joint group of representatives from the three congregations which was charged with managing issues of common concern. When, in 1639, the three original congregations – Beth Ya'acov, Neve Shalom, and Beth Israel – merged into one, called Talmud Torah, this leadership group was replaced by the *ma'amad*, the all-powerful lay governing board that ran the community's religious and secular affairs. Michael sat on the *ma'amad* for a term, in 1649, and took a turn on Talmud Torah's educational board as well.

Hannah Deborah, Spinoza's mother, was Michael's second wife. His first wife, Rachel, had died in 1627. Hannah herself was never very well, and she died in 1638, when Spinoza was only five years old. Michael, undoubtedly greatly in need of help in the home with five children, married the forty-year-old Esther Fernand in 1641. Esther would live only another twelve years; she died in October 1653. Michael himself followed her to the grave five months later. The household in which Spinoza grew up seems to have seen more than its fair share of sorrow.

Spinoza must have been an intellectually gifted youth, and he would have made a strong impression on his teachers as he progressed through the levels at the community's school on the Houtgracht. He probably studied at one time or another with all of the leading rabbis of Talmud Torah, including Menasseh ben Israel, an ecumenical and cosmopolitan rabbi who was perhaps the most famous Jew in Europe, and who was teaching in the elementary grades when Spinoza attended the school; the mystically inclined Isaac Aboab da Fonseca; and Saul Levi Mortera, the chief rabbi of the congregation whose tastes ran more to rational philosophy and who often clashed with Rabbi Aboab over the relevance of kabbalah.

Spinoza may have excelled in school, but, contrary to the story long told, he did not study to be a rabbi. In fact, he never made it into the upper levels of the educational program, which involved advanced work in Talmud. In 1649, his older brother Isaac, who had been helping his father run the family business, died and Spinoza had to cease his formal studies to take his place. When Michael died in 1654, Spinoza found himself, along with his other brother Gabriel, a full-time merchant, running the firm "Bento y Gabriel de Spinoza." He seems not to have been a very shrewd businessman, however, and the company, burdened by the debts left behind by his father, floundered under his direction.

Spinoza did not have much of a taste for the life of commerce anyway. Financial success, which led to status and respect within the Portuguese-Jewish community, held very little attraction for him. By the time he and Gabriel took over the family business, he was already distracted from these worldly matters and was devoting more and more of his energies to intellectual interests. Looking back a few years later over his conversion to the philosophical life, he wrote of his growing awareness of the vanity of the pursuits followed by most people (including himself), who gave little thought to the true value of the goods they so desperately sought.

After experience had taught me that all the things which regularly occur in ordinary life are empty and futile, and I saw that all the things which were the cause or object of my fear had nothing of good or bad in themselves, except insofar as [my] mind was moved by them, I resolved at last to try to find out whether there was anything which would be the true good, capable of communicating itself, and which alone would affect the mind, all others being rejected – whether there was something which, once found and acquired, would continuously give me the greatest joy, to eternity.

He was not unaware of the risks involved in abandoning his former engagements and undertaking this new enterprise.

I say that "I resolved at last" – for at first glance it seemed ill-advised to be willing to lose something certain for something then uncertain. I saw, of course, the advantages that honor and wealth bring, and that I would be forced to abstain from seeking them, if I wished to devote myself seriously to something new and different; and if by chance the greatest happiness lay in them, I saw that I should have to do without it. But if it did not lie in them, and I devoted my energies only to acquiring them, then I would equally go without it. (TIE, G II.5/C I.7)

By the early to mid 1650s, Spinoza had decided that his future lay in philosophy, the search for knowledge and true happiness, not the importing of dried fruit.

### CHEREM

At around the time of his disenchantment with the mercantile life, Spinoza began studies in Latin and the ancient classics, especially drama. Latin was still the lingua franca for most academic and intellectual discourse in Europe. Spinoza would need to know Latin for his studies in philosophy, especially if he intended on attending any university lectures, and would eventually compose his own philosophical works in that tongue. He had to go outside the Jewish community for instruction in these disciplines, and found what he needed under the tutelage of Franciscus van den Enden, a former Jesuit and political radical whose home seemed to function as a kind of salon for secular humanists, arch-democrats, and freethinkers. (Van den Enden himself was later executed in France for his participation in a republican plot against King Louis XIV and the monarchy.) It was probably Van den Enden who also first introduced Spinoza to the works of Descartes and other contemporary thinkers. While pursuing this secular education in philosophy, literature, and political thought at his Latin tutor's home, Spinoza probably continued his Jewish education in the *yeshiva* or academy, Keter Torah ("Crown of the Law"), run by Rabbi Mortera.

Although distracted from his business affairs by his studies, and undoubtedly experiencing a serious weakening of his Jewish faith as he delved ever more deeply into the world of pagan and gentile letters, Spinoza kept up appearances and continued to be a member in good standing of the Talmud Torah congregation throughout the early 1650s. He paid his dues and communal taxes, and even made the contributions to the charitable funds that were expected of congregants.

And then, on July 27, 1656 (the sixth of Av, 5416, by the Jewish calendar), the following proclamation was read in Hebrew from in front of the ark of the Torah in the crowded synagogue on the Houtgracht:

The *Senhores* of the *ma'amad* [the congregation's lay governing board] having long known of the evil opinions and acts of Baruch de Spinoza, they have endeavored by various means and promises, to turn him from his evil ways. But having failed to make him mend his wicked ways, and, on the contrary, daily receiving more and more serious information about the abominable heresies which he practiced and taught and about his monstrous deeds, and having for this numerous trustworthy witnesses who have deposed and born witness to this effect in the presence of the said Espinoza, they became convinced of the truth of this matter; and after all of this has been investigated in the presence of the honorable *chakhamim* ["wise men," or rabbis] they have decided, with their consent, that the said Espinoza should be excommunicated and expelled from the people of Israel. By decree of the angels and by the command of the holy men, we excommunicate, expel, curse, and damn Baruch de Espinoza, with the consent of God, Blessed be He, and with the consent of the entire holy congregation, and in front of these holy scrolls with the 613 precepts which are written therein; cursing him with the excommunication with which Joshua banned Jericho and with the curse which Elisha cursed the boys and with all the castigations which are written in the Book of the Law. Cursed be he by day and cursed be he by night; cursed be he when he lies down and cursed be he when he rises up. Cursed be he when he goes out and cursed be he when he comes in. The Lord will not spare him, but then the anger of the Lord and his jealousy shall smoke against that man, and all the curses that are written in this book shall lie upon him, and the Lord shall blot out his name from under heaven. And the Lord shall separate him unto evil out of all the tribes of Israel, according to all the curses of the covenant that are written in this book of the law. But you that cleave unto the Lord your God are alive every one of you this day.

The document concludes with the warning that "no one should communicate with him, not even in writing, nor accord him any favor nor stay with him under the same roof nor [come] within four cubits in his vicinity; nor shall he read any treatise composed or written by him."[3]

It was the harshest writ of *cherem*, or ostracism, ever pronounced upon a member of the Portuguese-Jewish community of Amsterdam. The *parnassim* sitting on the *ma'amad* that year dug deep into their books to find just the right words for the occasion.[4] Unlike many of the other bans issued by *ma'amad*, this one was never rescinded.

For us, trying to understand the event three and a half centuries later on the basis of very meagre documentary evidence, it is all a bit of a mystery. We do not know for certain why Spinoza was punished with such extreme prejudice. That the punishment came from his own community – from the congregation that had nurtured and educated him, and that held his family in such high esteem – only adds to the enigma. Neither the *cherem* itself nor any document from the period tells us exactly what his "evil opinions and acts [*más opinioins e obras*]" were supposed to have been, nor what "abominable heresies [*horrendas heregias*]" or "monstrous deeds [*ynormes obras*]" he is alleged to have practiced and taught. He had not yet

---

[3] The Hebrew text is no longer extant, but the Portuguese version is found in the Book of Ordinances (*Livro dos Acordos de Naçao e Ascamot*), in the Municipal Archives of the City of Amsterdam, Archives for the Portuguese Jewish Community in Amsterdam, 334, no. 19, fol. 408.

[4] The text used for the *cherem* had been brought back to Amsterdam from Venice by Rabbi Saul Levi Mortera almost forty years earlier, ostensibly to be used in case an intramural congregational dispute in 1619 could not be resolved amicably.

published anything, nor (as far as we know) even composed any treatise. Spinoza never refers to this period of his life in his extant letters, and thus does not offer his correspondents (or us) any clues as to why he was expelled.[5] All we know for certain is that Spinoza received, from the community's leadership in 1656, a *cherem* like no other in the period.

Writing many years after the fact, and claiming to have talked with Spinoza himself, his earliest biographer, Jean-Maximilian Lucas, relates that Spinoza was convicted "not of blasphemy, but only of a lack of respect for Moses and the law."[6] Perhaps Spinoza was violating the restrictions of the Jewish Sabbath or the dietary code of *kashrut* or some other aspect of *halakhah*, Jewish law. On the other hand, it has been argued that his "sins" were more secular in nature, and that Spinoza, who had gone over the heads of the community's governors and appealed to the Dutch authorities in order to escape his inherited debts, "had to be removed from the community because legal and financial interests were at stake."[7]

Neither of these explanations, however, appears to be sufficient to account for the singular venom directed at Spinoza in his *cherem*. Instead, what seems really to have been the offense behind the vicious *cherem* earned by Spinoza are not actions, either religious or legal, but rather, as the proclamation reads, *más opinioins* and *horrendas heregias*: "evil opinions" and "abominable heresies" – that is, ideas.

Three relatively reliable sources from the period tell us as much. In Lucas's chronology of the events leading up to the *cherem*, there was much talk in the congregation about Spinoza's opinions; people, especially the rabbis, were curious about what the young man, known for his intelligence, was thinking. As Lucas tells it – and this particular anecdote is not confirmed by any other source – "among those most eager to associate with him there were two young men who, professing to be his most intimate friends, begged him to tell them his real views. They promised him that whatever his opinions

---

[5] Spinoza's friends, who edited his works and letters for publication immediately after his death, seem to have destroyed all letters that were not of mainly philosophical (as opposed to biographical and personal) interest.

[6] Freudenthal 1899, p. 10.

[7] See Vlessing 1996, pp. 205–10.

were, he had nothing to fear on their part, for their curiosity had no other end than to clear up their own doubts."[8] They suggested, trying to draw Spinoza out, that if one read Moses and the Prophets closely, then one would be led to the conclusion that the soul is not immortal and that God is material. "How does it appear to you?", they asked Spinoza. "Does God have a body? Is the soul immortal?" After some hesitation, Spinoza took the bait.

I confess, said [Spinoza], that since nothing is to be found in the Bible about the non-material or incorporeal, there is nothing objectionable in believing that God is a body. All the more so since, as the Prophet says, God is great, and it is impossible to comprehend greatness without extension and, therefore, without body. As for spirits, it is certain that Scripture does not say that these are real and permanent substances, but mere phantoms, called angels because God makes use of them to declare his will; they are of such kind that the angels and all other kinds of spirits are invisible only because their matter is very fine and diaphanous, so that it can only be seen as one sees phantoms in a mirror, in a dream, or in the night.

As for the human soul, Spinoza reportedly replied that "whenever Scripture speaks of it, the word 'soul' is used simply to express life, or anything that is living. It would be useless to search for any passage in support of its immortality. As for the contrary view, it may be seen in a hundred places, and nothing is so easy as to prove it."

Spinoza did not trust the motives behind the curiosity of his "friends" – with good reason – and he broke off the conversation as soon as he had the opportunity. At first his interlocutors thought he was just teasing them or trying merely to shock them by express-ing scandalous ideas. But when they saw that he was serious, they started talking about Spinoza to others. "They said that the people deceived themselves in believing that this young man might become one of the pillars of the synagogue; that it seemed more likely that he would be its destroyer, as he had nothing but hatred and contempt for the Law of Moses." Lucas relates that when Spinoza was called before his judges, these same individuals bore witness against him, alleging that he "scoffed at the Jews as 'superstitious

---

[8] Freudenthal 1899, p. 5.

people born and bred in ignorance, who do not know what God is, and who nevertheless have the audacity to speak of themselves as His People, to the disparagement of other nations'."[9]

Then there is the report of Brother Tomas Solano y Robles. Brother Tomas was an Augustinian monk who was in Madrid in 1659, right after a voyage that had taken him through Amsterdam in late 1658. The Spanish Inquisitors were interested in what was going on among the former New Christians now living in northern Europe, most of whom had once been in its domain and still had converso relatives back in Iberia. They interviewed the friar, as well as another traveler to the Netherlands, Captain Miguel Pérez de Maltranilla, who had stayed in the same house in Amsterdam, and at the same time, as Brother Tomas. Both men claimed that in Amsterdam they had met Spinoza and a man named Juan de Prado, who had been expelled from the community shortly after Spinoza. The two apostates told Brother Tomas that they had been observant of Jewish law but "changed their mind," and that they were expelled from the synagogue because of their views on God, the soul, and the law. They had, in the eyes of the congregation, "reached the point of atheism."[10] According to Tomas's deposition, they were saying that the soul was not immortal, that the Law was "not true" and that there was no God except in a "philosophical" sense.[11] Maltranilla confirms that, according to Spinoza and Prado, "the law . . . was false."[12]

---

[9] Freudenthal 1899, p. 7.    [10] Revah 1959, pp. 32–3.

[11] The text of Brother Tomas's deposition (in Revah 1959, p. 32) reads as follows:

> He knew both Dr. Prado, a physician, whose first name was Juan but whose Jewish name he did not know, who had studied at Alcala, and a certain de Espinosa, who he thinks was a native of one of the villages of Holland, for he had studied at Leiden and was a good philosopher. These two persons had professed the Law of Moses, and the synagogue had expelled and isolated them because they had reached the point of atheism. And they themselves told the witness that they had been circumcised and that they had observed the law of the Jews, and that they had changed their mind because it seemed to them that the said law was not true and that souls died with their bodies and that there is no God except philosophically. And that is why they were expelled from the synagogue; and, while they regretted the absence of the charity that they used to receive from the synagogue and the communication with other Jews, they were happy to be atheists, since they thought that God exists only philosophically . . . and that souls died with their bodies and that thus they had no need for faith.

[12] The original text of Maltranilla's testimony is in Revah 1959, p. 67.

The community poet-historian David Franco Mendes is our final witness on this matter. Although he was writing many years later, his work undoubtedly represents a repository of communal record and memory. He insists, in his brief report on the case, that Spinoza not only violated the Sabbath and the laws governing the festivals, but also was filled with "atheistic" ideas, and was punished accordingly.[13]

"God exists only philosophically," "The Law is not true," and "The soul is not immortal." These are rather vague and indeterminate propositions, particularly the first two. Ordinarily, there is no more telling what is intended by them than what is meant by the notoriously ambiguous charge of "atheism." But in Spinoza's case we have some fair basis for knowing what he would have meant, for they are likely just the views that he would at least begin elaborating and arguing for in his written works within five years. To be sure, we cannot be certain that what we find in those writings is exactly what he was saying *vive voce* within the community. But the report by Lucas and the testimony by Brother Tomas indicate that the metaphysical, moral, and religious doctrines that are to be found in his mature philosophical works were already in his mind, and not necessarily in only an embryonic form, in the mid-1650s.

According to Lucas, Spinoza took his expulsion in good stride. "All the better," he quotes Spinoza as saying, "they do not force me to do anything that I would not have done of my own accord if I did not dread scandal . . . I gladly enter on the path that is opened to me."[14] By this point, he was certainly not very religiously observant, and must have had grave doubts about both the particular tenets of Judaism and, more generally, the value of sectarian religion. Besides the opportunity it afforded him to maintain the family business and earn a living, membership in good standing in the community seems to have mattered little to him.

### A PHILOSOPHER IN THE COUNTRY

Contrary to yet another myth about Spinoza's life – and, given the dearth of extant biographical information, there are many – after the

---

[13] Mendes 1975, pp. 60–1.          [14] Freudenthal 1899, p. 8.

ban the city magistrates did not exile him from Amsterdam at the urging of the rabbis. Although we do not know his exact address, and he almost certainly no longer resided in Vlooienburg, he seems to have continued to live in the city or just outside it from 1656 until 1661, when his surviving correspondence begins. He is also reported to have passed some time during this period studying philosophy (most likely of the Cartesian variety) at the University of Leiden, although his name does not appear on the list of matriculated students there.

There is also a widely accepted view that Spinoza was a loner, a solitary figure who just wanted to be left alone with his work. Nothing could be further from the truth. While he greatly valued his time and independence to pursue his studies, he did indeed have some very dear friends and a wider circle of admirers, acquaintances, and correspondents. Many of his closest and most lasting personal relationships developed in the period of his life immediately before and after the ban. The medical doctor Lodewijk Meyer, a liberal humanist with a strong interest in the arts; Jarig Jellesz and Pieter Balling, fellow-merchants whom Spinoza may have met at the Amsterdam Exchange; the grocer Simon Joosten de Vries; the radical thinker Adriaen Koerbagh; Jan Rieuwertsz, the bold publisher from whose press came many politically and religiously incendiary works, including those of Spinoza; and the physician-philosopher Johan Bouwmeester were perhaps his most devoted friends. What these men had in common, besides a taste for philosophy, was a suspicion of political and ecclesiastic authority and a heterodox approach to religion. Many were members of the dissident Reformed sects – Mennonites, Collegiants, Anabaptists, Quakers – that flourished in the laissez-faire environment of Amsterdam; a few probably had no religious beliefs whatsoever. They found in Spinoza a charismatic figure who could express with some sophistication the doubts they felt about the value of sectarian worship (and the major Christian denominations in particular) and the truths about God, nature, the human being, and politics that informed their intellectual outlook.

In the late 1650s, Spinoza, Meyer, Jellesz, and others formed the core of a reading group in Amsterdam that met regularly to discuss Cartesian and other philosophical matters. Later, after Spinoza's departure from Amsterdam, the group changed its focus and began to study Spinoza's own ideas as these emerged slowly from his writings in progress. They would forward to Spinoza questions about some difficult aspects of the manuscript he had sent them and that they had recently discussed, and he would reply with helpful clarifications. Writing to Spinoza in 1663, when the philosopher was no longer living in the city, De Vries informs him that as they go through the manuscript of the *Ethics*,

if it happens that one [of us] cannot satisfy the other[s], we have thought it worthwhile to make a note of it and to write to you, so that, if possible, it may be made clearer to us, and under your guidance we may be able to defend the truth against those who are superstitiously religious and Christian, and to stand against the attacks of the whole.[15]

Sometime in the late 1650s, Spinoza began work on a treatise on philosophical method, the *Treatise on the Emendation of the Intellect* (*Tractatus de intellectus emendatione*). His first extant original philosophical work, it was conceived as the preliminary part of a larger project. In the *Treatise*, Spinoza addresses some basic problems concerning the nature and varieties of knowledge and the proper means to achieving true understanding, all in the context of a broad conception of what constitutes "the good" for a human being. The way to emend the intellect, to "heal" and "purify" it and "render it capable of understanding things," Spinoza insists, is to discover a methodical and reliable way of distinguishing clear and distinct true ideas from the inadequate ones that so often mislead us. In this way, one can come to perceive how all things depend on fixed and eternal principles and, our ultimate goal, apprehend "the union that the mind has with the whole of nature."

Many of these issues would receive a deeper treatment in the more substantive remainder of the work, which at this point Spinoza calls simply "our Philosophy." Not yet written at the time he was composing the *Treatise*, this "Philosophy" (the envisioned core of which almost certainly constitutes much of the content of the *Ethics*) was to be an extensive and systematic inquiry into the mind, metaphysics, physics, morality, and other subjects. What seems to

---

[15] Letter 8, G IV.39/C I.190.

have happened, however, is that, for one reason or another, Spinoza decided in late 1659 or early 1660 to abandon the *Treatise* altogether and start over, this time working on what would become the *Short Treatise on God, Man and His Well-Being* (*Korte Verhandeling van God, de Mensch en des Zelfs Welstand*),[16] whose own methodological chapters overlap with much of the material in the *Treatise*. The *Short Treatise* contains in embryonic form many themes and ideas that will reappear in more mature versions and in a more orderly and perspicuous format in the *Ethics*. Despite its obvious shortcomings, the work represents Spinoza's first serious attempt to lay out what he takes to be the metaphysics of God and nature; the proper conception of the human soul; the nature of knowledge and freedom; the status of good and evil; and the human being's relationship to nature and the means to true happiness.

Spinoza began the *Short Treatise* while he was still living in Amsterdam. Sometime during the summer of 1661, however, he moved to Rijnsburg, outside of Leiden. He may have been directed to this small village by his Collegiant friends, since there was a vibrant practicing community of these "churchless Christians" there.[17] More likely, though, Spinoza chose Rijnsburg because it was a quiet place to pursue his occupations, yet close enough to Leiden for him to be able to travel there easily and keep up with acquaintances and developments at the university.

In the back room of the house in which he lodged in Rijnsburg, Spinoza set up his lens-grinding equipment. (The house still stands today, and its interior has been re-fitted with the accoutrements of Spinoza's residence, including his library and lens-grinding machine.) This was a craft he must have begun working on while still in Amsterdam, for by the time he settled in Rijnsburg he was fairly skilled at it. As early as the fall of 1661, he was known for making not just lenses but also telescopes and microscopes. Spinoza's friend Christian Huygens, the Dutch scientist and mathematician, commented in a letter to his brother that "the [lenses] that the Jew

---

[16] This treatise was not included in the Latin or Dutch collections of Spinoza's writings published by his friends after his death, and was only rediscovered in Dutch manuscripts in the nineteenth century.

[17] The phrase is from Kolakowski 1969.

of Voorburg has in his microscopes have an admirable polish."[18]
Spinoza may initially have taken up the production of lenses and
instruments to support himself – it was now, besides loans and
gifts from his friends, his chief source of income – but it also served
his own scientific interests. With his general enthusiasm for the
new mechanistic science of nature, Spinoza was fascinated by the
latest detailed explanations of the microphenomena of biology and
chemistry and the ever-improving observations of the macrophe-
nomena of astronomy, as well as by the mathematical principles of
optics that made such discoveries possible. Writing in 1665 to his
friend Henry Oldenburg, corresponding secretary to the Royal
Society in England, with evident delight about some new instruments he had heard of from Huygens, Spinoza notes that "he has
told me wonderful things about these microscopes, and also about
certain telescopes, made in Italy, with which they could observe
eclipses of Jupiter caused by the interposition of its satellites, and
also a certain shadow on Saturn, which looked as if it were caused
by a ring."[19]

Spinoza kept up with his friends in Amsterdam, who were soon
asking him for an accessible general introduction to the philosophy
of Descartes, on which they considered him an expert. Thus, in
1663, shortly after moving from Rijnsburg to Voorburg, a small
village not far from The Hague, he composed for their benefit the
only work that would be published in his lifetime under his own
name, *Parts One and Two of the Principles of Philosophy of René
Descartes Demonstrated According to the Geometric Method* (*Renati
Des Cartes Principiorum Philosophiae Pars I. & II.*, 1663). This was
based on some tutorials on the *Principles* that Spinoza had been
giving to a young man who was living with him for a time in
Rijnsburg, Johannes Casearius. In the written version, Spinoza
reorganized the metaphysics, epistemology, and basic physics of
Descartes's "textbook" of philosophy into a geometrical method
involving axioms, definitions, and demonstrated propositions. (By
this point, he had decided that the Euclidean format was the best
way to present these parts of philosophy.) To the published edition

---

[18] Huygens 1893, VI.181.          [19] Letter 26 G IV.159/C I.394.

of his lessons Spinoza added an appendix of "Metaphysical Thoughts" (*Cogitata Metaphysica*). In this he provides explanations of "more difficult questions" in metaphysics, occasionally revealing glimpses of some of his own ideas that he offers as corrections to the views of his philosophical mentor. The *Principles* brought Spinoza fame as an expositor of Cartesian philosophy, and (misleadingly, and much to the later chagrin of the Cartesians) earned him a reputation as a leading Cartesian himself.

## FROM ETHICS TO POLITICS

The exposition of Descartes temporarily distracted Spinoza from what was now his main occupation, a rigorous presentation of his own highly original philosophical thoughts. The *Short Treatise* clearly did not satisfy him, and by early 1662 he had aborted the incomplete manuscript in order to make yet another fresh start. Thus, most likely in the spring of 1662, Spinoza took up his pen to begin what would be his philosophical masterpiece, the *Ethics* (*Ethica*). Still, in essence, a treatise on "God, Man and His Well-Being," the *Ethics* was an attempt to provide a fuller, clearer, and more systematic layout in "the geometric style" for his grand metaphysical and moral philosophical project. He worked on it steadily for a number of years, through his move to Voorburg in 1663 and on into the summer of 1665. He envisioned at this point a three-part work, and seems to have had a fairly substantial draft in hand by June 1665. He felt confident enough of what he had written so far to allow a select few to read it, and there were Latin and even Dutch (translated by Pieter Balling) copies of the manuscript circulating among his friends.

We do not know how close to a final product Spinoza considered this draft of the *Ethics* when he put it aside, probably in the fall of 1665, to turn his attention to another, immediately more relevant project. At the time, he probably saw it as mostly complete but in need of polishing. It would be a good number of years, though, before Spinoza returned to his metaphysical-moral treatise to put the finishing touches on it, which included significant additions and revisions, no doubt in the light of further reading and reflection. This delay was due in part to circumstances of a political and personal nature that had begun to disturb the peace at Voorburg and in the United Provinces as a whole.

These were difficult years in the life of the young Dutch Republic. The long war for independence from Spain had finally come to a formal conclusion only in 1648, with the Peace of Münster. But this was quickly followed by a series of wars with England, from 1652 to 1654 and again from 1664 to 1667; increased tensions on other fronts, particularly with France and the German states; a virulent outbreak of the plague in 1663–4; and, perhaps most ominous of all, a heating up of the internal political squabbling that seemed constantly to rile the republic throughout the century.

Dutch politics in the seventeenth century can basically be characterized by two broadly drawn positions. On the one hand, there was the States General or republican party. The relatively liberal members of this camp favored a decentralized federation of quasi-sovereign provinces, each of which was in turn a federation of quasi-sovereign cities and towns. Real power on this scheme devolved to the local regents governing each municipality, such as the members of the wealthy professional and merchant families that took turns ruling Amsterdam for decades. The republicans tended to favor a laissez-faire attitude in politics, culture, and religion, including a general (but not unlimited) toleration in matters of faith. On the other hand, there were the Orangists, who sought a more centralized state under the leadership of the Stadholder, a quasi-monarchical position usually occupied throughout a number of provinces by the Prince of Orange. The Stadholder, in the Orangist scheme, would be the supreme ruler of the land and the commander-in-chief of the armed forces. The supporters of a strong Stadholdership also tended to be more conservative when it came to religion and cultural and social mores, and sought to impose a higher degree of conformity not only among the members of the Reformed Church, but in the Republic at large.

The passions behind this political division were fed by a corresponding battle in the ecclesiastic domain between two irreconcilably opposed factions of the Dutch Reformed Church. The Arminians were followers of Jacobus Arminius, a liberal theology professor at the University of Leiden; they were also called "Remonstrants" because of the remonstrance they had issued in 1610 setting forth their unorthodox views on certain sensitive theological questions, including a rejection of the strict Calvinist doctrines of grace and predestination. Because of their unwillingness to toe the party line, the Remonstrants were expelled from the Dutch Reformed Church in 1619 at the Synod of Dort. The representatives to the gathering reiterated their commitment to freedom of conscience in the Republic, but nonetheless insisted that public worship and office holding be restricted to orthodox Calvinists. There was a purge at all levels of the Church, and for a time the Counter-Remonstrants, as the conservative group came to be called, had the upper hand in the religious affairs of most provinces. The harassment of Remonstrants continued for a number of years, and although by the mid-1620s things had quieted down somewhat, there would be occasional flare-ups over the next five decades. By the middle of the century, Amsterdam itself had gained a reputation as a city favorable to Remonstrants.

The history of public affairs in the Dutch Golden Age is a series of pendulum swings back and forth between the two politico-theological camps, with the States General party finding its natural allies among Remonstrant sympathizers, and the Orangists getting support from the more orthodox Calvinists. Throughout the 1650s and 1660s, the liberals were in the ascendancy – the last dominant Stadholder in the major provinces, William II, had died in 1650, and would not be replaced until 1672, by William III – but there were troubling clouds on the political horizon.

What seems initially to have disturbed Spinoza's peace at Voorburg and occasioned his putting the *Ethics* aside in the fall of 1665 to begin composing a work on theology and politics was a dispute over succession in the local church. When the Reformed preacher in Voorburg died, the committee appointed to select his replacement chose a candidate who, if not himself of Remonstrant inclinations, was perceived to be at least tolerant of the Arminians. This angered the conservatives in town, who accused their colleagues of deliberate provocation. Spinoza seems to have sided with the liberal group, and may even have played a role in the controversy. Dutch politics being what they were, religious disagreements bled into political grievances and the dispute grew all out of proportion and became a rather nasty and divisive experience for the community. Spinoza himself was resentful of the whole affair, both of how he had been talked about and treated by a number of important people in town – he says they called him an atheist and a trouble-maker – and more generally of the way in which Reformed ministers, for whom he had never had much respect, tried to dominate civic matters in Voorburg and elsewhere.

Spinoza thus undertook to compose a treatise in which he would, in effect, argue for the separation of the secular and the sectarian, of reason and religion, and defend "the freedom to philosophize and to say what we think," which, he believes, "is in every way suppressed by the excessive authority and egotism of preachers."[20] It seems, in fact, to have been not so much a new project that Spinoza was beginning as a return to an old one, since we have some reason to believe that "theological-political questions" had already occupied his attention in the late 1650s and that he may even have written at that time an early draft of some of the material that would appear in what he was now calling the *Theological-Political Treatise* (*Tractatus Theologico-Politicus*).

In the *Theological-Political Treatise*, Spinoza intends to show that the Bible is not literally the work of God – or, more precisely, of Moses serving as God's amanuensis – but rather a very historical document composed and edited by ordinary human beings and transmitted in a very natural way over many generations. What we now have is, therefore, most likely a highly corrupt human product that has no greater claim to historical, philosophical, or theological truth than any other work of literature. What Scripture does contain that is "divine" are some very simple moral truths – that we should love God and our fellow human beings – that will guide us toward happiness and well-being.

Spinoza insists, moreover, that the proper method for interpreting Scripture is the same as that used to investigate nature. Following the Baconian procedure, one should examine the evidence imme-diately at hand – that is, the text itself – compile the relevant data by comparing passages, and draw justified general conclusions

---

[20] Letter 30.

from them. He believes that grasping the true meaning of Scripture requires one to study its language, the personalities of its authors, editors, and audiences, the context of its composition, and the record of its transmission. The real touchstone for understanding Scripture is Scripture itself and its history, not what reason (i.e., philosophy and science) or authority dictates as true.

In this way, Spinoza sought to undermine the general authority of Scripture and, consequently, to weaken the position of those ecclesiastics who elevate Scripture into a sacred object and worship its every word and who, claiming to be the sole and specially gifted interpreters of Scripture, rely on it to bolster their own pretensions to power. The conclusion of Spinoza's argument is that religion is one domain, where the concern is with faith and obedience, and philosophy and science a completely separate domain, where the goal is truth and knowledge. Religion, therefore, has no right to prescribe limits to philosophy, much less to interfere with the secular affairs of the state. On the contrary, the secular leaders of the state are to exercise control over religious worship so as to insure that it poses no harm to civic well-being. The treatise offers as strong and eloquent a plea for toleration and secularism as has ever been expressed.

As he argues for these general principles, Spinoza, showing great erudition, addresses a number of important questions about Jewish religion and history, including the status and validity of Jewish law (which he claims is no longer binding upon contemporary Jews); the divine election of the Jewish people (it consists only in what was natural political good fortune for an extended period of time, and not any kind of metaphysical or moral superiority over other peoples); and the virtues, vices, and devolution of the Hebrew state, from Moses down to the destruction of the Second Temple. He also looks at the nature of prophecy (he believes that the prophets just happened to be gifted storytellers with particularly vivid imaginations) and of miracles (he denies that, if by 'miracle' one means a supernaturally caused event that is an exception to the course of nature, there are any such things). Finally, Spinoza considers the origins of the state and the grounds of political obligation. At the basis of any legitimate polity is a convention – a social contract – by which people unite and agree to give up the unbridled pursuit of self-interest for the sake of peace and security. Political power and ecclesiastic authority are to remain distinct, and while the political sovereign is to regulate the public practice of religion, religious leaders are to play no role whatsoever in political affairs. This is the clear lesson to be learned from the downfall of the ancient Hebrew kingdom, wherein power was ultimately divided between the king and the priests, who usurped secular prerogatives, and it was one which Spinoza felt his Dutch contemporaries would do well to heed.

If Spinoza sincerely thought that his "treatise on Scripture" would, as he said to Oldenburg in 1665, allow him to silence those "who constantly accuse me of atheism" and dispel the impression that he denied all religion, then he was in for a rude awakening.[21] In fact, he can have been under no illusions about the reception his ideas would face. The *Theological-Political Treatise* is an astoundingly bold and radical work. When it was published in 1670 – anonymously, and with a false publisher and city on the cover – it generated an enormous outcry in the Netherlands and elsewhere. The book, the identity of whose author was no real secret, was attacked by theologians, political leaders, academics, and lay people. Calvinists, Remonstrants, Collegiants, Lutherans, and Catholics all agreed that it was a subversive and dangerous work. There were formal condemnations and bannings from city councils, provincial assemblies, and church bodies. The delegates to the Synod of South Holland concluded that it was "as vile and blasphemous a book as the world has ever seen." Even Thomas Hobbes, not one to be squeamish when it came to political and theological controversy, was taken aback by Spinoza's audacity. According to his biographer, the English philosopher claimed that the *Treatise* "cut through him a bar's length, for he durst not write so boldly."[22]

The *Treatise* is also a very angry work. The decision to publish it sooner rather than later came from a personal loss that Spinoza suffered in 1669. His friend Adriaan Koerbagh, in a series of provocative books with remarkably Spinozistic themes, had undertaken to attack the irrationality of most religions, with their superstitious rites and meaningless ceremonies. Taking a swipe at trinitarianism,

---

[21] Letter 30.          [22] As reported in Aubrey 1898, I.357.

Koerbagh had argued that God is one being, not three. He also insisted, however, that God is nothing but the substance of the universe. In Koerbagh's view, the real teaching of God, the "true religion," is simply a knowledge of and obedience to God and a love of one's neighbor. Koerbagh was also a radical democrat and warned of the dangers of the ecclesiastic encroachment upon civic political power.

Despite the fact that Koerbagh offered a strong defense of the republican principles of Johan de Witt, the Grand Pensionary of the States of Holland and, in the absence of a Stadholder, the effective political leader of the Dutch Republic, there was little De Witt could do – or may even have wanted to do – to protect him from the counter-attack of his conservative opponents. One of Koerbagh's mistakes, besides putting his name on the covers of his books, was to write in Dutch rather than, like Spinoza in the *Theological-Political Treatise*, hide behind the veneer of academic Latin. Koerbagh was arrested and, after a short trial, sentenced to ten years in prison, to be followed by ten years in exile. He did not last long in confinement, however. His health took a serious and rapid turn for the worse, and he died in October 1699, just nine months after being sentenced.

This was an enormous blow to Spinoza. It represented not only the loss of a close friend, but also a violation of the highest principles of freedom and toleration to which his homeland was dedicated. Koerbagh's treatment at the hands of the magistrates and the religious authorities who pressed them to prosecute him was a dangerous collusion between church and state. It gave Spinoza the impetus he needed to put the final touches on the *Theological-Political Treatise* and begin preparing it for publication. To his mind, putting forth his case on the proper relationship between religion and the state had become a matter of pressing personal and public importance.

## CALM AND TURMOIL IN THE HAGUE

When work on the treatise was behind him and the book in press, Spinoza moved from Voorburg to The Hague. He may have begun to tire of life in the country, and desired easier access to the intellectual and cultural life of the city. With his many friends and

acquaintances in town, he would have found it much more convenient to live there rather than commute in from the village.
Once settled in the house of Hendrik van der Spyck, a painter,
Spinoza went back to work on the *Ethics* and his expanding
correspondence, and dealt calmly with the storm generated by
the *Theological-Political Treatise*, including halting the publication
of a Dutch translation that his friends were preparing.

He seems to have had a friendly, even intimate relationship with
his landlord's family. They had many good things to say about
Spinoza to Johannes Colerus, the Lutheran preacher of their congregation and another early biographer of the philosopher. Spinoza
apparently spent a good deal of time in his room, working on either
his lenses or his writing, or perhaps just reading. "When he was at
home, he was troublesome to no one . . . When he tired of his
investigations, he came down and spoke with his house companions
on whatever was going on, even about trivial matters." For diver-
sion, he liked to collect spiders and have them fight each other, or
throw flies into their webs, creating battles, which so entertained
him "that he would break out laughing." Far from being the
morose, anti-social recluse of legend, Spinoza was, when he put
down his work, gregarious and possessed of a pleasing and even-
tempered disposition. He was kind and considerate, and enjoyed
the company of others, who seem in turn to have enjoyed his. He
appears, in fact, to have lived just the kind of reasonable, self-
controlled life – involving moderating the passions rather than
letting them overwhelm one – that he presents in the *Ethics* as the
ideal for human flourishing.

His conversation and way of life were calm and retiring. He knew how to
control his passions in an admirable way. No one ever saw him sad or
merry. He could control or hold in his anger and his discontent, making it
known only by a sign or a single short word, or standing up and leaving
out of a fear that his passion might get the better of him. He was,
moreover, friendly and sociable in his daily intercourse.

If the housewife or other members of Van der Spyck's household
were sick,

he never failed to console them and to encourage them to endure that
which, he told them, was the lot assigned to them by God. He exhorted the

children of the house to be polite and to be respectful of their elders and to go to public worship often.[23]

Even Pierre Bayle, the czar of the seventeenth-century Republic of Letters who excoriated Spinoza for his "atheistic philosophy," took note of the virtues of Spinoza's personal character and his blameless lifestyle, using this as evidence of the fact that someone who remains unconvinced of Christian truth can still lead a good and upright existence.[24]

What Spinoza earned from his lens-grinding had always been supplemented by the generosity of his friends. But all the evidence suggests that Spinoza's personal needs were not very great to begin with and that he led a frugal life. "Not only did riches not tempt him, but he even did not at all fear the odious consequences of poverty . . . Having heard that someone who owed him two hundred florins had gone bankrupt, far from being upset by it, he said, while smiling, 'I must reduce my daily needs to make up for this small loss. That is the price,' he added, 'of fortitude.'"[25] His daily meals were simple – he liked a milk-based gruel with raisins and butter and preferred to drink beer – and his furnishings "sober and humble." He dressed plainly and without much fuss (at least according to Colerus, who notes that "in his clothing he was simple and common"[26]). He did not have many expenses, and, Lucas says, although he did not oppose "honest pleasures," those of the body "touched him little."[27]

While deeply engaged in his main metaphysical-moral and theological-political projects, Spinoza nonetheless found time for a number of less philosophical undertakings in the last decade of his life. He composed a short treatise on the rainbow, examining the geometry of the optics behind the phenomenon, and also produced for the benefit of his friends an introductory grammar of Hebrew, the *Compendium grammatices linguae Hebraeae.* The dating of these works is uncertain, and neither was published until after his death.

---

[23] See Freudenthal 1899, pp. 57–61.
[24] See the article on Spinoza in his *Dictionnaire historique et critique.*
[25] This is from Lucas's biography; see Freudenthal 1899, p. 16.
[26] Freudenthal 1899, p. 59.
[27] Freudenthal 1899, p. 20.

Without question, however, his major preoccupation during his early years in The Hague, from 1670 to 1675, was revising the *Ethics* and readying it for publication. He concentrated especially on reworking material from what had been an extensive Part Three but that he was now organizing into Parts Three, Four, and Five. This included much of his moral psychology, his account of human bondage to the passions, and the picture of the "free human being." It is almost certain that much of what Spinoza has to say in the *Ethics* of a political and social nature and on religion and true freedom underwent significant revision after 1670. The latter parts of the manuscript that he picked up after a hiatus of at least six years now had to be recast in the light not just of his reading in the intervening period – including Hobbes's *Leviathan*, which was translated into Dutch and Latin in the late 1660s (Spinoza could not read English) – but, more importantly, of the theory of the state and civil society that he himself set forth in the *Theological-Political Treatise*. On the other hand, given what appears to be a general continuity in his metaphysical, moral, and political thinking between the early 1660s and the early 1670s, it is unlikely that the additions or changes made to the work after his move to The Hague represented any significant revision of his basic underlying doctrines. The political implications of his theory of the human being and human motivation may have become clearer and more elaborate after his completion of the *Theological-Political Treatise*, but they could never have been very far from his mind even when he began the geometrical presentation of his system in 1662.

In the midst of this work, Spinoza saw the United Provinces experience what was undoubtedly the worst year of its brief existence, the *annus horribilis* of Dutch history. Disaster struck in 1672 in the form of an invasion by the army of Louis XIV. France and the Netherlands had participated in an uneasy alliance ever since the Franco-Dutch treaty of 1662. Louis was initially useful to the Dutch in their second war against England, and had even helped to restrain threats to the Republic from the east from the prince-bishop of Münster. But always lurking in the background behind the professed amity were tensions over French ambitions toward the Spanish Netherlands. Louis sought to expand his dominion into the southern Low Countries, which, two centuries earlier, had belonged to the Duke of Burgundy. When, in the mid-1660s, a substantially weakened Spain began withdrawing its forces from its Flemish and Wallonian possessions, the King of France saw that the opportunity was ripe to make his move. In addition to these territorial issues between the two nations, there was a low-level campaign of hostilities on the economic front. The French, concerned by the increasing share that Dutch exports – such as cloth, herring, tobacco, and sugar – were assuming in their market, imposed harsh tariffs on all foreign imports, which greatly antagonized Dutch producers and traders and had them clamoring for retaliatory measures. The intense competition between the recently founded French East and West Indies Companies and their more established Dutch counterparts served only to push the anger and resentment, not to mention the anxiety, of the Dutch public to the breaking point.

Through a series of French alliances, by 1672 the Dutch found themselves surrounded by hostile states. Louis seemed intent not just on taking the Spanish Netherlands but also in defeating the Dutch Republic itself and transforming it into a monarchy. In April, Louis declared war on the Republic; he was soon followed by England, the prince-bishop of Münster, and the Elector of Cologne.

There had always been great division among the Dutch over how to respond to France's threatening behavior. De Witt believed that nothing could be gained by war, and all along argued against military intervention. His Orangist opponents, on the other hand, insisted on a strong response and clamored for the return of the Stadholder to take command of the armed forces. On the eve of the French invasion, they effectively won the debate and William III, now reaching his majority, was appointed Stadholder in Holland and other provinces.

Things did not go well for the Dutch in the early months of the war. As a consequence, De Witt was in serious trouble. Public sentiment was running strongly against him, as he was accused of military incompetence, financial improprieties, and even of plotting to hand the Republic over to its enemies so that he could rule it on their behalf. By June, after an assassination attempt, he had resigned the position of Grand Pensionary. Soon thereafter, his brother, Cornelis, was arrested, allegedly for plotting against the life of the Stadholder. Although Cornelis was acquitted, when Johan came to retrieve him from prison, the brothers found themselves trapped inside by an angry mob. By the end of the day, they were dead, hung up and literally torn apart by the crowd.

Spinoza was stunned and outraged by these acts of barbarity, perpetrated not by some roving band of thieves but by a crowd of ordinary citizens. He had to be restrained by his landlord from rushing out into the street and placing a placard – reading *Ultimi barbarorum* [roughly translated: "You are the greatest of barbarians!"] – near the site of the atrocity.

Spinoza also mourned the sudden end of the period of "True Freedom," with its liberal republican principles and generally tolerant atmosphere. Regents seen as sympathetic to the De Witts were replaced by individuals who were unequivocally Orangist and favorably disposed to the aims of the orthodox Calvinists. Seemingly overnight, political power became more centralized as it moved back from the towns and the provincial States to the Stadholder and the States General, over which William had great influence. Consequently, it became easier for the authorities to exercise a broader and more consistent control over what was said and done in the Republic.

These changes in the political winds probably account for the fact that, after 1672, Spinoza found himself once again the object of attack. He was now vilified not only by political, academic, and theological conservatives, especially the Voetian camp in the Reformed Church – so-called because it was united behind the orthodox firebrand Gisbertus Voetius, dean of the University of Utrecht and one of Descartes's most implacable foes – but also by those from whom he might have expected some support. The Voetians' doctrinal opponents in the Church, known as Cocceians (because they were followers of Johannes Cocceius, a theology professor at Leiden who was fairly liberal in his interpretation of the demands of Calvinism), were equally vociferous in condemning the *Theological-Political Treatise*. They were joined by their natural intellectual and political allies among the moderate Cartesians in the universities, who turned on Spinoza and other like-minded individuals (such as his friend Lodewijk Meyer, whose book *Philosophy, Interpreter of Scripture* was often condemned in the same breath as Spinoza's *Treatise*). It was, in part, a defensive maneuver, as Spinoza and Meyer were generally perceived to be nothing more than radical Cartesians. Thus, through their attacks, the academic Cartesians, afraid that the backlash against Spinoza would undermine their own tenuous position, hoped to distance themselves from Spinozistic ideas and distinguish themselves in the minds of their enemies from the more "dangerous" strains of freethinking infecting the Republic. Spinoza saw through their strategy. He notes in a letter to Oldenburg that "the stupid Cartesians" denounce his opinions "in order to remove suspicion from themselves."[28]

In the midst of the campaign against him that began after De Witt's murder, Spinoza must have been pleased to learn that some people, at least, appreciated his philosophical talents. In February, 1673, Spinoza was invited by Karl Ludwig, Elector of Palatine, one of the German imperial states, to take up a chair in philosophy at the University of Heidelberg. Spinoza was flattered by the invitation, and gave it serious consideration. He was, however, reluctant to make such an extreme change in his living situation and to interrupt his work by taking on formal duties. Moreover, while the letter of offer had promised him "the most extensive freedom in philosophizing," it also stipulated that he not abuse this "to disturb the publicly established religion." Spinoza was troubled by this ambiguous phrase, and expressed his reservations in a letter to Johann Fabricius, Karl Ludwig's adviser, a stern Calvinist and the holder of a chair in theology at Heidelberg.

I do not know within what limits the freedom to philosophize must be confined if I am to avoid appearing to disturb the publicly established religion. For divisions arise not so much from an ardent devotion to religion as from the different dispositions of men, or through their love of contradiction that leads them to distort or to condemn all things, even those that are stated aright. Now since I have already experienced this while leading a private and solitary life, it would be much more to be feared after I have risen to this position of eminence. So you see, most Honorable Sir, that my reluctance is not due to the hope of some better fortune, but to my love of peace, which I believe I can enjoy in some measure if I refrain from lecturing in public.[29]

---

[28] Letter 68.     [29] Letter 48.

After thinking it over for a month, Spinoza decided – probably wisely – to decline the position.

That summer, Spinoza received another invitation, one that required him to make a trip behind enemy lines. The city of Utrecht had been captured by the French in June, and the highly cultured Prince of Condé, the commanding officer of Louis XIV's forces, set up his headquarters there. While occupying the city, he sought to surround himself with intellectuals and courtiers and recreate the kind of salon atmosphere that he enjoyed back home in Chantilly. His second-in-command, Jean-Baptiste Stouppe, wrote to Spinoza asking him to join the circle in Utrecht, and even offered to get him a pension from Louis if only Spinoza would dedicate one of his books to the French monarch. Spinoza declined the offer of a pension, but did accept the invitation to come to Utrecht. Thus, in July 1673, he found himself traveling through dangerous and ravaged country to enter French-controlled territory. Spinoza probably did not get to meet Condé himself, who had been called away from Utrecht before Spinoza's arrival and may not have returned until after his departure some weeks later, but he nonetheless mingled among the writers and artists whom the Prince had gathered in his entourage.

It was a trip that did not endear Spinoza to his Dutch compatriots. The whole affair only added to their suspicions about his loyalties, and he was now seen not only as blasphemer of religion but also a traitor. "They considered him a spy," Colerus tells us,

and mumbled that he corresponded with the French over state affairs. Because his landlord became worried about this, and was afraid that they would break into his house to look for Spinoza, Spinoza calmed him with these words: "Do not be afraid! I am not guilty, and there are many people at the highest office who know well why I have gone to Utrecht. As soon as they make any noise at your door, I will go out to the people, even if they should deal with me as they did with the good De Witt brothers. I am an upright republican, and the welfare of the state is my goal."[30]

Spinoza's claim that there were individuals in high places who knew why he had made the trip to the enemy's camp has given rise

---

[30] Freudenthal 1899, pp. 64–5.

to the speculation that perhaps he was on an official diplomatic mission, possibly carrying some overture to peace negotiations from the government at The Hague to the head of the French army. It seems highly unlikely, however, that Spinoza was in the employ of the Dutch government. These were the days of the Orangists, not the De Witts. Even if the Stadholder or the States were inclined to communicate with the French, they would not have entrusted so sensitive a task to someone they perceived as an enemy of the Republic.

Spinoza was not, of course, an enemy of the Republic. All of his writing is directed toward the virtue and well-being not just of his fellow human beings, but also of the political society they composed and upon which they depended. He had a special affection for the Dutch Republic in particular, similar to Socrates's love for the Athens that put him to death two thousand years earlier. Each state, through its democratic culture and intellectual cosmopolitanism, nourished a philosopher who, once he turned his critical eye upon his own society and the lives led by others, would find himself the object of great ire.

## FINAL YEARS

By early July, 1675, Spinoza was sufficiently satisfied with his progress on the *Ethics* to decide it was finally time to publish it. The manuscript of which he had been so protective as to allow only a select few to see it – and even then only on the condition that they not talk about it to others – was, it seemed, about to be revealed to the public. He made the trip to Amsterdam toward the end of the month and handed a fair copy over to Rieuwertsz. It is unclear whether Spinoza was planning to withhold his name from the title page, as he had done with the *Theological-Political Treatise*. It is unlikely, however, that he any longer felt the need to take such precautions. Much had happened in the fifteen years since he began the work, particularly the five years since the appearance of the *Treatise*, and there would be very little mystery about who its author was.

Also, the political situation being what it was, there was very little to be gained at this point by anonymous publication. By the fall of

1674, the Dutch had turned the war around and forced a French evacuation from Utrecht and other towns. This strengthened the hand of the Orangists, and William and his supporters came down hard on those republicans who resisted his consolidation of powers. Whereas liberal regents and much of the merchant class wanted to end hostilities quickly and get back to the political and economic *status quo ante*, the Stadholder party insisted on continuing the war until France was finally defeated and taught a lesson. With the Orangists having their way in most matters political and military, and the Voetians enjoying a similar ascendancy in the theological domain, the rules of the game had changed considerably since 1670. There was no reason to think that simply by publishing a treatise anonymously one would be saved from a fate like that of the more brazen Koerbagh.

Despite the obvious risks he was taking, Spinoza felt confident and everything seemed to be on track during the summer of 1675. He stayed in Amsterdam for two weeks. But no sooner had Spinoza begun overseeing the production of his book than he abruptly stopped the printing. Back in The Hague by early September, he explained to Oldenburg, who had been pressing Spinoza to make public his writings for a long time, the reasons for his decision ultimately not to publish the *Ethics*:

While I was engaged in this business, a rumor became widespread that a certain book of mine about God was in the press, and that in it I endeavor to show that there is no God. This rumor found credence with many. So certain theologians who may have started this rumor seized the opportunity to complain of me before the Prince and the magistrates . . . Having gathered this from certain trustworthy men who also declared that the theologians were everywhere plotting against me, I decided to postpone the publication I had in hand until I should see how matters would turn out, intending to let you know what course I would then pursue. But the situation seems to worsen day by day, and I am not sure what to do about it.[31]

Part of what must have troubled Spinoza was the resolution against him issued by the consistory in his city of residence in June of that year. The Reformed leaders in The Hague had already

---

[31] Letter 68.

condemned the *Theological-Political Treatise* five years earlier. But this time their attack seemed more personal and ominous. At an ordinary gathering of the assembly, the members of the consistory, whose discussion was entered into the record of their proceedings under the simple label "Spinoza," noted that

as the consistory understands that the most blasphemous opinions of Spinoza are beginning to spread more and more, as much in this town as elsewhere, each of the members of this body is earnestly asked to see what they can learn about this, whether there is any other book by him that might happen to be in press, and what danger further lies here, in order to report back about it to this gathering and then, after a finding, to do something about it.[32]

Although this did not deter Spinoza from leaving for Amsterdam a month later with his plans to publish the *Ethics* intact, it must have weighed heavily upon his mind. More worrisome than the occasional broadside from the preachers, which he had come to expect, were, as his letter to Oldenburg indicates, the intimations that the secular authorities might, at the instigation of the theologians, be preparing to act once again. Spinoza was well served by his informants regarding the less-than-friendly murmurings about the content of his forthcoming book. From The Hague, Theodore Rijckius wrote to an influential friend on August 14 that

there is talk among us that the author of the *Tractatus Theologico-Politicus* is about to issue a book on God and the mind, one even more dangerous than the first. It will be the responsibility of you and those who, with you, are occupied with governing the Republic, to make sure that this book is not published. For it is incredible how much that man, who has striven to overthrow the principles of our most holy faith, has already harmed the Republic.[33]

If the point of publishing the *Theological-Political Treatise* before the *Ethics* had been to prepare the way for his extreme metaphysical and moral views by first setting out the arguments for freedom of philosophizing, Spinoza badly miscalculated. In fact, given Spinoza's distaste for controversy and his guarded character – the motto on his signet ring was *Caute*, "be cautious"

---

[32] Freudenthal 1899, pp. 147–8.    [33] Freudenthal 1899, p. 200.

– the *Treatise* in effect made the publication of the *Ethics* impossible in his lifetime. It would not appear in print until 1677, when his friends brought out his previously unpublished writings in Latin and Dutch posthumous editions, the *Opera posthuma* and *Nagelate Schriften.*

Throughout the years, as he moved from one place to the next, Spinoza continued to visit Amsterdam and, in turn, to receive visitors from his home town and elsewhere, including Oldenburg, De Vries, and Huygens. Among the guests in his lodgings in The Hague in 1676 was the philosopher Gottfried Wilhelm Leibniz, who was passing through the Netherlands on his way back to Germany after a sojourn of four years in Paris. While in France, Leibniz learned something of Spinoza's ideas from their mutual friend, Ehrenfried Walther von Tschirnhaus. Tschirnhaus, in fact, had brought a manuscript copy of the *Ethics* with him when he came to Paris from Amsterdam, with explicit orders not to show it to anyone without first asking Spinoza. Leibniz was anxious to see the work, and he had Tschirnhaus write to Spinoza to get permission to show it to him; Spinoza, unsure of Leibniz's motivations despite the fact that they had briefly corresponded some years earlier, said no. Still, Leibniz and Tschirnhaus clearly talked about the contents of the *Ethics*, and when Leibniz came to see Spinoza in The Hague, he took the opportunity to question Spinoza about his views on philosophical, political, and scientific topics. They met numerous times over the course of several weeks. Leibniz says that

I saw [Spinoza] while passing through Holland, and I spoke with him several times and at great length. He has a strange metaphysics, full of paradoxes. Among other things, he believes that the world and God are but a single substantial thing, that God is the substance of all things, and that creatures are only modes or accidents. But I noticed that some of his purported demonstrations, that he showed me, are not exactly right. It is not as easy as one thinks to provide true demonstrations in metaphysics.[34]

---

[34] Freudenthal 1899, p. 206.

Leibniz found his discussions with Spinoza immensely fruitful, and the contact between these two great thinkers of the seventeenth century was clearly of great consequence for Leibniz's own philosophical development.

The meetings with Leibniz, stimulating and pleasant as they were, distracted Spinoza from his work on what would be the last, albeit unfinished project of his short life. Spinoza must have begun the *Political Treatise* (*Tractatus Politicus*) no later than the middle of 1676. It is, in some respects, a sequel to the *Theological-Political Treatise*. If the 1670 treatise establishes the basic foundations and most general principles of civil society, regardless of the form which sovereignty takes in the state – whether it be a monarchy, an aristocracy, or a democracy – the new, more concrete work concerns more particularly how states of different constitutions can be made to function well. Spinoza also intended to show that, of all constitutions, the democratic one is to be preferred. No less than the *Theological-Political Treatise*, the composition of the *Political Treatise* is intimately related to the contemporary political scene in the Dutch Republic. Spinoza treats a number of universal political-philosophical themes with an immediate historical relevance, even urgency.

He had barely begun the section on democracy, however, when his health began to fail him. He seems to have suffered from respiratory ailments for most of his life. These were undoubtedly exacerbated by years of inhaling the glass dust produced by his lens-grinding. Although he took to his bed often during the winter of 1676–7, he was reportedly unprepared for the quickness of his decline; he did not even compose a will. According to Colerus's account of Spinoza's last day, which he learned about directly from the philosopher's landlord, neither Spinoza nor anyone else had a clue that he would not even last the afternoon.

When the landlord came home [from church] at around four o'clock [on the day before], Spinoza came downstairs from his room, smoked a pipe of tobacco and spoke with him for a long time, particularly about the sermon that was preached that afternoon. He went to bed soon afterwards in the forechamber, which was his to use and in which he slept. On Sunday morning, before church, he came downstairs again, speaking with his landlord and his wife. He had sent for a certain doctor L.M.

from Amsterdam [almost certainly Lodewijk Meyer], who ordered them to buy an old cock and to cook it up that morning, so that Spinoza might, that afternoon, have some broth, which he did. And when the landlord returned with his wife, he ate it with a good appetite. In the afternoon, the landlord's family went back to church, and Dr. L.M. stayed with him alone. But when they came back from church, they heard that Spinoza had died at around three o'clock, in the presence of the doctor, who just that evening returned to Amsterdam by nightboat, not even seeing to the care of the deceased.[35]

Spinoza died quietly on Sunday, February 21, 1677. He was buried four days later in the cemetery at the New Church, in The Hague.

---

[35] Freudenthal 1899, pp. 95–6.

# CHAPTER 2

# *The geometric method*

## SEARCH FOR A METHOD

The most striking thing that any reader approaching the *Ethics* for the first time notices is its unusual, even forbidding appearance. Rather than the even-flowing prose broken up into familiar paragraphs and organized into manageable chapters that one expects from a classic, reader-friendly treatise, one finds, instead, an intimidating array of definitions, axioms, propositions, demonstrations, and corollaries. It is almost as if one has stumbled upon a mathematical or scientific text rather than a philosophical masterpiece. Although it lacks the rigorous symbolic notation of the calculus, the *Ethics* nonetheless at first glance looks more like Newton's *Mathematical Principles of Natural Philosophy* than Descartes's *Meditations on First Philosophy* (all three were originally written in Latin).

It is not just neophytes who have been put off by the format of the *Ethics*. The famous French philosopher Henri Bergson, writing early in the twentieth century, insists that "the formidable apparatus of theorems and the tangle of definitions, corollaries, and scholia, this intricate machinery and this crushing power are such that the newcomer, in the presence of the *Ethics*, is struck with admiration and terror as if standing before an armored dreadnought."[1] More recently, one seasoned Spinoza scholar refers to the work's presentation as a "charmless apparatus of demonstrations,"[2] and suggests that Spinoza would have been better off without such an unnecessarily formal encumbrance.

---

[1] Bergson 1934, p. 142.    [2] Bennett 1984, p. 16.

In fact, Spinoza thought long and hard about how best to present his philosophical ideas. He experimented with different formats, and his writings exhibit a variety of well-worn styles, including direct exposition, dialogue, and autobiographical meditation. Around 1660, he began serious work on a full-scale treatment of his metaphysical, epistemological, and ethical ideas, the *Short Treatise on God, Man and His Well-Being*. The work was divided in the traditional way into parts and chapters. But by late 1662, Spinoza abandoned the treatise and started over again, this time with a completely new mode of presentation. What seems especially to have bothered him about the *Short Treatise* was the inadequacy of its relatively straightforward literary approach for making his ideas clear, orderly, and convincing. In fact, in the extant manuscript of the work is found an "Appendix," which contains a small number of the treatise's main metaphysical theses organized into formal propositions and demonstrations, prefaced by seven axioms. This represents Spinoza's first tentative steps toward adopting a more rigorous format, and were probably elements of an early draft of Part One of the *Ethics*.

His ultimate abandonment of the *Short Treatise* is foreshadowed in a letter from September 1661. Writing to his friend Henry Oldenberg, the corresponding secretary of the Royal Society in England, Spinoza speaks of his desire to establish with the utmost certainty the most basic truths about God and substance, and is at this time already insisting that "I can think of no better way of demonstrating these things clearly and briefly than to prove them in the geometric manner and subject them to your understanding" (Letter 2, G IV.8/ C I.166). Clearly, by this point Spinoza had come to the realization that the best way to go about communicating his ideas for maximum effect was to use the *mos geometricus*, the "geometrical method," or to present them, as the subtitle of the *Ethics* indicates, *ordine geometrico demonstrata*, "demonstrated in geometric order."

He was aware of the problems that this unusual format would cause for readers who are not used to seeing metaphysical and moral questions so treated. "It will doubtless seem strange that I should undertake to treat men's vices and absurdities in the geometric style" (E, III, Preface, G II.138/C I.492). Oldenberg himself – and this should provide some comfort to the modern reader struggling to make sense of the *Ethics* – after reading the brief, geometrically formatted sketch of some propositions drawn from the *Short Treatise* that Spinoza sent him in the September 1661 letter, found it difficult to figure out what Spinoza was trying to say. "I have received your very learned letter, and read it through with great pleasure. I approve very much your geometric style of proof, but at the same time I blame my own obtuseness that I do not follow so easily the things you teach exactly" (Letter 3, G IV.10/C I.168). Gottlieb Stolle, a German scholar of the early eighteenth century, even claimed that working with the geometric method was so taxing for Spinoza that it ruined his health and led to his early death.[3] This is, of course, nonsense, but it does create a touching picture of the heroic Spinoza, so committed to discovering the truth and, just as importantly, making it accessible and convincing to others that he is willing to sacrifice his own well-being in the struggle to meet an exacting standard. In a less romantic vein, whatever else one might say about the geometrical format, pro or con, one thing is certain: Spinoza's choice of it was not casual or accidental, but the result of a deliberate calculation.

The model for certain knowledge in the seventeenth century was mathematics. Its propositions or theses were clearly formulated, its demonstrations (when properly attended to) indubitable, and its methods (when properly employed) foolproof. Euclid's *Elements*, the most famous paradigm for the discipline, begins with twenty-three basic definitions ("A point is that which has no part," "A line is a breadthless point"), five postulates ("That all right angles are equal to one another,") and five "common notions" or axioms ("Things that are equal to the same thing are also equal to one another", "If equals be added to equals, the wholes are equal"). With these simple tools in hand as assumed premises, Euclid proceeds to prove a great number of propositions about plane figures and their properties, some of them extremely complex. (The first proposition of Book One, for example, lays out the method for constructing an equilateral triangle on a finite straight line; the fifth proposition states that in an isosceles triangle the angles at the base are equal to one

---

[3] Freudenthal 1899, pp. 224–8.

another. By Book Ten, he is demonstrating how to find two rational straight lines that are commensurable in square only.) The demonstration of each proposition uses – besides the definitions, postulates, and axioms – only propositions that have already been established. No unproven theorems are introduced into the demonstrations; nothing is presupposed except what is self-evident, accepted as a stipulation or demonstrably known. In this way, the results are guaranteed to be absolutely certain.

With this model in mind, Spinoza hoped to fulfill and even expand upon Descartes's own dream of maximum certainty in the sciences. Like his intellectual mentor, he thought that philosophy (understood broadly to include much that today would more properly fall under the natural and social sciences) could reach a degree of precision and indubitability that approximated if not equaled that achieved by mathematics. Spinoza wanted to do for metaphysics, epistemology, physics, psychology, and even ethics what Euclid had done for geometry. Only in this way could philosophy, the discipline that must prescribe for human beings the path to happiness and well-being, become truly systematic and its conclusions guaranteed to be valid. The means for accomplishing this goal was literally to put metaphysics and the other subjects in the exact same form in which Euclid had organized his material. As Spinoza proclaims in the preface to Part Three of the *Ethics*,

I shall treat the nature and powers of the Affects, and the power of the Mind over them, by the same Method by which, in the preceding parts, I treated God and the Mind, and I shall consider human actions and appetites just as if it were a Question of lines, planes, and bodies. (G II.138/C I.492)

Despite his passion for extending mathematical certainty to other disciplines, Descartes himself was not very fond of using the geometric order in non-mathematical domains. He is willing to do so to oblige his friend Marin Mersenne, who had asked him to "set out the entire argument [of the *Meditations*] in geometrical fashion." But Descartes notes that "I am convinced that it is the *Meditations*" – with their analytic, not synthetic or demonstrative, method – "which will yield by far the greater benefit."[4] Spinoza had a stronger

---

[4] Replies to the Second Set of Objections [to the *Meditations*], AT VII.159/CSM I.113.

faith in the "geometrical fashion" than Descartes did, and even went to the trouble of revising substantial parts of Descartes's *Principles of Philosophy* and present them *in ordine geometrico* to help himself tutor a young man and further the studies of his own friends in the Cartesian philosophy.

## PHILOSOPHICAL TRUTH AND GEOMETRICAL EXPOSITION

The *ordo geometricus* certainly does not represent the way and order in which Spinoza *discovered* his truths. It was not, that is, Spinoza's *method* of *doing* philosophy (as opposed to his method of presenting philosophical discoveries). To be sure, Spinoza did believe that the proper method of philosophical inquiry will yield necessary and indubitable results. For Spinoza, as for a good number of other philosophers in the period, the search for knowledge must be the search for absolutely certain truths by a systematic and proven method. Descartes, for example, defines 'method' as "reliable rules which are easy to apply, and such that if one follows them exactly, one will never take what is false to be true or fruitlessly expend one's mental efforts, but will gradually and constantly increase one's knowledge until one arrives at a true understanding of everything within one's capacity."[5] His method includes dividing a difficulty into parts and then proceeding in an orderly manner from knowledge of the simpler elements up to knowledge of the most complex. Similarly, Spinoza says that "the true method is the way that truth itself . . . should be sought in the proper order," according to "certain rules as aids," until one arrives at a knowledge of the "objective essences of things" (TIE, G II.15–16/C I.18–19).

But method should be distinguished from the ultimate form taken by the presentation of its results. Spinoza did not go about discovering his principles about God, the human being, and everything else by starting with a few definitions, axioms, and propositions and then seeing what he could deduce from them a priori. The theses of the *Ethics* may be capable of being organized into a purely deductive format, one that reveals the necessary connections between them. But that does not mean that one is to do philosophy

---

[5] *Rules for the Direction of the Mind*, AT X.372/CSM I.16.

just as one does mathematics. Rather, what Spinoza believed was that, at the very least, with the geometric format the products of rule-guided philosophical inquiry could be convincingly presented, with maximum persuasive force and (ideally) leaving no room for reasonable dissent. For no one who accepts the starting points of an argument and then fully grasps the subsequent steps of a rigorous, geometric-like proof could possibly deny the conclusion. The clarity and distinctness of presentation would reveal the truths of metaphysics, psychology, and ethics in a perspicuous and convincing manner.

Does this mean that the geometric format, however valuable it may be for what it can accomplish, is still nothing for Spinoza but a mere manner of presentation, a kind of rhetorical flourish? Could Spinoza just as well have used some other, non-Euclidean format in the *Ethics*? We know that he favored the *mos geometricus* for its perspicuity and persuasiveness, for its ability to show convincingly how one thing follows from another and its efficiency in leading one to a clear and distinct perception of the truth. Having alighted upon the geometrical order and thus abandoning the *Short Treatise* to begin anew with the *Ethics*, Spinoza all but confesses that he found it to be the superior format for making known his ideas. But is that all that recommended it to him? Is there no necessary connection between *what* Spinoza is saying in the work and *how* he is saying it?

This is certainly a possibility. One could argue that the geometrical format is nothing but synthetic window-dressing for ideas that could have – and, some insist, *should* have – been offered in another manner. Indeed, one prominent Spinoza scholar argues that there is no meaningful relationship whatsoever between form and content in the *Ethics*. "There is no logical connection between the substance of Spinoza's philosophy and the form in which it is written, his choice of the Euclidean geometrical form is to be explained on other grounds." What those other grounds are, on this reading, amounts to nothing but a pedagogical choice: "to delineate the main features of an argument and to bring them into high relief. [The geometrical method] was used for the same reason that one uses outlines and diagrams."[6] The *mos geometricus* is thus only a teaching or communicating device, an extrinsic garb that can be used for expositing any

---

[6] Wolfson 1934, 55. See also Joachim 1901, p. 12.

number of philosophies (as Spinoza surely knew, having himself once dressed Descartes's philosophy in it).

On the other hand, one could argue that there is in fact a close, even *necessary* relationship between Spinoza's subject matter and the format in which he presents it, such that the geometric model is the only one suitable for conveying his ideas. On this interpretation, Spinoza's philosophy *demands* that it be written in the form in which it appears in the *Ethics*, as Spinoza himself discovered in abandoning the *Short Treatise*.[7]

The argument for such an essential relationship between form and content in the *Ethics* must rely on a distinctive and important feature of Spinoza's thought: his necessitarianism. As we shall see, for Spinoza there is no contingency in Nature. Everything is necessitated by causes to be such as it is. Moreover, Spinoza claims that the causal determinism that governs all things in Nature derives "from above," as it were, from Nature's eternal and infinite principles (i.e., from God). All beings in Nature – and there is nothing that is not a part of Nature – follow with an absolute, indeed geometrical necessity from God (or Nature).

> I think I have shown clearly enough that from God's supreme power, or infinite nature, infinitely many things in infinitely many modes, i.e., all things, have necessarily flowed, or always follow, by the same necessity and in the same way as from the nature of a triangle it follows, from eternity and to eternity, that its three angles are equal to two right angles.
> (E, IP17s)

This being the case, the argument runs, it would seem that Spinoza has no real choice in how to present his philosophy. If he wants to exhibit the strictly mathematical necessity that (he claims) governs reality and show that all things "flow" from God, he must employ a geometrically formatted series of demonstrations that reveal the logically necessary connections that unite (in the proper order) propositions about those things with propositions about God. If things in Nature really do follow from God just as the properties of a geometric figure follow from the nature of that figure, then the

---

[7] See Gueroult 1968, 15. Gueroult insists that the "geometric prolixity" of the *Ethics* forms a unity with its doctrines and captures Spinoza's conception of adequate knowledge, a centerpiece of the work.

geometric method applied to metaphysics, physics, and human nature would seem to be uniquely qualified for Spinoza's purposes.

This view of the relationship between geometric order and philosophical ideas is a much more interesting and potentially fruitful way of looking at Spinoza's use of the *ordo geometricus* than the one that sees only a extrinsic connection between the two. It is also a more plausible reading. Since we know that Spinoza gave a good deal of attention to *how* he should communicate his ideas, it is highly unlikely that his adoption of the geometric mode of presentation for his philosophy bears no connection whatsoever with the content of that philosophy, a philosophy whose central metaphysical doctrine is the geometrical necessity that governs Nature itself. Indeed, Spinoza explicitly tells us that the goal of philosophical method is to make the order and connection of ideas in the mind mirror the order and connection of things in reality. This means that one must arrive in one's thought at a proper alignment of truths, and especially perceive the logical dependence that some truths have on others (representing the causal dependence that their objects have on other things).

As for order, to unite and order all our perceptions, it is required, and reason demands, that we ask, as soon as possible, whether there is a certain being, and at the same time, what sort of being it is, which is the cause of all things, so that its objective essence may also be the cause of all our ideas, and then our mind will . . . reproduce Nature as much as possible. For it will have Nature's essence, order, and unity objectively.
(TIE, G II.36/C I.41)

Thus there does indeed seem to be an intimate relationship between form and content in the *Ethics*. The *ordo geometricus* is not just a convenient and particularly persuasive way for Spinoza to present his ideas. If, as Spinoza tells us, Nature is ordered with mathematical necessity, then so must our ideas also be ordered with mathematical necessity. For the most part, a person originally acquires ideas about things haphazardly, by the uncritical means of the senses and everyday experience. The geometric format of the *Ethics* is, by the force of its reasoning, supposed to lead the reader to the correct re-arrangement of his ideas so that they, in their new, geometrically rigorous connections, match up with the order of reality itself. One who follows the work's arguments carefully will experience the kind of emendative therapy for the mind that one recent scholar has seen as an important function of the geometric method.[8]

I would like, however, to suggest a slight but significant modification to this way of reading the format of the *Ethics*, one that should be regarded as a friendly amendment to the interpretation. I would not go so far as to insist that Spinoza's thought *demands* or *necessitates* a literally Euclidean style. Rather, I would say instead that his philosophy finds its most adequate (but not necessarily only) expression in that mode of presentation. The system elaborated in the *Ethics* requires that the reader come to see the quasi-mathematical necessity inherent among things, and especially the way all things depend on God or Nature. It thus demands that the deductive connections among its truths (mirroring the chain of causes in Nature) be clearly exhibited. While the *ordo geometricus* is especially well suited for this purpose, there is no necessary reason why that format is the only way to convey this information.[9]

Despite the difficulty of the work and the forbidding character of its style, Spinoza clearly believed that anyone – and we are all endowed with the same cognitive faculties – with sufficient self-mastery and intellectual attentiveness can perceive the truth to the highest degree. We may think that the geometric format gets in the way of this goal. Spinoza thought that it brought it closer to realization.

THE ELEMENTS

Like Euclid in the thirteen books of his *Elements*, Spinoza begins each part of the *Ethics* with a set of definitions and axioms. These are followed by a series of propositions and their respective demonstrations. The demonstration of each proposition relies only on the definitions, axioms, and already demonstrated propositions that precede it. Thus, the first proposition of Part One is supposed to

---

[8] See Garrett 2003.
[9] See Allison 1987, pp. 42–3, for a discussion of this more moderate way of seeing the relationship between philosophical content and geometric form in the *Ethics*.

follow only from two of the definitions of Part One, while proposition five is demonstrated through definition three, axiom six, and propositions one and four. This is intended to guarantee that each proposition is established on a solid foundation, without the importation of any unproven claims and unwarranted assumptions that might weaken its argument. There are also corollaries to many of the propositions, each requiring its own separate demonstration, as well as more discursive scholia meant to explain or comment upon the subject at hand. Let us look at each of these elements in turn to discover the role that it plays in Spinoza's overall project.

## Definitions

The definitions are the bedrock of Spinoza's system. They lay down the basic elements of his ontology, or theory of what there is (for example, God, substance, attribute, mode); they explain the items of his theory of knowledge and psychology (idea, affect); they indicate the natures of some of the relations in which those basic things can stand to each other (cause, "conceived through"); and they give the reader an understanding of the general characteristics that may belong to them (infinite, eternal, free, good, evil).

The definitions also serve a dynamic function. They provide the impulse that puts the machine into motion and they are a part of the grease that allows it to keep going. The definitions are the initial point of departure for Spinoza's overall argument, and make it possible for the demonstrations to get started in the first place; without the definitions, proposition one of Part One could never be established. And they are used, along with already demonstrated propositions, in the demonstrations of subsequent propositions.

A definition delineates the essence of a thing – what it is to be a substance; what it is to be a cause, etc. It allows one to deduce the properties that necessarily belong to its object. "We require a concept, or definition, of the thing such that when it is considered alone, without any others conjoined, all the thing's properties can be deduced from it" (TIE, G II.35/C I.40).[10] From the definition of a

---

[10] See also IP16; and Letter 83.

circle, one can deduce that all the lines drawn from the center to the circumference are equal. From the definition of substance, it must be possible to derive all the properties (eternity, infinitude, uniqueness, existence) that necessarily belong to any substance.

In order to do this kind of work, a definition must spell out its content in a perspicuous manner using accessible terms. It must, above all, be clear and conceivable. "A bad definition," Spinoza says in a letter to his friend Simon Joosten de Vries around 1663, "is one that is not conceived" (Letter 9, G IV.44/C I.194). Definitions must also be relatively simple and basic – simple and basic, that is, relative to the rest of the system. Understanding a definition must not require appealing to any subsequent elements in the system; Spinoza cannot employ in his definitions in Part One terms that are themselves not defined until Part Two.

There are two ways to think about what the status of a definition is. On the one hand, a definition can be purely stipulative, a kind of convention or setup about what something is to mean in a given context. The definitions of words, and most obviously technical terms, are like this. When Euclid says that "a point is that which has no part" or "a line is a breadthless length," he can be read as meaning something like the following: "for my purposes, this is how I shall understand the term." On this conception of definition, it makes no sense to ask whether the definition is true or false. A stipulative definition can, in fact, be purely arbitrary. It simply is to be taken as an explication of the term being defined. The only requirement is that in the subsequent context the term is used consistently.

On the other hand, a definition may purport to describe the way something really is in itself. This is the case with definitions of things, as opposed to definitions of words. Understood in this way, definitions are indeed bearers of truth value. The definition of a dog or a lion will be true just in case it accurately captures what a dog or a lion really is. While stipulative or "nominal" definitions are free and self-contained, so to speak, and do not pretend to be anything other than a kind of agreement that fixes what the meaning of a term will be, "real" definitions are intended to be accurate representations of things that, while not necessarily actually existing – the unicorn has a definition – are objective beings with a reality outside and independent of the definition itself.

What is the status of Spinoza's definitions in the *Ethics*? Are they real or are they nominal? When Spinoza offers his definition of 'substance' or 'cause,' is he saying that this is what a substance or a cause truly is, and anyone who thinks otherwise is wrong? Or is he instead saying "let us assume, for the sake of argument and without caring whether it really is in fact the case, that a substance is such and such, and a cause is such and such"?

Spinoza is quite aware of the distinction between the two different kinds of definitions, as is clear in the letter that he wrote to De Vries. De Vries, who was a member of the "Spinoza circle" in Amsterdam that was working through a draft of early parts of the *Ethics*, had asked Spinoza to clarify for the reading group how they should understand his definitions. "We did not agree about the nature of definition," De Vries writes, and they are especially confused as to whether a definition needs to be certain and true or can be arbitrary and even false (Letter 8). Spinoza replies that "you are in these perplexities because you do not distinguish between different kinds of definition – between one which serves to explain a thing whose essence only is sought, as the only thing there is doubt about, and one which is proposed only to be examined. For because the former has a determinate object, it ought to be true. But the latter does not require this." For example, he continues, if someone were to ask for a definition of Solomon's temple, one ought to reply with a true description, one that accurately depicts Solomon's structure. On the other hand, if one is simply forming for oneself the idea of a temple one wants to build, then it would not make any sense to complain that the conception is false. In such a case, one may validly draw all kinds of conclusions from one's "definition" – such as how much wood and stone one would have to purchase in order to build such a temple – even though the conception itself has no basis in reality.

Will anyone in his right mind tell me that I have drawn a bad conclusion because I have perhaps used a false definition? Or will anyone require me to prove my definition? To do so would be to tell me that I have not conceived what I have conceived, or to require me to prove that I have conceived what I have conceived. Surely this is trifling.

He concludes that "a definition either explains a thing as it is [in itself] outside the intellect – and then it ought to be true . . . or else it explains a thing as we conceive it or can conceive it – and then it . . . need not, like an axiom, be conceived as true" (Letter 9, G IV.42–3/ C I.194).

On the face of it, one might think that Spinoza's definitions are of the nominal and arbitrary variety. Most of them begin with the locution "By *x*, I understand . . .", making it seem as though Spinoza is simply stipulating what the meaning of each term is to be, without implying that this is either a true definition or how others understand it. As he says to De Vries, with regard to his definition of substance in Part One, "I say that this definition explains clearly enough what I wish to understand by substance, or attribute" (Letter 9, G IV.45/C I.195). Moreover, in the letter he seems particularly concerned to show that the validity of the conclusions that one draws from a definition (functioning as a premise: "Let us build a temple of such and such dimensions") is not affected by the fact that the definition is arbitrary or even false. Perhaps, then, we should look at the entire structure of the *Ethics* as simply Spinoza's attempt to show what can be derived from some basic but not necessarily true starting points.

And yet, I believe it is fairly clear that Spinoza does not look at the matter this way. He does not take himself only to be showing what are the extended implications of a number of stipulated but not necessarily true definitions. On the contrary, he sees the *Ethics* as laying out the truth. The book is about reality: its nature, its structure, its operations, and the implications of these for human happiness. In Part One, he is not just saying: "If you will assume for the sake of argument that this is what 'substance,' 'God' and 'attribute' are, then it will follow that God is the only substance and is identical with Nature." Rather, he is saying: "This is how 'substance,' 'God' and 'attribute' *should* be understood, if defined truly; and therefore it is the case that God is the only substance and is identical with Nature."

Naturally, one will want to know *how* Spinoza can be so sure – and, more importantly, how he can persuade us – that these definitions are true. Because they are definitions, he does not immediately provide any arguments for them. One possibility is that the definitions are "proven" by their consequences. Spinoza believes that one acquires greater knowledge of a cause by coming to a greater knowledge of its effects: "Knowledge of the effect is nothing but acquiring a more perfect knowledge of its cause" (TIE, G II.34/C I.39). Thus, the more one sees how much follows from a given set of definitions, which in Spinoza's argument function as causes, and especially how much of reality they can explain, the greater is one's knowledge of those starting points.

Ultimately, however, Spinoza seems not to be troubled by the epistemological worry of how to justify his definitions. In this regard, he is different from Descartes, who believed he needed to validate his clear and distinct ideas by appealing to the benevolence and veracity of the God who created him with his faculty of thinking. For Spinoza, the truth of a true definition, like the truth of any true idea, is something that it wears on its sleeve. "He who has a true idea at the same time knows that he has a true idea, and cannot doubt the truth of the thing" (E, IIP43). It seems that Spinoza thinks that the definitions are self-evidently true.

### Axioms

The axioms that Spinoza provides at the beginning of Parts One, Two, Four, and Five of the *Ethics* are, like all axioms, general principles about things. These fundamental and abstract statements express common ontological and epistemological truths. Although, given their broad scope, the axioms apply to all particulars that fall under them, Spinoza is elsewhere careful to warn that from an axiom alone one cannot derive any particular truth about the existence and nature of an individual thing. "From universal axioms alone the intellect cannot descend to singulars, since axioms extend to infinity, and do not determine the intellect to the contemplation of one singular thing rather than another" (TIE, G II.34/C I.39).

While Spinoza says that the axioms include "eternal truths" (Letter 9, G IV.43/C I.194), it is clear that not all of them have this exalted status. Some of the axioms are indeed a priori principles; others, however, are simply matters of fact. A number of the axioms seem to be governed by logic alone: "Whatever is, is either in itself or in another" (IA1), "What cannot be conceived through another must be conceived through itself" (IA2). Others appear to derive immediately from experience: "Man thinks" (IIA2), "We feel that a certain body is affected in many ways" (IIA4), "Each body moves now more slowly, now more quickly" (IIA2′). There are axioms that offer insight into some basic metaphysical categories – "From a given determinate cause the effect follows necessarily" (IA3), "If a thing can be conceived as not existing, its essence does not involve existence" (IA7) – as well as axioms that specify the requirements of knowledge: "A true idea must agree with its object" (IA6). Some axioms even state basic laws of nature: "If two contrary actions are aroused in the same subject, a change will have to occur, either in both of them, or in one only, until they cease to be contrary" (VA1).

While foundational for the purposes of Spinoza's deductive demonstrations of his propositions, axioms are not necessarily as basic as the definitions. In fact, the axioms sometimes seem to require the definitions. An axiom from Part Two, for example, "All bodies either move or are at rest" (IIA1′), certainly depends on the definition of 'body' that Spinoza offers at the beginning of that part.

Unlike definitions, which Spinoza concedes in principle may or may not be true, an axiom must be true. For the purposes of demonstration, it may not make much difference whether or not one sees the truth of a definition, as long as one accepts it as a starting assumption; but it certainly does make a difference whether or not one sees the truth of an axiom. As Spinoza insists, again to De Vries, "[a definition] differs from an axiom and a proposition in that it need only be conceived, without further condition, and need not, like an axiom [and a proposition] be conceived as true" (Letter 9, G IV.43/C I.194). There are no stipulative or nominal axioms. To accept an axiom is to accept it as a truth.

Spinoza also believes that the truth of an axiom is not something that requires independent proof, but should be evident to any sufficiently attentive mind. That is to say, an axiom is self-evident, indubitable on its own terms. No one who gives proper consideration to an axiom and its constituent items can reasonably deny it. This may mark another possible difference from definitions, which, as we have seen, can acquire support from the consequences derived from them.

One wonders, though, whether the distinction between definition and axiom is sometimes arbitrary. For example, why could not definition eight of Part One – "By eternity I understand existence itself, insofar as it is conceived to follow necessarily from the definition alone of the eternal thing" – have been expressed as an axiom: "If the existence of a thing can be conceived to follow necessarily from its definition, then that thing is eternal"? Is it because Spinoza regards such a definition of eternity as potentially contentious, and thus not endowed with the self-evidence of an axiom?

## Propositions

The propositions of the *Ethics* are the meat of the system. They are the substantive philosophical conclusions – about God, Nature, and the human being – that Spinoza hopes to establish. The variety and number of propositions in the work is remarkable. There are 259 of them (not counting corollaries) and they range over ontology, epistemology, psychology, political philosophy, and ethics. They are also highly original and, to his Cartesian and other contemporary readers, very unorthodox. Spinoza may have thought that the definitions and axioms are self-evident to the attentive and rational mind, but he most certainly did not believe this to be true of the propositions as well.

Each proposition is essentially a theorem stating a basic, relatively simple (but by no means easily interpretable) claim. "Except God, no substance can be or be conceived" (IP14). "The first thing that constitutes the actual being of a human mind is nothing but the idea of a singular thing which actually exists" (IIP11). "A desire that arises from reason cannot be excessive" (IVP61). Some of the propositions seem eminently plausible, either philosophically ("The essence of things produced by God does not involve existence" [IP24]) or empirically, from ordinary experience ("He who imagines that what he hates is destroyed will rejoice" [IIIP20]; "Love and desire can be excessive" [IVP44]). Other propositions are wildly counterintuitive and require a lot of explaining ("Whatever is, is in God, and nothing can be or be conceived without God" [IP15]).

Every proposition is accompanied by a demonstration, which is supposed to establish its truth. (The proposition, once demonstrated, is also thereby now fit to be used as a premise in the demonstrations of subsequent propositions.) Some are also followed by corollaries – closely related theorems and their respective demonstrations – and scholia, more informal discussions in which Spinoza, often in a fit of clarity, elaborates on particular themes outside the rubric of "our cumbersome Geometric order" (IVP18s). A good deal of interesting, important and accessible philosophical material is found in the scholia, as well as in the appendices that follow Parts One, Three, and Four of the work. It is in these that the reader can often find a good clue as to what Spinoza is really getting at.

These, then, are the elements of Spinoza's deductive system. By the end of the work, all of Spinoza's propositions are, through their respective demonstrations, to be taken as established not just with a high degree of probability, but with absolute and objective certainty. Spinoza does not pretend to offer merely a valid argument for an internally consistent set of claims. Rather, he believes that the *Ethics* represents a sound argument for what is the philosophical truth.

Although the geometric format serves well to capture the rigorously deductive nature of Spinoza's reasoning, it should not be mistaken for an a priori argument. Many of the elements, as I have noted, have an empirical origin, either in the senses or in the imagination; and it certainly should not be thought that Spinoza believed that he could logically deduce the actual state of the world at a given time from his first principles alone. As we shall see throughout this study, Spinoza's use of the *ordo geometricus* also gives rise to some pressing philosophical questions about what Spinoza is in fact entitled to claim to have proven.

# CHAPTER 3

# On God: substance

Writing in the *Treatise on the Emendation of the Intellect,* Spinoza says that our well-being and happiness, indeed our ultimate perfection, consists in a certain state of knowing. Above all, we need to understand ourselves and the nature and powers of the human mind. But, he insists, this will come about only when we understand the natural order of which we are indelibly a part, and especially the highest causes from which all things bodily and spiritual follow.

> Since it is clear through itself that the mind understands itself the better, the more it understands of Nature, it is evident from that that this part of the Method will be more perfect as the mind understands more things, and will be most perfect when the mind attends to or reflects on knowledge of the most perfect Being. (TIE, G II.16/C I.19)

The highest good for a human being is the knowledge of God and Nature.[1]

Establishing this conclusion with demonstrative certainty is the main project of the *Ethics.* And in Part One, Spinoza takes the first step of his project by proving the most general and important metaphysical truths about God and Nature. His startling conclusion is that, in fact, God and Nature are one and the same thing. Rather than speaking of 'God and Nature,' as if they are distinct, we should in fact speak of 'God or Nature,' *Deus sive Natura,* where the two words are simply different ways of referring to one subject. This

---

[1] In this book, I will use "Nature" (upper case) when referring to what Spinoza identifies as God, that is, the universe considered as a necessarily existing, infinite, eternal substance; I will use "nature" (lower case) when referring to what we ordinarily think of as nature, that is, the items and processes that take place in the empirical world around us, which Spinoza will claim is brought about by Nature and exists at the level of its "modes."

controversial, even (to his contemporaries) incendiary phrase, which appears in the Latin (but not the more accessible Dutch vernacular) posthumous edition of his writings, would confound and incite Spinoza's readers for centuries, as they sought to understand just what exactly he means by this identification. Is he saying that God is the whole of Nature? Is God only certain universal aspects of Nature? Is God somehow hidden within Nature but nonetheless distinct from it, as certain mystics might claim? Spinoza's partisans and critics seem to have found it especially difficult to determine whether what Spinoza is offering is a devious atheism, with God reduced to nothing more than Nature, or the most pious theism of Western philosophy, where God is to be found everywhere. While his contemporary ecclesiastic opponents opted for the former reading and condemned him for blasphemy, the Romantics would favor the latter and see him as a kindred spirit. The German poet Novalis, for example, called Spinoza "a God-intoxicated man"; to Goethe, Spinoza was *theissimus*.

Part One is perhaps the most difficult portion of the *Ethics*, not the least because of its technical vocabulary. Its crucial first fifteen propositions are where Spinoza presents the basic elements of his picture of God. Essentially, Spinoza's goal in IP1–15 is to establish that God is the unique, infinite, necessarily existing (that is, self-caused) substance of the universe. There is only one substance in the universe; it is God; and everything else that is, is "in" God. We will see that, although its metaphysical conclusions are abstruse and the particular demonstrations for the propositions highly challenging, the overall argument of IP1–15 is, in fact, quite simple and elegant.

## SUBSTANCE, ATTRIBUTE, AND MODE

The definitions with which Spinoza begins Part One constitute the fundamental metaphysical language of his philosophy. Some of the definitions are idiosyncratic, and thus it is important to understand the particular way in which he will be employing the terms being defined, although the full meaning and implications of each definition do not really appear until they are put to use in the subsequent propositions.

Definition Three is about substance (*substantia*), the most basic metaphysical category of all and one that would be familiar to his contemporary philosophical readers:

By substance I understand what is in itself and is conceived through itself, i.e., that whose concept does not require the concept of another thing, from which it must be formed.

The notion of substance goes back to ancient Greek philosophy. Aristotle, whose own conception of substance would be of enormous influence in the history of philosophy, defined it as the ultimate subject of predication which is itself not predicated of anything, or that to which properties belong but which is itself not a property of something else. A substance, in this primary sense, is basically a self-subsisting individual thing. "A substance – that which is called a substance most strictly, primarily, and most of all – is that which is neither said of a subject nor in a subject, e.g., the individual man or the individual horse . . . a primary substance is neither said of a subject nor in a subject."[2] We predicate things of a horse – that it is strong, or large, or grey – but we do not predicate the horse itself of anything. Aristotle also defines a substance as that which underlies and persists throughout all changes, just as an individual human being is at one time pale and another time (after lounging in the sun) dark.

Descartes, who is Spinoza's most proximate and influential source for his metaphysical framework, inherits the logical and ontological aspects of substance in the Aristotelian conception. A substance for Descartes is the subject and sustainer of properties that is not itself the property of something else. The term substance, he says, applies to "every thing in which whatever we perceive immediately resides, as in a subject, or to every thing by means of which whatever we perceive [properties, qualities, etc.] exists."[3] Descartes often seems more concerned, however, with the fact that a substance is what is self-subsistent: "By substance we can understand nothing other than a thing which exists in such a way as to depend on no other thing for

[2] *Categories* 2a10, 3a5.
[3] Replies to the Second Set of Objections, AT VII.161/CSM II.114.

its existence."[4] For Descartes, this means that, strictly speaking, only God is a substance, since only God has the requisite absolute ontological independence: God depends on nothing for His existence, while all other things depend on God for their continued existence. Descartes is, however, willing to grant that finite, created things (such as the human soul) are substances in an "equivocal" or secondary sense, since they "need only the concurrence of God in order to exist."[5]

When Spinoza defines a substance as that which is "in itself," he is clearly employing the self-subsistence criterion of substance. A substance is that which is truly ontologically independent, and that is not in or dependent upon something else for its being. It is, in a word, an individual thing in the truest sense. To use an example that Spinoza himself would ultimately, once the full implications of his definition are clear, have to reject, an individual horse can be seen as a substance because its being is independent of the being of any other creature. (By contrast, the color of the horse cannot exist by itself, without a subject in which to inhere, but is dependent upon the thing whose color it is.) Spinoza also introduces in his definition an epistemological or conceptual component that corresponds to the ontological requirement: a substance is that which can be conceived or understood on its own terms, without any appeal to the concept of anything else. If $x$ is a substance, then one can have a complete idea of $x$ – one that tells me exactly and fully what $x$ is and why it is as it is – without needing also to have an idea of some other substance $y$. The content of my concept of $x$ does not include or refer to the concept of any substance $y$. Again, to use what will ultimately prove to be an un-Spinozistic example, I can have a complete concept of any particular horse without having to think of some other horse, or tree, or human being, or any substantial thing.

The example of the horse is un-Spinozistic because Spinoza will go on to say that in fact God is the only substance. In doing so, he is drawing out the full implications of his Cartesian understanding of

[4] *Principles of Philosophy* I.51.
[5] *Principles of Philosophy* I.52.

substance. In effect, he is saying to Descartes: I agree that a substance is essentially what exists in such a way that it depends on nothing else for its existence; but then, as you yourself admit, strictly speaking only God is a substance; and I, in order to be fully consistent, refuse to concede to finite things even a secondary or deficient kind of substantiality.

Definition Four concerns what Spinoza calls 'attributes': "By attribute I understand what the intellect perceives of a substance as constituting its essence." An attribute is the most general and underlying nature of a thing. It is the thing's principal property – or, better, the nature that underlies all of its properties. Descartes had claimed that the attribute of mind or spiritual substance is thought or thinking, and the attribute of body or material substance is extension or three-dimensionality. The attribute of a substance, as its essence, is the determinable nature of which all of the particular properties of the thing are determinate manifestations. Thought is a determinable nature of which particular thoughts or ideas are determinate expressions. Extension is a determinable nature of which particular shapes or figures are determinate expressions. To speak of the attribute of a substance is to refer to the most general *kind* of thing that it is. In fact, the attribute is so important for making a substance what it is in the most basic sense that if two substances have different attributes, then, as Spinoza states in IP2, they have absolutely nothing in common with each other – neither as the kinds of things they are nor (since all of a thing's properties are simply determinations of its attribute) through their properties.

Two questions are raised by Spinoza's definition of attribute. The first question is whether there is a real distinction between substance and attribute. Is the substance some natureless thing or substratum underlying the attribute, or is it simply the attribute itself? The definition makes it seem as if substance is some featureless *x* to which the attribute belongs. The thinking substance, or *res cogitans* (Descartes's "thinking thing") would then be some unqualified and inaccessible *res* beneath the *cogitans*. Descartes himself is sometimes not clear about this. He does, at one point, suggest that the substance is the underlying subject for the attribute: "In addition to the attribute which specifies the substance, one must think of the substance itself which is the substrate of that attribute."[6] His considered position, however, is that while there is a *conceptual* distinction between substance and attribute (I can conceive separately what it is to be a substance and what it is to be an attribute), there is not a *real* distinction between them. Substance and attribute are in reality one and the same – the *res cogitans* is not *res* + *cogitans*, but rather *cogitans* itself considered as a *res*. "Thought and extension . . . must . . . be considered as nothing else but thinking substance itself and extended substance itself."[7] The thinking nature *is* thinking substance; extension or material nature *is* matter, the extended substance.

Spinoza, too, identifies a substance with its attribute. In the *Ethics*, he says that "there is nothing outside the intellect through which a number of things can be distinguished from one another except *substances or, what is the same, their attributes*, and their affections" (IP4d, my italics). In an early letter (1661), Spinoza defines 'attribute' in the same epistemological terms that will form a part of the definition of 'substance' in the *Ethics*: "By attribute I understand whatever is conceived through itself and in itself, so that the conception of it does not involve the conception of another thing" (Letter 2, G IV.7/C I.165). In another letter a few years later, in 1663, after he had begun work on the *Ethics*, Spinoza confirms that the more extended *Ethics* definition of substance, now including not just epistemological independence but ontological independence as well, is also applicable to attribute.

By substance I understand what is in itself and is conceived through itself, i.e., whose concept does not involve the concept of another thing. I understand the same by attribute, except that it is called attribute in relation to the intellect, which attributes such and such a definite nature to substance. (Letter 9, G IV.45/C I.195)

The words 'substance' and 'attribute,' he insists in this letter, are two names for the same thing, just as the names 'Israel' and 'Jacob' refer to the same Biblical individual. Each name simply stresses a different feature of the thing named: 'substance' refers to its ontological

---

[6] "Conversation with Burman," §25.
[7] *Principles of Philosophy* I.63.

status, its "thing-hood," while 'attribute' refers to the fact that it has a distinctive character or nature.

The second question raised by Spinoza's definition of attribute is not so easy to resolve. Notice that in the definition, Spinoza speaks of "what the intellect perceives of a substance, as constituting its essence." This has led some commentators to believe that the attribute is not itself a real thing or nature, but rather simply a way of perceiving things. This "subjectivist" reading of 'attribute' would make an attribute nothing more than a perspective upon reality, and not a real ontological feature of reality itself. By contrast, according to the "objectivist" reading, attributes are real aspects of the world, not merely conceptual projections onto it. Things in Nature, on this realist account, truly are distinguished by their different natures. At this point, the question of the status of attributes and the debate between the subjectivist and objectivist readings can only be suggested; a more thorough discussion and proposed resolution will have to wait until we are further along in the examination of Spinoza's metaphysics.

The third category of Spinoza's ontology is 'mode.' ID5 states: "By mode I understand the affections of a substance, or that which is in another through which it is also conceived." A mode or affection of a substance is like the property of a thing. It is a particular and determinate way in which the thing exists. The exact shape and size of an individual human body are modes (or modifications) of that body; specific thoughts or ideas in the human mind are modes of that mind. As such, the modes of a thing are concrete manifestations of the attribute or nature constituting the thing. They therefore cannot be conceived without also conceiving the attribute or nature that underlies them. One cannot understand the circularity of a ball without conceiving what it is to be a circle (or extended in a circular way), which in turn cannot be understood without conceiving what it is to be extended, or what extension itself is. In this way, the meaning of IP1 – "A substance is prior in nature to its affections" – becomes clear. What Spinoza has in mind in this, the first proposition of the work, are both the ontological and the epistemological priority of substance over its modes, since modes are dependent upon the substance to which they belong for their being and their being understood.

Two other elements in Spinoza's preliminary materials of Part One need to be highlighted here. First, there is the claim made in IA3 that

From a given determinate cause the effect follows necessarily; and conversely, if there is no determinate cause, it is impossible for an effect to follow.

The second part of this axiom is simply a claim of universal causality: nothing happens without a determinate cause; there are no spontaneous or uncaused events.[8] The first part of the axiom represents *causal necessitarianism*: the relationship between a cause and its effect is a necessary one. In fact, Spinoza's claim here, as we shall see, will turn out to be quite strong. He believes that the necessity that is found between a cause and its effect is a *logical* necessity. If $x$ is the cause of $y$, then if $x$ occurs it is logically impossible that $y$ not occur.

Second, there is the all-important IA4: "The knowledge of an effect depends on, and involves, the knowledge of its cause." This is the principle of *causal rationalism*. To know something, to have a true and adequate conception of it, is to understand how it came about and why it is as it is and not otherwise. That is, to know something is to know its aetiological history, to have a sufficient explanation of it in causal terms. This axiom plays a crucial role throughout the *Ethics*, as Spinoza will go on to claim that obtaining the most perfect knowledge of things in the world around us – the knowledge that is the key to our well-being – involves knowing their higher causes in Nature, up to and including God itself.

## "THERE CANNOT BE TWO OR MORE SUBSTANCES OF THE SAME NATURE" (IP5)

The first fourteen propositions of Part One are meant to establish that God – an infinite, necessary, uncaused, indivisible being – is the only substance of the universe. The overall argument is stunning in its economy and efficiency, with the simple and elegant beauty

---

[8] It would seem that this claim is evidence that Spinoza subscribes to the principle of sufficient reason; but for a critical discussion of this, see Carraud 2002, chapter 3.

peculiar to a well-crafted logical deduction. First, Spinoza will establish that there cannot be two or more substances having the same nature or attribute (IP1–5). Then, he will prove that there necessarily is a substance with infinite (i.e., all possible) attributes, namely (by definition) God (IP6–11). It follows, in conclusion, that the existence of that infinite substance precludes the existence of any other substance. For if there *were* to be a second substance, it would have to have *some* attribute or essence. But since God has *all* possible attributes, then the attribute to be possessed by this second substance would be one of the attributes already possessed by God. But it has already been established that no two substances can have the same attribute. Therefore, there can be, besides God, no such second substance (IP14).

The first key premise of the argument is IP5: "In nature there cannot be two or more substances of the same nature or attribute." If there is a substance having a certain nature, *a*, then there cannot be any other substance having *a* as its nature. In other words, there cannot be two substances of the kind *a*.

On the face of it, this seems odd. We would ordinarily think that there can be many things of the same kind – for example, many things having the human nature. But, Spinoza would reply, the human nature is not what he means by an attribute; it is not ontologically basic enough. What, then, about Thought? Descartes considered it to be a principal attribute or nature of things, and so does Spinoza. And it certainly seems possible that there can be a plurality of thinking substances – in fact, Descartes himself says that there are a great many substances all having the attribute Thought, namely, all the souls that will ever exist. Spinoza agrees that there have been and will be many thinking things, many souls or minds all sharing the same nature, but as we shall see he denies that they are true substances.

Spinoza's demonstration for IP5 relies on the ways in which we can distinguish and individuate things. If there were two or more distinct substances – something he will eventually deny – then (by IP4) there are only two ways they could be distinguished from each other: either they differ in terms of their underlying natures (their attributes) or they differ in terms of their properties that express those underlying natures (their modes or affections). If they differ in terms of their attributes – with substance *x* having attribute *a* and substance *y* having attribute *b* – then the proposition holds, since there would not be more than one substance having an attribute.

If there were two or more distinct substances, they would have to be distinguished from one another either by a difference in their attributes or by a difference in their affections. If only by a difference in their attributes, then it will be conceded that there is only one [substance] of the same attribute.

It is worth noting an important objection that the philosopher-Gottfried Wilhelm Leibniz, one of Spinoza's contemporaries, made to Spinoza's argument at this point. Spinoza is assuming that if two substances have an attribute in common, then they cannot be distinguished from each other by their attributes; and thus, conversely, that if they can be distinguished from each other by their attributes, then they must not have an attribute in common. Leibniz insists, in his 1678 comments on the posthumous edition of Spinoza's writings, that this train of reasoning is valid only if one is also assuming that a substance cannot have more than one attribute. "There seems to be a concealed fallacy here. For two substances can be distinguished by their attributes and still have some common attribute, provided they also have others peculiar to themselves in addition."[9] If a substance is limited to one attribute, then it can be granted that if two substances are distinguishable from each other by a difference in their attributes, it must be because they do not (and cannot) have an attribute in common. On the other hand, if substance *x* has only attribute *a* and if substance *y* has only attribute *a*, then of course by attributes alone there is no way to distinguish *x* from *y*. But, Leibniz insists, if a substance can have two or more attributes, then it would seem possible for two substances both to be distinguishable from each other *and* to share an attribute. For example, if substance *x* has attributes *a* and *c* and substance *y* has attributes *b* and *c*, then although *x* and *y* have an attribute in common (i.e., *c*), they are still distinguishable from each other (by virtue of their possessing, respectively, *a* and *b*).

---

[9] Leibniz 1999, VI.4b, p. 1768.

Leibniz is right, it would seem, and Spinoza can reply only that he is indeed assuming that a substance has only one attribute. This is Descartes's view, and it would be perfectly reasonable for Spinoza to appeal to such a principle. This would be problematic for Spinoza's project, however, since very soon (IP9) he will need to claim that substance can have many – in fact, infinite – attributes.

The second way that substances can be distinguished from each other is by means not of a difference in their attributes but a difference in their modes or properties – the way we might distinguish, for example, one horse from another not by virtue of their being horses but by their "accidental" characteristics, such as their color or size. Spinoza then goes on to argue that

since a substance is prior in nature to its affections (by IP1), if the affections are put to one side and [the substance] is considered in itself, i.e. (by ID3 and IA6), considered truly, one cannot be conceived to be distinguished from another, i.e. (by IP4), there cannot be many, but only one [of the same nature or attribute], q.e.d.

The reasoning here is not entirely clear, but with some work I think Spinoza's meaning comes through. Assume for the sake of argument that there are indeed two substances that have the same nature or attribute (since we are now dealing with a distinction between substances based not on attributes but on modes). The way they are supposed to be distinguished, then, is by the different ways in which that nature is modified or manifested in each thing – the affections. But what does it mean to take the affections and "put [them] to one side," and why should it be permissible in the context of this argument to do that? That would seem, on the face of it, to be a clear case of begging the question. If you can simply "put to one side" those aspects by which two things are supposed to differ, well, then, of course there will no longer be any distinction between them. Is Spinoza here guilty of such spurious reasoning?

In fact, what Spinoza seems to have in mind is that since the modes or properties of a substance are only ways in which the attribute or nature is being expressed, then it is really the attribute that we should be looking at. Any difference at the level of modes/ affections can be explained and understood only at the more basic level of attributes, since modes are conceived through the substance or attribute of which they are the modes. Notice from the demonstration of IP1 that the "priority" of substance over its affections to which Spinoza appeals in the demonstration of IP5 is supposed to follow from ID3 and ID5. ID3 says that substance is conceived through itself, and ID5 says that the modes or affections of a substance are "in" the substance (or, which is the same thing, its attribute) and conceived through it. But if the modes can be conceived only through the substance/attribute of which they are the modes, then any distinction at the level of modes must be a function of a "prior" distinction at the level of attribute. This is why the affections can be "put to one side and [the substance] considered in itself." But in the argument for IP5, we are assuming that *there is no difference of attribute* under the difference of modes; and so, when the modes are put to the side, what remains is undifferentiated attribute, one single nature devoid of any numerical or qualitative variety. Thus, contrary to our initial assumption, there cannot be two substances having the same attribute and differing only in their modes, since (with the modes put aside) there are no grounds for claiming that what we have are *two* substances.[10]

With IP5, Spinoza has established the uniqueness of any substantial nature. Every substance is unique in its kind; there is no other substance like it. If there is a thinking substance, then there is only one thinking substance. If there is an extended or material substance, then there is only one extended or material substance. In the end, there will be only one substance, period, constituted by an infinite number of attributes. It will be a thinking substance, an extended substance, and so on, for all other possible (but to us unknown) natures.

### SUBSTANCE IS NECESSARILY EXISTING, ETERNAL, AND INFINITE

Spinoza now turns to a number of essential features of substance. Some of these are traditional, such as the claim that substance has true ontological independence; some are novel, such as the claim

---

[10] IP5 is so important that Spinoza offers a second demonstration for it, in the second scholium to IP8.

that substance necessarily exists and is infinite. When put together, they add up to a highly idiosyncratic picture of reality, one that has posed difficulties for Spinoza's interpreters for centuries.

IP6 says that "one substance cannot be produced by another substance," and its corollary concludes – on the basis of the claim already established that there is nothing in nature except substances and their affections – that therefore "a substance cannot be produced by anything else." Substance, in other words, must be totally uncaused. This is because two things can be causally related to each other only if they have something in common (IP3 – this is what might be called a "causal likeness principle"); for if they have nothing in common, one could not be understood through the other, and Spinoza's causal rationalism demands that if one thing is the effect of another, then the former must be able to be understood through the latter. But IP5 has already established that no two substances can have the same nature or attribute. And this means that no two substances can have anything whatsoever in common, since everything about a substance is explained by its attribute. Two substances that differ in essential attribute certainly cannot have anything in common at the level of affections, since affections just are modes of the attribute. A causal relationship with something outside itself is thus ruled out for substance. (The causal rationalism lies behind a second argument that Spinoza provides for IP7: if a substance were caused by another substance – or by anything else whatsoever – then the knowledge of it would depend on the knowledge of something else. But then the substance would be conceived not through itself, as ID3 demands, but through something else, i.e., its cause.)

Like Descartes before him, Spinoza thus makes ontological independence the hallmark of substance. Unlike Descartes, however, Spinoza is not willing to compromise and say that there is a secondary degree of substantiality, whereby a finite thing can be caused by an infinite substance and still qualify as a substance, just as long as it is not dependent for its being on some other finite thing. Spinoza will stand by the most rigorous understanding of this aspect of what it is to be a substance.

Now if substance is not caused by something outside itself, and if there must always be some cause or reason for the existence of a thing (as we know from Spinoza's commitment to the principle of universal causality), and if the cause or reason for the existence of anything must lie either in some external circumstances or in the nature of the thing itself,[11] it follows that the cause of the existence of substance must be the nature of substance itself. Or, as Spinoza puts it in IP7: "It pertains to the nature of a substance to exist." Substance exists because such is its nature. But this is just to say that substance *necessarily* exists.

It might be objected that all that Spinoza has proven here is that *if* a substance exists, then it exists necessarily, but not that necessarily, substance exists. However, given its ontological independence from anything else, the only reason why a substance would not exist would have to lie in its nature – that is, its nature would have to contain some inherent contradiction, such as is contained in the nature of a square circle. But we are assuming all along that, whatever else may be true of a substance, at the very least its nature is a self-consistent and possible one. Therefore, since there is no reason either within or outside the substance that prevents it from existing, it necessarily exists.

Substance, then, is self-caused. Spinoza's proof for the (necessary) existence of substance recalls St. Anselm's (and Descartes's) famous ontological proof for God's existence, which starts from the concept of God and concludes, in a completely logically deductive or a priori manner, that God necessarily exists because it cannot be conceived as not existing. Like that theological proof, Spinoza argues that anyone who truly conceives of substance and recognizes all of the proper implications of that conception must conclude that substance exists.

If someone were to say that he had a clear and distinct, i.e., true, idea of a substance, and nevertheless doubted whether such a substance existed, that would indeed be the same as if he were to say that he had a true idea, and nevertheless doubted whether it was false (as is evident to anyone who is sufficiently attentive). (IP8s2, G II.50/C I.414)

It follows, as well, that substance must be eternal. If substance is not caused to be by something else but its existence is a necessary consequence of its own nature; and if, as Spinoza insists, there is

---

[11]  Spinoza makes this claim in IP8s2 (G II.50/C I.415).

nothing either within or outside that nature that can prevent its existence, then for substance there is no beginning or end to its existence. In fact, Spinoza's definition of 'eternity' explicitly links it to necessary existence: "By eternity I understand existence itself, insofar as it is conceived to follow necessarily from the definition alone of the eternal thing" (ID8). The existence of substance is not just everlasting or "sempiternal" – that is, a durational existence or an existence in time that simply has no beginning or end. Since existence follows from the nature of substance just as having three angles follows from the nature of a triangle, the existence of substance is "conceived as an eternal truth," a truth that is outside all time and duration.

At the level of substance, then, there is no coming-to-be or ceasing-to-be. Substance abides eternally and indivisibly beneath all the motions and changes and beginnings and endings that take place among things and their properties in the observable world. Spinoza cautions the reader not to make the common and tempting mistake of ascribing to substance features that belong only to the realm of its modes or affections.

> I do not doubt that the demonstration of IP7 will be difficult to conceive for all who judge things confusedly, and have not been accustomed to know things through their first causes – because they do not distinguish between the modifications of substances and the substances themselves . . . So it happens that they fictitiously ascribe to substances the beginning which they see that natural things have . . . But if men would attend to the nature of substance, they would have no doubt at all of the truth of IP7. Indeed, this proposition would be an axiom for everyone, and would be numbered among the common notions. For by substance they would understand what is in itself and is conceived through itself, i.e., that the knowledge of which does not require the knowledge of any other thing.
>
> (IP8s2, G II.49/C I.412–13)

It may seem that Spinoza has gone well beyond anything that previous philosophers had been willing to say about substance. Descartes's finite thinking substances, including human minds, are created and exist in time, but are no less substantial for all that. But, again, Spinoza's conclusions about substance result only from taking the traditional conception of substance – "what is in itself" – to its logical limits.

In IP8 and IP9, Spinoza turns to the infinitude of substance. But before we look at these propositions, it will be helpful to refer to a distinction that Spinoza introduces in the definitions of Part One. In ID2 and ID6, Spinoza distinguishes between that which is infinite in its own kind and that which is absolutely infinite. Something can be limited only by something else of the same kind or nature; and something is infinite in its own kind if there is nothing else of the same kind or nature that limits it. Thus, a bodily substance can be limited only by another bodily substance. But if, as IP5 implies, there is just one bodily substance, then that bodily substance is unlimited and is thus infinite in its kind. It does not follow, however, that the bodily substance is absolutely infinite or unlimited, since there may be much of reality that does not belong to its nature (or, in Spinoza's terms, "we can deny infinite attributes of it"). By contrast, something is absolutely infinite if every possible positive reality belongs to its nature ("if something is absolutely infinite, whatever expresses essence and involves no negation pertains to its essence"). An absolutely infinite being encompasses everything that is real.

In the proof for IP8 – "Every substance is necessarily infinite" – Spinoza argues that a substance cannot be finite, because then it would have to be limited by something else of the same attribute or nature. But we know from IP5 that there is nothing else of the same attribute or nature as any substance. Therefore, any substance "exists as infinite". This is fine as it stands, and the demonstration is relatively straightforward. But the proposition is, for Spinoza's purposes, relatively weak. For it should be clear that all that he has established by this is that a substance with one attribute is infinite only in its own kind, since there is no other substance of the same nature or attribute to limit it. And this means that it is still possible that there are a great many substances, each with one attribute, each necessarily existing, each eternal, and each infinite in its own kind (because each is unique in its kind). What Spinoza intends ultimately to show, however, is that there is, in fact, only one substance, and that all attributes or natures belong to or constitute this one substance. The infinitude of substance that Spinoza wants and needs to do this is not relative infinitude but absolute infinitude. He must establish that there is a substance that is not just infinite in its own kind, but absolutely infinite. This will be undertaken in IP9-11.

In a letter to his friend Lodewijk Meyer in 1663, Spinoza addresses some "difficulties" and ambiguities in the notion of infinitude. He contrasts those things that are "infinite by their nature and cannot in any way be conceived to be finite" with other things that are infinite "by the force of the cause in which they inhere", and with still other things that are really only "indefinite, because they cannot be equated with any number, though they can be conceived to be greater or less" (Letter 12, G IV.60–1/C I.205). The true infinitude of substance, once Spinoza has established that there is an infinite substance, will be of the first kind, what medieval philosophers referred to as absolutely infinite being. For Spinoza, this means that an infinite substance will have infinite attributes or natures, that is, all possible attributes or natures.

Nothing in nature is clearer than that each being must be conceived under some attribute, and the more reality, or being it has, the more it has attributes which express necessity, or eternity, and infinity. And consequently there is nothing clearer than that a being absolutely infinite must be defined . . . as a being that consists of infinite attributes, each of which expresses a certain eternal and infinite essence. (IP10s)

Each attribute is infinite in its own kind, since there is no other attribute like it to limit it. Substance itself, however, is absolutely infinite, and thus possesses an (absolute) infinity of attributes, each of which is infinite in its own kind.

Now we have cognizance of only two of these attributes, Thought (the nature of mental things) and Extension (the nature of material things). Thus, if we take Spinoza at his word, and I see no reason why we should not, then when he speaks of infinite attributes he is saying that there are an infinite number of attributes that are unknown (and perhaps in principle unknowable) to us. As hard as it is for us to conceive what these other attributes might be, and as odd a position as this appears, I believe it is, nonetheless, Spinoza's view. To be sure, it is possible that by "infinite attributes" Spinoza means not "infinitely many", but simply "all."[12] On this reading, it

[12] See Allison 1987, p. 58.

would be compatible with Spinoza's conception of the infinitude of substance that there are only two attributes – namely, the two known to us – and that they all (i.e., both) belong to substance. But while for Spinoza "infinite attributes" clearly does imply "all attributes," and while this is, as we shall see, all that he needs for his argument for the uniqueness of God as substance to go through, much of what he says strongly suggests that he also holds the more robust thesis that there are infinitely many attributes, all but two of them unknown to us.[13]

Spinoza goes out of his way to insist that although each of these attributes or natures is or exists "in itself" and is conceivable by itself and independently of any other attribute or nature – for example, Extension or Matter does not depend on Thought, and one does not need to conceive of Thought in order to conceive of Extension or Matter, and vice versa – it is not the case that each attribute is a distinct substance. It is by no means absurd, he says, to attribute many attributes to one substance. If substance is (absolutely) infinite, then it has infinite natures or attributes. Or, since substance is not some featureless substratum distinct from its attributes, perhaps it is better to say that substance consists in or is constituted by infinite natures or attributes.

This does not mean that substance is an aggregate or complex whole of which the attributes are parts into which it can be divided. Spinoza argues explicitly against the divisibility of substance (IP12, IP13). Among other reasons, he insists (in IP13s) that if substance could be divided into parts, then each part of a divisible infinite substance would have to be a finite substance; and this would be inconsistent with the demonstrated truth (IP8) that every substance is infinite.[14] The attributes are indeed elements making up the

---

[13] See KV, I.7 (G I.44/C I.88). For an extended discussion of why only two of the attributes are known to us, see the correspondence between Spinoza and Tschirnhaus (through Schuller, in Letters 63–64). I discuss this issue on pages 141–2 below.

[14] Here the ambiguity of 'infinite' comes back to haunt Spinoza. IP8 says only that substance is infinite in its own kind, whereas the argument in IP13 against the divisibility of substance seems to rely on a premise (falsely attributed to IP8) that substance must be absolutely infinite. The division of an infinite substance into finite substances contemplated by IP13 would presumably be a division of an absolutely infinite substance into substances each of which is, while not absolutely infinite, at least infinite in its own kind, and this is not ruled out by IP8.

absolutely infinite substance, but none can be removed or separated from the totality that is the substance itself, not even in principle. Each attribute is in itself and is conceived through itself. But for Spinoza this implies that each attribute necessarily exists, and from this it follows that no attribute could exist without the others. Thus, the division of substance is absolutely impossible and the unity of the attributes as substance is guaranteed.[15]

Substance thus encompasses all possible realities or ways of being and unifies them into one system. Spinoza will identify this infinite substance with Nature itself, and with God.

## "EXCEPT GOD, NO SUBSTANCE CAN BE OR BE CONCEIVED"

With the exception of ID6, God has not yet made an appearance in the *Ethics*. God is completely absent from the first ten propositions. And there is certainly nothing in these propositions that even hints at the theologically bold – and, to Spinoza's critics, shocking – culmination toward which we are heading. Everything so far has been about substance and attribute, basic metaphysical categories that would have been very familiar to Spinoza's contemporaries (especially those schooled in Cartesian philosophy) and all fairly abstract. Even Spinoza's definition (ID6) of God as "a being absolutely infinite" would not have aroused any concerns among the more conservative members of his audience. However, with IP11, the careful reader will begin to get a clearer (and, if he is wedded to the traditional conception of God and its relationship to the world, perhaps troubling) sense of the direction things are about to take.

In IP11, Spinoza offers a series of proofs of God's existence. All three of the proofs piggy-back on what has already been demonstrated about substance, and each makes its case by identifying God with an absolutely infinite substance – that is, "a substance consisting of infinite attributes."

---

[15] See Curley 1988, pp. 27–30. However, it still remains somewhat mysterious how Spinoza believes the unity of substance to be compatible with the plurality of attributes, something that Margaret Wilson calls simply "a very difficult problem" (1999a, p. 166).

The first proof takes the ontological proof for the existence of substance and transforms it into a proof for God's existence simply by substituting 'God' for 'substance,' a substitution permitted by the definition of God as an infinite substance. God necessarily exists, this proof concludes, because it is impossible to conceive that God does not exist. For to conceive that God does not exist is to assert that God's essence does not involve existence. But it has been shown by IP7 that the nature of substance involves existence, and God is a substance, albeit one that happens to be (by definition) infinite.

The second proof also argues to the claim that God necessarily exists and similarly relies on what has already been established about substance, along with the principle of sufficient reason. For everything there must be a cause or reason why it either exists or does not exist, and this cause or reason must lie either in the nature of the thing or outside it. If there is no cause or reason, either within the nature of the thing or outside it, to prevent it from existing, then the thing necessarily exists. Now there can be nothing outside of God's nature to prevent God from existing, since any such thing would either have to have the same nature as God – in which case it is being conceded that God exists – or it would have to have a different nature from God. And a substance that has a different nature from God can neither cause God to exist nor prevent God from existing (presumably because of IP3, the causal likeness principle, although Spinoza does not cite this proposition in the proof). Nor can there be something about God's nature itself that prevents God from existing, since that would mean that God's nature involves a contradiction. And Spinoza insists that "it is absurd" to think that the nature of an "absolutely infinite and supremely perfect Being" involves a contradiction, for then it most certainly would not be a supremely perfect being. Therefore, since there is no cause or reason either within or external to God's nature that prevents God from existing, it follows that God necessarily exists.

The third proof in IP11, unlike the first two, takes as one of its premises the claim that something actually exists – namely, ourselves. Thus, as Spinoza acknowledges, this proof proceeds a posteriori, although it is not your typical a posteriori proof from effect to cause. And although it works from a premise about a matter of fact,

Spinoza believes that that proof still establishes that God necessarily exists. The proof as it appears in the text is somewhat too compact for its own good, and so I shall try to add some clarity to the reasoning I believe he has in mind.

To be able to exist is, Spinoza says, to have power; to be able not to exist is to lack power. He offers this as a self-evident maxim. Moreover, if something exists, then it necessarily exists, either because it is necessary in itself (because existence follows from its essence) or because its existence is necessitated by some external cause: either way, if something exists, then it is not able not to exist. Now if finite beings presently (necessarily) exist but an absolutely infinite being does not, then finite beings would be more powerful than an absolutely infinite being. For the non-existing absolutely infinite being would obviously be able not to exist (which is to lack power), while the presently existing finite beings (either by virtue of their natures or their causes) would not be able not to exist. But it is absurd to think that finite beings are more powerful than an absolutely infinite being. So either nothing presently exists or an absolutely infinite being also presently exists. We know that the former is not the case, since we ourselves, who are finite beings, exist. Therefore, an absolutely infinite being – by definition, God – necessarily exists.

Fortunately, Spinoza does not seem to regard this third proof as being as important to his overall argument as the first two proofs.

By the end of IP13, Spinoza has established that there is an absolutely infinite substance (i.e., a substance consisting in infinite attributes); that this substance necessarily exists; that it is, as substance, indivisible; and that it is eternal. He has also reminded the reader that this infinite eternal substance is just what we understand by 'God.' Everything is now in place for Spinoza to establish that God is the *only* substance in Nature. In fact, what he is going to conclude is that God just *is* the one, necessarily existing, eternal, infinite substance of Nature (IP14), and that everything else is "in" this substance, which he calls God or Nature (IP15).

The demonstration of the first of these two propositions, which represents a culmination of sorts of the first stage of Spinoza's metaphysical project, is brief and neat. IP14, "Except God, no substance can be or be conceived," follows directly from IP5 (according to which no two substances can have the same attribute) and IP11 (which says that there is a substance with infinite attributes). For a substance with infinite attributes is a substance to which all possible natures or realities belong. Its existence, which has been determined to be necessary, therefore precludes the existence of any other substance. This is because any substance other than God would have to have *some* nature or attribute, and it would have to be a nature or attribute that is already possessed by God (since God possesses all attributes); but this would violate IP5, since two substances would then have the same attribute. In the corollary to IP14, Spinoza clarifies for the reader just what he takes himself to have established: "God is unique, i.e., in Nature there is only one substance."

The demonstration of IP15 – "Whatever is, is in God, and nothing can be or be conceived without God" – is equally short. Modes or affections, by definition, must exist in and be conceived through the substance which they modify. And there is and can be nothing that is neither a substance nor a mode. But because God is the only substance, whatever else exists besides God/infinite substance must be a mode, and therefore must exist in God. Thus, whatever is "can be in the divine nature alone, and can be conceived through it alone." Everything, that is, is "in" God.

And this is where our troubles begin.

### GOD AND THINGS

The idea that God is the only substance in Nature, and in fact is identical with Nature itself (or some fundamental part of Nature) is something that had been a part of Spinoza's thinking for some years, although he struggled with ways to express this most basic metaphysical truth. In the *Short Treatise*, we find him claiming that "Nature consists of infinite attributes, of which each is perfect in its kind. This agrees perfectly with the definition one gives of God . . . [A]ll these attributes which are in Nature are only one, single being, and by no means different ones." This is what explains "the unity which we see everywhere in Nature" (G I.22–23/C I.68–70). Nature is one because the substance of it is one, and everything in Nature is a mode or affection of that one substance. "Nature," he says, "which comes from no cause, and which we nevertheless know to exist, must necessarily be a perfect being, to which existence belongs."

The various strands in this doctrine are more clearly laid out and argued for in the *Ethics*, and to that extent the later work represents a vast improvement over the aborted *Short Treatise*. But even in the *Ethics* it is still exasperatingly unclear what Spinoza means by saying that "whatever is, is in God." What can it mean to say that something is *in* God? There are many ways in which something can be *in* something else: it can be the way in which parts are in the whole that they compose, or the way in which an object is in a container that holds it (which is akin to the way in which Newton, for example, conceived of things to be in absolute space), or the way in which properties or qualities belong to a subject (such as wisdom is in Socrates or hardness is in the rock).

It is important to keep in mind the "things" about which we are speaking. The things that are supposed to be *in* God or Nature precisely as modes or affections are *in* substance just are all of those familiar items that populate our world and that we, in our pre-Spinozistic and unphilosophical way of thinking, took to be substantial in their own right: physical objects (trees, chairs, human bodies) and human minds or souls. Like Aristotle (and, to a degree, Descartes), we believed that these were things that were "in themselves," things in which other items (such as properties) existed but which themselves did not exist in anything else. Now Spinoza seems to be telling us that, in all metaphysical rigor, we were wrong. But then what is the correct way to conceive of the ontological status of these items?

One popular interpretation of Spinoza's conception of the relationship between substance (God or Nature) and its modes (everything else that exists) is perhaps also the most natural way to think of it. According to this interpretation, for Spinoza things are in God in the sense of being properties or states or qualities of God. They inhere in God as in a subject or substratum. This makes Spinoza's account of the substance–mode relationship similar to that of Descartes, for whom the modes of a substance are the properties that inhere in it – or, more precisely, in its principal attribute or nature – and for that reason are predicable of it. For Spinoza, then, just as motion is a state of the moving body, so the moving body itself would be a property or state of God (in one of God's infinite attributes, Extension). And just as my thought at this moment is a property or state of my mind, so my mind is a property or state of God (in another of God's infinite attributes, Thought). The moving body and my mind just *are* God's nature (or, more precisely, nature*s*) existing or expressing itself in one way (mode) or another. As Spinoza says in IP25c, "Particular things are nothing but affections of God's attributes, or modes by which God's attributes are expressed in a certain and determinate way."

This is how the prominent seventeenth-century intellectual Pierre Bayle read Spinoza. Bayle admired Spinoza's character, but abhorred his philosophy, "the most monstrous that could be imagined, the most absurd, and the most diametrically opposed to the most evident notions of our mind." Bayle was offended in particular by what he took to be Spinoza's conception of God and of God's relationship to things. According to Spinoza, Bayle says,

There is only one being, and only one nature; and this nature produces in itself by an immanent action all that we call creatures . . . It produces nothing that is not its own modifications. There is a hypothesis that surpasses all the heap of all the extravagances that can be said. The most infamous things the pagan poets have dared to sing against Venus and Jupiter do not approach the horrible idea that Spinoza gives us of God.[16]

Bayle objected that if things and their properties are themselves nothing but properties of God and therefore predicable of God, then a number of unacceptable conclusions follow. First, there is the logical problem that God would have incompatible properties. The happy person and the sad person would equally be states of God, and thus God would itself be both happy and sad; this, Bayle insists, is absurd. Second, there is the theological problem that God itself would be subject to change, division, and motion, since the things that are modes of God are divisible and are constantly changing and moving. Spinoza's God is thus "a nature actually changing, and which continually passes through different states that differ from one another internally and actually. It is therefore not at all the

---

[16] Bayle 1965, p. 301.

supremely perfect being, 'with whom is no variableness, neither shadow of turning' (James 1:17)."[17] This is not just a theological problem, but also a question of philosophical consistency in Spinoza's system, since Spinoza himself seems to say that God is immutable and not subject to change (IP20c2). Finally, and (in Bayle's eyes) most problematic of all, God would be the ultimate subject of all the thoughts and intentions and actions of human beings, including not only all of our loves, hates, and desires, but also the most evil thoughts and deeds conceivable. "Here is a philosopher who finds it good that God be both the agent and the victim of all the crimes and miseries of man."[18] When one person kills another, God is, on Spinoza's account, the true author of the crime, or so Bayle would have it.

Bayle, seeing these as the necessary implications of Spinoza's view of God, basically concluded "so much the worse for Spinoza."[19] Other, more recent commentators have said "so much the worse for that reading of Spinoza." Surely, one might think, Spinoza could not have held a theory that had such clear and obviously problematic philosophical and theological consquences. Moreover, one scholar has claimed, it is simply odd to regard the items that we think of as "things" and as real individuals (houses, chairs, human souls) as actually being properties or states of something else. That seems to be quite a serious category mistake, one of which Spinoza should not be accused.

Spinoza's modes are, prima facie, of the wrong logical type to be related to substance in the same way Descartes' modes are related to substance, for they are particular things, not qualities. And it is difficult to know what it would mean to say that particular things inhere in substance . . . What it would mean to say that one thing is predicated of another is a mystery that needs solving.[20]

For those who would reject Bayle's reading, a second interpretation of what Spinoza means by saying that "whatever is, is in God" is made possible by a subtle but important change in his approach as

[17] Bayle 1965, p. 308.　　　[18] Bayle 1965, p. 311.
[19] A more recent (but idiosyncratic) version of this way of reading Spinoza can be found in Bennett 1984.
[20] Curley 1969, p. 18.

of IP16.[21] The language so suggestive of properties inhering in a substratum gives way to a new kind of model. IP16 says that "from the necessity of the divine nature there must follow infinitely many things in infinitely many modes." The relationship between God and things, or substance and modes, is now described in causal terms. The shift is not total, since Spinoza will continue to refer to particular things as "affections of God's attributes" (for example, in IP25c), but it is something that cannot be ignored. In the demonstration of IP18, God is described as "the cause of all things"; in IP24, we are told that things are "produced" by God; and IP28 describes the ways in which things have been "determined" by God or by God's attributes. On this model, God or substance is not the subject in which things inhere as properties, but rather the infinite, eternal, necessarily existing (uncaused) cause of all things. More particularly, God's attributes can be seen as the universal causal principles of everything that falls under them – which, as we now know, is absolutely everything. The attribute of Extension just is the nature of extension and involves the laws governing all material things (including the truths of geometry, since geometrical objects just are extended objects); and the attribute of Thought just is the nature of thought and involves the laws governing all thinking things (understood, perhaps, as the laws of logic). Nature is governed by a necessary order as the active ground of all things, and to speak of God or substance just is, on this second interpretation, to refer to that universal causal framework. Support for this kind of reading can be found in texts like IP15s, where Spinoza seems to identify being *in* God with being causally generated by certain laws: "All things, I say, are in God, and all things that happen, happen only through the laws of God's infinite nature and follow (as I shall show) from the necessity of his essence." In a letter to Jacob Ostens, in which Spinoza replies to charges made against him by Lambert Van Velthuysen, he seems to reduce the ontological relationship between God and the world to a causal claim when he says that "it is the same, or not very different, to

---

[21] This interpretation was first offered in Curley 1969, and reiterated in Curley 1988. See also Allison 1987, chapter 3.

assert that all things emanate necessarily from God's nature and that the universe is God" (Letter 43, G IV.223/SL 239).

There is something to be said for both of these readings of the relationship between substance and mode (or God and things) in Spinoza's metaphysics. Each of them must also face some difficult although not necessarily insuperable questions. There are, of course, the puzzles that Bayle raises for the "subject/property inherence" model. But Spinoza could reply to the first objection that it is certainly not the case that God has the incompatible properties in absolutely the same respects, which is what would be required in order to generate the alleged contradiction. Just because God is happy in so far as God is one person and God is sad in so far as God is another person, it does not follow that God itself is both happy and sad in the same respect – for it is explicitly specified that God is happy and sad in *different* respects. And while Spinoza does indeed say that "God, or all of God's attributes, are immutable" (IP20c), this does not mean that there is and can be no change in God; rather, it is a claim about the permanence of the existence and the nature of each attribute. Spinoza is saying that despite the variability at the level of modes, the attributes themselves do not change. As for Bayle's third objection, based on the apparent impiety of making God the cause of evils, Spinoza, as we shall see, both argues that 'good' and 'evil' do not refer to anything real in nature and refuses to concede that God has any moral characteristics that need to be respected in the first place; therefore, he would not be very troubled by this objection. Nor may Spinoza have been bothered by the oddity of thinking of ordinary things as properties of something else.

The second, causal interpretation must take care to do justice to Spinoza's understanding of the precise nature of God's causal relationship to things. God (or Nature) is, above all, the ultimate and general efficient cause of all things, the active agent whose power explains their coming into being. This much is absolutely true, certain, and non-negotiable about Spinoza's account. No matter which interpretation of the substance/mode relationship that one adopts, one must preserve the special *causal* relationship that exists between God and things. The question that divides the two interpretations is, is it also a relationship of *inherence*?

The second interpretation says no to this question. But – and here is the problem – Spinoza insists that God or substance is also the *immanent* cause of its modes. "God is the immanent, not the transitive, cause of all things" (IP18). An immanent cause is ordinarily understood to be a cause whose effects belong to or are a part of itself (much as the mind can be said to be the cause of its own ideas). A transitive cause, on the other hand, brings about effects that are ontologically distinct from itself (as the baseball is the cause of the broken window and the sun is the cause of the melted ice). It might seem that unless we think of the things causally brought about by God as properties or states of God – that is, unless we adopt the first, "inherence" interpretation – we will be unable to explain God's causation of things as an immanent causation, as Spinoza demands.

The demonstration for God's immanent causation in IP18, however, relies exactly on the claim that our competing interpretations are fighting over: "Everything that is, is in God." Thus, it would seem, we cannot use the immanence of IP18 itself to argue for one interpretation of that problematic phrase over another; that would be begging the question. But can the second interpretation, which rejects the inherence model, still make sense of immanent causation? Perhaps it can, if it can interpret immanence in such a way that it does not imply that the effect belongs to the cause as its state or property.

One important and distinguishing feature of immanent causation is the inseparability of cause and effect. Without the continued existence and operation of the cause, the effect would cease to exist. Medieval philosophers called this *causalitas secundum esse*, or causality with respect to being, and contrasted it with *causalitas secundum fieri*, or causality with respect to becoming (or coming into being).[22] The sun is a *causa secundum esse* of its light and heat; when the fusion reactions in the sun stop, so will their effects. By contrast, a builder is a *causa secundum fieri* of a house. Once the house is built, the builder does not need to continuously work to keep the house in being; rather, the completed house (the effect) has an ontological independence from the activity of the builder (the cause). Now

---

[22] See St. Thomas Aquinas, *Summa Theologiae* I, q. 104, a1.

Spinoza certainly does think that God stands to all things in a relationship of *causalitas secundum esse*. In the corollary to IP24, he insists that "God is not only the cause of things' beginning to exist, but also their persevering in existing, or (to use a Scholastic term) God is the cause of the being [*causa essendi*] of things." It may be, then, that all that Spinoza means by calling God the immanent cause of all things is to stress that it is a relationship of *causalitas secundum esse*, and that God's causal activity is ongoing and necessary with respect to the continued existence and operation of everything else, without also implying that everything else is *in* God in the way in which properties inhere in a subject.[23]

There may also be another way to have immanence without inherence. If, as the second interpretation stresses (but the first interpretation must accept as well), God is the cause of all things, it follows – from IA4: "The knowledge of an effect depends on, and involves, the knowledge of its cause" – that everything must ultimately be conceived through God. This, in fact, is one of the ultimate conclusions of the *Ethics*. And given what Spinoza sees as the logical relationship between the concept of the effect and the concept of the cause through which it is conceived (as we shall examine in chapter 4), it also follows that the concept of the effect is logically contained in and follows from the concept of the cause. But then this means that everything is *in* God just in the way in which the consequent is *in* its antecedent(s) or logical ground. The immanence in question is therefore logical immanence. *A* is in *B*, in this sense, just in case *A* is logically implied by *B*.[24] This is a rather weak understanding of the way in which things might be *in* God, however, and may not capture the intended ontological boldness of Spinoza's claim. Moreover, given Spinoza's discussion of immanence in the *Short Treatise*, where he says that "[God] is an immanent and not a transitive cause, since he does everything in himself, and not outside himself" (G I.35/C I.80), it may appear difficult to sustain immanence without inherence.

---

[23] It is not clear to me how Curley intends to preserve immanence. He does say that, on his view, we should think of God as producing and acting "on things other than God" (Curley 1988, p. 38).

[24] See Curley 1969, chapter 2.

### GOD OR NATURE

Something very important hinges on this question of how to interpret the *in* of IP15, "Whatever is, is *in* God." One of the most difficult and persistent questions raised by Part One of the *Ethics* is just how to understand Spinoza's identification of God with Nature. There can be no question that the identity he has in mind is a literal and numerical one. He is denying that God is anything distinct from Nature, whether one understands this to mean "distinct from and outside Nature" (as a transcendent God is ordinarily conceived) or even "distinct from but within Nature," as a kind of supernatural element within nature. As Spinoza says in a letter to Henry Oldenburg of April 1662, "I do not separate God from nature as everyone known to me has done" (Letter 6, G IV.36/C I.188). When he is well along in the *Ethics*, Spinoza will employ his infamous phrase: "That eternal and infinite being we call God, or Nature" (IVP4, G II.213/C I.548). The *sive* of *Deus, sive Natura*[25] is clearly the 'or' of identification: "God, that is, Nature", or "God, or – which is the same thing – Nature."

But what is the extent of the identification of the two? This is what is not clear. Is God the whole of Nature, the entire universe and everything in it? Or is God just some fundamental, unchanging, eternal, and universal aspects of Nature? On the first interpretation of the relationship between God/substance and modes, whereby all things inhere in God as properties, God must be identical with the whole of Nature, including all of its contents. This is because the properties or states of a thing *are* the thing, existing in particular manner. Thus, God is both the universal elements of Nature – substance, its attributes, and whatever they involve – as well as all of the things that are (immanently) caused by and belong to those natures, right down to the lowest level of particularity. God is material nature (Extension) and its most general features, as well as every particular material thing and state of a material thing that expresses that nature; God is thinking nature (Thought) and its most general features, as well as every individual "idea" or mind that

---

[25] At IV, Preface (G II.206/C I.544), Spinoza says *Deus, seu Natura*.

expresses that nature, and all of the particular ideas had by these; and so on for every attribute.

On the second interpretation, whereby the relationship between God and particular things is a more external one, God/substance is identified only with the attributes, the universal natures and causal principles that govern all things. Particular things are not literally and numerically identical with God, since they are not *in* God in the way in which properties are in a subject, but only necessarily and eternally causally generated by (and thus perpetually dependent upon) God. God is the invisible but active dimension of Nature, its essences and laws. All of the rest, including the visible furniture of the world, is but an effect of God's powers.

Now Spinoza certainly does recognize active and passive aspects of Nature. There is, in fact, an important distinction that he draws in IP29s, one that shows that the term 'Nature' is, when left unqualified, ambiguous.

> I wish to explain here . . . what must be understood by *Natura naturans* [literally: naturing Nature] and *Natura naturata* [natured Nature] . . . [B]y *Natura naturans* we must understand what is in itself and is conceived through itself, or such attributes of substance as express an eternal and infinite essence, i.e., God, insofar as he is considered as a free cause.
> But by *Natura naturata* I understand whatever follows from the necessity of God's nature, or from any of God's attributes, i.e., all the modes of God's attributes insofar as they are considered as things which are in God, and can neither be nor be conceived without God.[26]

According to the purely causal interpretation of God's relationship to things, God is to be identified not with all of Nature, but solely with *Natura naturans*. God is only substance and its attributes. Everything that follows from or is caused by – or, to use the passive participle employed by Spinoza, *natured* by – substance (that is, absolutely everything else) belongs to *Natura naturata*, and is thus distinct from (albeit dependent upon) God. According to the

---

[26] To refer back to my earlier remark about the use of the terms 'Nature' and 'nature,' when Spinoza is speaking of *Natura naturans*, he is referring to Nature (God or substance), whereas when he is speaking of *Natura naturata*, he is referring in part to nature (the things and processes in the world around us).

substance/property inherence interpretation, favored by Bayle, God is both *Natura naturans* and *Natura naturata.*

Despite the neatness and sophistication of the causal interpretation, it must be granted that, in the light of this distinction between *Natura naturans* and *Natura naturata,* there is certain advantage to the reading according to which God is identical to the whole universe, in both its active invisible and passive visible aspects. Spinoza identifies *Deus* with *Natura.* Thus, when he tells us that *Natura* includes both a *naturans* aspect and a *naturata* aspect, the natural conclusion would seem to be that *Deus* is to be identified with both of these. God is both the active and the passive dimensions of Nature, what causes (or "natures") and what is caused (or "natured"). If, as IP29s claims, *Natura naturans* just is God, "insofar as he is considered as a free cause," it would seem to follow that *Natura naturata* is also God, in so far as he is considered in some other way.

With his identification of God and substance and the consequent doctrine of immanence, Spinoza has departed a good way from the traditional conception of God. The Judeo-Christian God is a transcendent being. It is ontologically distinct from the world. Even after bringing the world into being, and despite various trends of immanency in Jewish and Christian mystical thought, the Judeo-Christian God essentially stands outside its creation. For Spinoza, on the other hand, whether we identify God with the whole of Nature or only with certain fundamental and universal features of Nature, God literally *is* Nature. Or, to put it another way, God is in Nature not as something distinct from Nature but contained within it, as some forms of pantheism may hold, but just as elements of Nature itself are, by definition, in Nature. As we shall see in the next chapter, this is only the beginning of Spinoza's theological radicalism in the *Ethics.* His campaign against the anthropomorphizing of God takes an even more extreme – and, to his critics, disturbing – turn when he addresses the details of God's causal relationship to the modes of Nature's attributes, or particular things.

CHAPTER 4

# On God: necessity and determinism

In the late summer of 1661, the Englishman Oldenburg was one of the earliest visitors to Spinoza's small house in Rijnsburg. These initial meetings, in which the two talked about philosophy and science, led to an extended and fruitful correspondence (interrupted for a time by the Anglo-Dutch war). In his letters, Oldenburg was constantly encouraging Spinoza to publish his metaphysical ideas, although as the true nature of those ideas became clearer and clearer to Oldenburg, especially after the publication of the *Theological-Political Treatise* in 1670, he started to have some serious misgivings about them. Writing to Spinoza some years later, in November 1675, Oldenburg takes note of those passages in the *Theological-Political Treatise* "which have proved a stumbling-block to readers," especially "reasonable and intelligent Christians." He is referring in particular, he adds, "to those [passages] which appear to treat in an ambiguous way of God and Nature, which many people consider you have confused with each other" (Letter 71).

Spinoza, naturally, is curious as to what passages Oldenburg has in mind that might appear "to undermine the practice of religious virtue" (Letter 73). In a follow-up letter, Oldenburg makes his meaning clear:

You appear to postulate a fatalistic necessity in all things and actions. If this is conceded and affirmed, they say, the sinews of all laws, all virtue and religion are severed, and all rewards and punishments are pointless. They consider that whatever compels or brings necessity to bear, excuses; and they hold that no one will thus be without excuse in the sight of God. If we are driven by fate, and if all things, unrolled by its relenting hand, follow a fixed and inevitable course, they do not see what place there is for blame and punishment. (Letter 74)

In his reply, Spinoza gets right to the point and does not hide his opinion. Indeed, he tells Oldenburg that the deterministic doctrine that is troubling him is the centerpiece of the work of which Oldenburg has had glimpses over the years but that Spinoza does not yet dare to publish – that is, the *Ethics*.

> I see at last what it was that you urged me not to publish. However, since this is the principal basis of all the contents of the treatise which I had intended to issue, I should here like to explain briefly in what way I maintain the fatalistic necessity of all things and actions.
> In no way do I subject God to fate, but I conceive that all things follow from God's nature in the same way that everyone conceives that it follows from God's nature that God understands himself.
>
> (Letter 75, G IV.311–12/SL 337)

The second half of Part One of the *Ethics* presents both the large-scale or global features of Spinoza's determinism and the details of the ways in which any particular finite thing is causally brought about. Whether it is indeed a necessitarianism, or what Oldenburg calls "fatalism," is something we will have to investigate.

## CAUSAL NECESSITY

God or Nature is the uncaused substance that is the primary and universal efficient cause of everything else. Because, as we know from IA3 ("From a given determinate cause the effect follows necessarily"), causes necessitate their effects, this means that God is the necessary and necessitating ground of everything else. As Spinoza says in IP16, "from the necessity of the divine nature there must follow infinitely many things in infinitely many modes." Whatever else there is in the cosmos, whether among the most general features of nature or among particular things, it is causally necessitated to be as it is, either directly by God/Nature/substance itself, or indirectly by God/Nature/substance along with its more proximate effects.

Ordinarily, causal necessity is distinguished from logical or absolute necessity. It is one thing to say that an effect follows necessarily from its cause; it is quite another to say that the connection between two items is logically necessary. First, logical necessity would seem to be something that holds primarily between propositions, not things. Second, even if we put this problem aside – since we can always translate talk of things into talk of truths about those things – causal relationships would seem to be necessary only with what might be called natural or nomological (law-based) necessity. If one thing in nature is the cause of another, it is because that is how nature just happens to work, or because the laws of nature dictate that the two items should be so related. Thus, while we may regard it as unnatural or contrary to some law of nature for the one to happen without the other – for example, for water to freeze at a temperature higher than 32 degrees Fahrenheit – we do not think that it is logically inconceivable (unless we are also willing to grant that nature and its laws are themselves logically necessary). Surely, as Hume so clearly points out, just because $a$ is the cause of $b$, it does not follow that jointly positing $a$ and denying $b$ (that is, conceiving $a$ to occur but not $b$) generates a logical contradiction (as would be the case if we both posited $a$ and denied $a$).

Spinoza, by contrast, believes that causes necessitate their effects with the same kind of necessity by which the premises in a valid argument logically entail their conclusion, or the necessity by which one mathematical truth follows from another. Thus, for Spinoza, if one thing is the cause of another, then it is absolutely necessary that the one follow the other. In the demonstration for IP16, just after claiming that "from the necessity of the divine nature there must follow infinitely many things," Spinoza identifies that way in which things follow from any of God's natures with the way in which properties necessarily follow from the essence or definition of a thing. Each attribute is a nature or expresses an infinite essence. The modes of that attribute follow from that nature or essence with the same degree of logical necessity with which having three angles follows from the nature or essence of a triangle. As he says in IP17s2,

I have shown clearly enough (see IP16) that from God's supreme power, or infinite nature, infinitely many things in infinitely many modes, i.e., all things, have necessarily flowed, or always follow, by the same necessity and in the same way as from the nature of a triangle it follows, from eternity and to eternity, that its three angles are equal to two right angles.

Thus, even if one were to insist that one state of affairs necessitates another only because the laws of nature say it must be so,

Spinoza could grant this but then reply (as we shall see) that nature and its laws are themselves absolutely necessary – and therefore anything that follows from them must also be absolutely necessary.

Now Spinoza sometimes says things that have led commentators to see in his thought a distinction between causal necessity and logical necessity.[1] For example, in IP33s1, he states that "[a] thing is called necessary either by reason of its essence or by reason of its cause. For a thing's existence follows necessarily either from its essence and definition or from a given efficient cause." However, it would be wrong to read this as laying out a distinction between two *kinds* of necessity: logical or metaphysical vs. causal. Rather, Spinoza is simply explaining that there are two ways in which something becomes necessitated – either "internally," because of its essence (and this is the way in which God or substance and its attributes are necessary); or "externally," because of its antecedent conditions (the way in which everything else is necessary). The necessity itself in each case is the same, and it is absolute. In the "Metaphysical Thoughts" appended to his exposition of Descartes's *Principles of Philosophy*, Spinoza writes that "if men understood clearly the whole order of Nature, they would find all things just as necessary as are all those treated in Mathematics" (CM, G I.266/C I.332). A clearer statement of the identity of causal or natural necessity with logical or mathematical necessity cannot be imagined.

As we shall see, one consequence of this account of the necessity by which things follow from God or Nature is that there is no contingency for or in the universe. If Leibniz says that this is the best of all possible worlds, Spinoza's retort is that this is the *only* possible world.

INFINITE MODES

When it comes to writing philosophical dialogues, Spinoza is no Plato. He does experiment with that literary form, however, and in the *Short Treatise* Spinoza uses the conversation between Erasmus

[1] See, for example, Curley and Walski 1999.

and Theophilus to begin his exploration of the nature of God's causal relationship to the rest of the universe. "I heard you say," Erasmus begins, "that God is a cause of all things, and moreover, that he can be no other cause than an *immanent* one. If, then, he is an *immanent cause* of all things, how could you call him a remote cause? For that is impossible in an immanent cause." In his reply, Theophilus, Spinoza's spokesman, draws a distinction that will play an important role in the subsequent discussion and, more importantly, in the elaboration in the *Ethics* of the different ways in which God relates causally to things. "When I said that God is a remote cause, I said that only in respect to those things [which do not depend on him immediately and not those things] which God has produced immediately (without any circumstances, by his existence alone)" (G I.31/C I.76).

This distinction between what follows immediately from God and its attributes and what follows only mediately from them is crucial to understanding the structure of Spinoza's universe, especially the status of infinite and finite things and the dynamic relations that govern them. Spinoza is going to argue that from the attributes – the eternal, infinite, and necessary foundations of Nature – there follows a number of equally infinite and necessary features of the universe. Some of these follow as a kind of spontaneously generated, co-eternal, and inseparable effect from the power of God or Nature alone; these are Nature's first effects. Others follow from Nature only in conjunction with these first effects. They, too, are necessary and eternal; but, unlike the first effects, they do not follow from substance and its attributes alone.

It is in IP21 through IP23 that Spinoza reiterates the *Short Treatise*'s claim that there are two ways in which something can follow from or (which is the same thing) be generated by God's attributes: immediately and mediately. IP21 states that "all things which follow from the absolute nature of any of God's attributes have always had to exist and be infinite, or are, through the same attribute, eternal and infinite." IP22, by contrast, says that "whatever follows from some attribute of God insofar as it is modified by a modification which, through the same attribute, exists necessarily and is infinite, must also exist necessarily and be infinite." IP23 makes the same case but in the opposite direction: "Every mode which exists necessarily and is infinite has necessarily had to follow either from the absolute nature of some attribute of God, or from some attribute, modified by a modification which exists necessarily and is infinite."

These necessary and infinite things that follow from God's attributes, whether they follow from the absolute nature of the attribute itself or from the attribute in so far as it is modified by something, have come to be known as the "infinite modes." Those infinite modes that do follow directly from the absolute nature of an attribute are the "immediate infinite modes." Those infinite modes that follow from an attribute only in so far as it is already modified by some mode (that is, by an immediate infinite mode) are the "mediate infinite modes."

The immediate infinite modes (the subject of IP21) consist in what is directly and necessarily caused or entailed by the absolute nature of each attribute. They are the most universal and basic principles that govern all of the other things which belong to that aspect of the universe represented by the attribute. To get some idea of what Spinoza has in mind here, it is useful to turn to his earlier writings. In the *Treatise on the Emendation of the Intellect*, Spinoza speaks of "those fixed and eternal things [that] . . . because of their presence everywhere, and most extensive power, they will be to us like universals, or genera of the definitions of singular changeable things, and the proximate causes of all things" (G II.37/C I.41). In the *Short Treatise*, Spinoza says that these are the very first elements of *Natura naturata*, the principal and most proximate effects of God or substance's – i.e., *Natura naturans*'s – causal power: "God is the proximate cause of those things that are infinite and immutable, and which we say he has created immediately" (KV I.3, G I.36/C I.81). "Turning now to universal *Natura naturata*, or those modes or creatures which immediately depend on, or have been created by God . . . We say, then, that these have been from all eternity, and will remain to all eternity, immutable, a work truly as great as the greatness of the workman" (KV I.9, G I.48/C I.91).

This, of course, is all very vague. The only way to understand what Spinoza is talking about is to have some concrete information about what exactly these immediate infinite modes are and how they are supposed to function. Unfortunately, Spinoza is not very forthcoming – in the *Ethics* or elsewhere – with details about the infinite modes.[2] It is thus extremely difficult to figure out what the content is of the immediate and the mediate infinite modes under each attribute. Commentators have wrestled with this problem for generations, and still no consensus has emerged. Still, there are a number of possible ways of making sense of what Spinoza is saying.

The immediate infinite mode under the attribute of Thought is what Spinoza, responding in Letter 64 to a request for clarification from Tschirnhaus, calls "absolutely infinite intellect."[3] This could be read as Spinoza's way of referring to God's power of thinking, or – since he rejects such abstractions as powers or faculties – God's infinite activity of thinking. Infinite thinking would thus be the first actualization of the attribute of Thought generated by the power that is essential to Nature or substance. However, by itself this seems a little too spare to capture what Spinoza has in mind, since any thinking – even infinite thinking – would have to be a thinking *of* something. A more fruitful reading is that the immediate infinite mode in Thought is God's actual thinking of everything.[4] That is, the absolutely infinite intellect is the infinite and eternal set of adequate ideas composing God's intellect. It is, in essence, a perfect knowledge of everything.[5] A passage from the *Short Treatise* suggests as much:

As for Intellect in the thinking thing, this too is a Son, product or immediate creature of God, also created by him from all eternity, and remaining immutable to all eternity. Its sole property is to understand everything clearly and distinctly at all times. (KV I.9, G I.48/C I.92)

---

[2] The references that do exist occur in the *Ethics* at IP21–3; the *Short Treatise* I.3, 8, 9; and Letter 64. Leibniz, for one, finds the notion confusing. In his comments on the *Ethics*, he laments the lack of specificity. "I wish he had given an example of such a modification" (Leibniz 1999, VI.4b, p. 1773).

[3] In the *Short Treatise*, he simply calls it "Intellect."

[4] In Letter 32, to Oldenburg, he does describe God's infinite intellect as "an infinite power of thinking [*potentiam infinitam cogitandi*]," but not as a bare power that is not directed at some object. Thus, he says that this infinite power of thinking "contains within itself the whole of Nature ideally, and whose thoughts proceed in the same manner as does Nature, which is in fact the object of its thought" (G IV.173–4/SL 194–5).

[5] In IP32c2, Spinoza suggests that the immediate infinite mode of Thought is "will and intellect," when he says that "will and intellect are related to God's nature as motion and rest [the immediate infinite mode in Extension] are . . ."

It may be possible to add still a little more detail here. In IP24 and IP25, Spinoza distinguishes between the essences of things and the existence of things and claims that both depend eternally on God: "God is the efficient cause, not only of the existence of things, but also of their essence." In the light of this, we can postulate something that will have to wait until later for full explanation: that the eternal adequate ideas composing the absolutely infinite intellect, because they follow from the attribute of Thought alone and are generated by the power of Nature (*Natura naturans*) itself, are essences in Thought. The absolutely infinite intellect is a collection of ideas constituted by God's infinite thinking of the eternal essences of things. Moreover, each eternal idea of the essence of a thing is itself an essence. And what eternal ideas are the essences of is, as we shall see in subsequent chapters, all of those other things in the attribute of Thought that are not eternal but rather stand in time or duration – namely, actually existing ideas or minds. (Later in the *Ethics* Spinoza will refer to the eternal ideas as eternal minds.) The ideas in infinite intellect thus constitute simultaneously (a) an eternal knowledge of the eternal essences of things in all the other attributes (and this might be labeled its "horizontal" dimension), and (b) the eternal essences of actually existing ideas or minds in the attribute of Thought (its "vertical" dimension). This interpretation is supported by the fact that in the *Ethics* itself, Spinoza both refers to the immediate infinite mode of Thought as "God's idea" (IP21), and identifies "God's eternal and infinite intellect" as a collection of eternal minds or ideas (IV40s).[6]

The immediate infinite mode under the attribute of Extension, Spinoza says, is what he calls "motion and rest" (Letter 64). Again, it is not entirely clear what this means. One possibility is that what is entailed by the nature of extension (the attribute) is just mobility. Whatever is extended is thereby necessarily mobile. And yet, Spinoza seems to have in mind something stronger than this. In the *Short Treatise* (I.9), he says that the immediate infinite mode in Extension is motion itself. Thus, it could be that what follows from the nature of extension alone, as an attribute of substance, is that motion and

---

[6] This kind of reading is offered by Gueroult 1968, I.309–24.

rest belong necessarily to an extended universe (or, more precisely, to the essence of an extended universe, since at the level of immediate infinite modes it is not yet a question of existence). Whatever is extended essentially partakes of motion and rest.

This is certainly a plausible reading. It is suggested by the first two axioms in the digression into physics that appears after IIP13, axioms which are supposed to establish some first principles within Extension, or "premise a few things concerning the nature of bodies." A1′ says "All bodies either move or are at rest"; and A2′ states "Each body moves now more slowly, now more quickly." Moreover, in Lemma 4 in this section, Spinoza argues that simply from the fact that all bodies "involve the concept of one and the same attribute" it follows that bodies are now in motion and at rest.

If this reading is indeed what Spinoza has in mind, then it would be a highly un-Cartesian thing for him to claim, as he well knew.[7] For Descartes quite clearly says that while extension by itself is mobile (i.e., capable of being put into motion), actual motion does not follow from the nature of extension alone; there must be some cause outside extension that puts motion into matter. For Descartes, this transcendent cause is either God or some finite mind.[8] On Spinoza's account, by contrast, Extension itself causes motion, in just the way that substance and its attribute immanently and immediately cause its most general mode. He can defend this claim because in his view substance (and, necessarily, its attributes), as *Natura naturans*, is essentially dynamic and has an intrinsic power to act; this point is neatly summarized in IP34, where Spinoza says that "God's power is his essence itself." Since God is substance, and not an efficient cause external to substance (as it is on Descartes's account); and since the attributes constitute God's natures, this proposition says in effect that the power belongs to substance and its attributes. In the attribute of Extension, the power of God or substance gets expressed immediately as motion (just as that power gets expressed immediately in Thought as thinking).

---

[7] See Letter 83, where he responds to the objection from Tschirnhaus that matter defined as extension cannot involve motion and rest.

[8] See, for example, *Principles of Philosophy* II.36.

This reading of the immediate infinite mode in Extension does raise a crucial question, however. Spinoza is going to insist (in Part Two) that there is a parallelism between the attributes. What is true in one attribute must be true in all the others. Thus, one would think that if the immediate infinite mode in Thought is constituted by the totality of eternal ideas, or (which is the same thing) the essences of minds, then the immediate infinite mode in Extension will have to be constituted by the totality of eternal bodies, or the essences of bodies. But where in the notion of "motion and rest" itself can we find a diversity of body-essences corresponding to the diversity of idea-essences in Thought? In fact, there may be a way of maintaining this parallelism, at least to some degree, on this reading. Bodies for Spinoza are nothing but parcels of extended matter whose parts maintain among themselves a stable ratio of motion and rest. The essence of any particular body will therefore represent some finite extension involving a degree of motion and rest. The attribute (Extension) and its immediate infinite mode (motion and rest) are thus sufficient to provide the conditions for any possible body, and the essence (but not the actual existence) of any body will therefore be virtually contained in the immediate infinite mode of Extension.[9] Of course, this is purely speculative, and it is unclear how Spinoza would have actually answered this question.

There is yet another way to think of the immediate infinite modes, one that has found some currency in the recent literature and that is actually quite appealing for its clarity. In the *Treatise on the Emendation of the Intellect*, Spinoza, when speaking of what appear to be the immediate infinite modes, adopts the language of laws:

The essences of singular, changeable things are not to be drawn from their series, or order of existing, since it offers us nothing but extrinsic denominations, relations, or at most circumstances, all of which are far from the inmost essence of things. That essence is to be sought only from the fixed and eternal things, and at the same time from the laws inscribed in these things, as in their true codes, according to which all singular things come to be, and are ordered. (G II.36–7/C I.41)

---

[9] Gueroult, by contrast, feels that the parallelism breaks down at this level (1968, I.323–4).

On this reading, what follows immediately and directly from the attributes (which can be read as "the fixed and eternal things" in this passage) are laws of nature that are "inscribed" in them. Thus, when Spinoza identifies the immediate infinite mode in Extension as "motion," this is to mean that from the attribute of Extension, which expresses the nature of matter, there immediately follows a supreme principle (or perhaps a number of supreme principles) about motion in extended things. In particular, what follows from the attribute of Extension are the most universal laws governing the ways in which matter moves – possibly the first physical lemmas introduced after IIP13, or a principle regarding the conservation of motion (or the conservation of the proportion of motion and rest) in the universe.[10] Similarly, from the attribute of Thought, there immediately follow certain laws about thinking things – for example, the rules of logic or the laws of psychology. Thus, the initial laws of motion can be deduced from the nature of extended or material things alone, and the laws of thinking can be similarly derived from the nature of thought itself.[11]

If there is debate over what exactly the immediate infinite modes are, there is even more uncertainty surrounding the *mediate* infinite modes. These are the modes that follow not directly and immediately from the absolute nature of the attribute – that is, from the absolute nature of the attribute considered absolutely and in itself – but from "some attribute of God insofar as it is modified by a modification which, through the same attribute, exists necessarily and is infinite." The mediate infinite modes, that is, follow from the attribute taken together with its immediate infinite mode.

There is not a single hint in the *Ethics* itself as to what the mediate infinite modes in Extension and Thought might be. And when Spinoza does offer some information as to their respective contents, the mystery only deepens. In a letter from July 1675, his friend Georg Hermann Schuller, acting on behalf of Tschirnhaus, had

---

[10] Descartes, at least, regarded the conservation principle as the supreme law of motion, following solely from the nature of the first cause (God) and the nature of matter, and from which other, more specific laws can be derived; see *Principles of Philosophy* II.36–42.

[11] This interpretation was first offered by Curley 1969 (pp. 59–61) and 1988 (pp. 45–7). It is also defended by Yovel 1991.

asked for some "examples of those things immediately produced by God, and of those things produced by the mediation of some infinite modification" (Letter 63). We have seen that, in reply, Spinoza offers absolutely infinite intellect as an example of an immediate infinite mode in Thought, and motion and rest as an immediate infinite mode in Extension. But he offers only one example of a mediate infinite mode: "the face of the whole universe [*facies totius universi*]" (Letter 64). Although he does not tell Schuller whether this is an example of a mode in Extension or in Thought, it presumably lies in Extension, since he refers Schuller to the physical digression in Part Two (the scholium to Lemma 7 after IIP13) for some clarification.

'The face of the whole universe' might refer to a number of things. On the one hand, Spinoza could mean the totality of all existing material things – the existing finite modes of Extension – taken as an infinite and eternal series; that is, all of corporeal nature. This would be the series of existing bodies that durationally realize the eternal essences of bodies that, as we saw, can be regarded as the contents of the immediate infinite mode in Extension.[12] In this way, the mediate infinite mode in Extension would be the entirety of the contents of the physical universe – all particular bodies and all their relations throughout all time – considered as an eternal, infinite set and as an individual in its own right, one that, as he remarks to Schuller, "although varying in infinite ways, yet remains always the same." What remains always the same throughout the variations and thus gives the physical universe its individuality is, presumably, the overall proportion of motion and rest among those ever-changing material things. In the scholium to which he refers Schuller in his letter, Spinoza discusses "how a composite individual can be affected in many ways, and still preserve its nature." The discussion begins by considering the way in which a particular body that is composed of many simpler parts (each of which is a body in its own right) preserves its identity and individuality through various internal changes because its component parts nonetheless maintain a particular ratio of motion and rest among themselves. Proceeding

---

[12] Gueroult 1968, I.309–24.

upwards, through more composite individuals made up of such composite bodies, and so on, one finally reaches the material universe itself as the ultimate composite individual: "We shall easily conceive that the whole of nature is one Individual, whose parts, i.e., all bodies, vary in infinite ways, without any change of the whole Individual" (IIL7, G II.101–2/C I.461–2).[13]

If this is the proper way to understand Spinoza's reply to Schuller, then what Spinoza is saying in the *Ethics* is that from the nature of Extension (the attribute) taken in conjunction with motion and rest (the immediate infinite mode, containing at least virtually the essences of all physical things), what follows is the whole of physical nature, with all of its rich variety. Take matter, add motion, and you get a world of particular individuals. The individuals themselves may undergo change, through the transfer of motion, but the super-individual that they together constitute – the physical universe itself, understood as an overall proportion of motion and rest in matter – is eternal and immutable (as an infinite mode must be).

On the other hand, if we adopt the nomological reading of the infinite modes, whereby the immediate infinite modes are the most universal laws of nature, then the higher mediate infinite modes – those which follow most proximately from the immediate infinite modes, and which in turn give rise to lower-level mediate infinite modes – could be seen as subordinate laws of nature. Under Extension, this would be the particular rules governing the transfer of motion among bodies in collision. The "face of the whole universe" would then be the system of all these subordinate physical laws, not the particular individuals covered by them.[14] Like Descartes before him, Spinoza's claim would be that from the nature or laws of Extension itself, along with some supreme laws of physics (the immediate infinite mode), he can deduce all of the other laws of corporeal nature. These secondary laws would be the immutable and necessary features of the material world, the eternal "face" of the universe. Together, they govern and make possible the particular interactions among finite things. The world of existing finite things itself, the infinite set of all the particulars that make up the universe,

---

[13] See Allison 1987 (pp. 71–2) and Giancotti 1991.
[14] See Yovel 1991, p. 88.

would presumably, on this reading, be yet another, lower-level mediate infinite mode, one that follows from the attribute of Extension, the supreme laws of nature that constitute the immediate infinite mode, and the subordinate laws of nature that represent the higher-level mediate infinite modes.[15]

Now this much trouble has been caused when Spinoza *does* tell us what the mediate infinite mode is. Consider how much more trouble ensues when he does not. Indeed, a good deal of time and energy has been devoted to trying to figure out just what the mediate infinite mode under the attribute of Thought is. One scholar, in a cry of frustration, suggests that the effort is "useless."[16] But in fact, with all the rest of the picture filled in, it does not seem so impossible to determine with some plausibility what this final element might be. If the mediate infinite mode in Extension ("the face of the whole universe") is the world of actually existing bodies, an infinite whole of finite modes that realizes in duration the extended essences constituting the immediate infinite mode, then the mediate infinite mode in Thought should be the world of actually existing minds or ideas, also an infinite whole of finite modes (of Thought) that realize in duration the essences that constitute Thought's immediate infinite mode. If we were in an expansive mood, we could even say that 'the face of the whole universe' refers not only to the infinite series of finite modes in Extension, but also to the infinite series of finite modes – particular ideas or minds – in Thought. The latter is as much a part of the "face" of the universe as the former. But even if we reject this dual identification of Spinoza's enigmatic phrase, and however we ultimately want to understand what each of the infinite modes is, what is certain is that among them, at the bottom (so to speak), is the world of actually existing things. The infinite collection of bodies and the

---

[15] In what follows, I shall try, when I can, to accommodate the two ways of reading what the infinite modes are for Spinoza: both the reading that treats the immediate infinite mode as a collection of essences that corresponds to the collection of existents in the mediate infinite mode, and the reading that treats it as specifying certain laws that give rise to subordinate laws and then, ultimately, existing things in the mediate infinite modes. My hope is that this will not prove confusing to readers, and that they will be able to choose one strand or the other through which to make sense of what Spinoza is saying.

[16] Giancotti 1991, p. 106.

infinite collection of ideas or minds that make up this temporal existence will be the lower-most of the mediate infinite modes, the ones that follow from everything else within each attribute. It is the ontologically final stage of what one scholar calls the "cascade" of effects that follow from God or Nature.[17]

FINITE MODES

This examination of the contents of the infinite modes brings us, finally, to the domain of finite modes. In general, finite modes are particular things. They include both the individual eternal essences of particular things (which, on the interpretation above, is what is found in the immediate infinite modes) and the actually existing particular things (found within the mediate infinite modes) that instantiate those essences in time. The former are eternal finite modes, and the latter are durational or temporally existing finite modes. (Spinoza defines 'duration' as the "indefinite continuation of existence" (IID5).) More particularly, when Spinoza uses the phrase "singular thing" or "particular thing," or speaks of a "certain and determinate way" in which an attribute of God is expressed, he can be referring either to the essences of individual bodies and minds or to actually existing bodies or minds in nature.

The finite modes in the attribute of Extension – the material aspect of the universe – are individual bodies. The finite modes in the attribute of Thought – the mentalistic aspect of the universe – are ideas or minds. They are all modes because they are "in" substance in just the way we have determined all things are "in" God for Spinoza: they belong to God or Nature as its immanent effects. "Particular things are nothing but affections of God's attributes, or modes by which God's attributes are expressed in a certain and determinate way" (IP25c). Everything, no matter what it is, is in Nature in the sense of being an immanently generated part of Nature. Nothing – not even human beings, as we shall see – stand outside of the causal system of Nature. Whatever is, is in Nature and is brought about by Nature's principles.

---

[17] Gueroult 1968, I.9.

Moreover, because the series of finite modes under any attribute is itself an infinite mode of that attribute, following from causes that are infinite, this means that the series of finite modes is itself infinite. That is, there are an infinite number of finite modes within each series. The minds in Thought constitute an infinite series, as do the bodies in Extension. There is no first mind or first body; every mind has a place in an infinite chain of minds and every body has a place in an infinite chain of bodies.

The infinite modes have an essential causal role to play with respect to finite modes in Spinoza's system. Without the infinite modes, particular things would not be such as they are. The natures and laws that derive from Extension and Thought are essential to the explanation of particular bodies and ideas/minds, respectively. Bodies are what they generally are and behave as they generally do because of the nature of extension and the laws of motion, and similarly for minds and the principles of Thought.

But there is more to the explanation of a particular thing than its infinite and eternal causes. These principles are, in themselves, too general to specify anything in particular; they are just natures and laws, and so they underdetermine finite modes, and especially what is to happen in duration, in the domain of temporal existence. The complete cause of any singular thing or event must in fact lie in a combination of antecedent conditions among other singular things or events and the natures and laws that relate those antecedent conditions to their effects. The nature of matter and the laws of motion alone will not dictate that a window being struck by a ball will be broken; we also need some facts about the hardness and velocity of the ball that has been thrown at it, which in turn requires some facts about the arm throwing the ball, which in turn requires some facts about the strength of the person whose arm it is, and so on ad infinitum.

To put this in Spinoza's technical language, while the infinite modes – including the mediate infinite mode that is the infinite series of existing finite modes – follow from the absolute nature of an attribute, either immediately or mediately, the individual finite modes themselves do not, since then they would be not finite but infinite. "What is finite and has a determinate existence could not have been produced by the absolute nature of an attribute of God;

for whatever follows from the absolute nature of an attribute of God is eternal and infinite" (IP28d). Actually existing finite modes, as limited and durational beings, come into being at a certain point in time and cease to exist at a certain point in time. And what causes them to come into being and to cease to exist, as well as to have the particular effects they do, are both God or Nature and an infinite number of other, antecedent finite things. Or, to state this more accurately, since everything is in some way God, every finite thing is caused to be as it is and to have the effects that it does by both (a) God as substance and as modified by infinite modes, and (b) God as modified by finite modes. This is the upshot of IP26 and IP28. IP26 says that

A thing which has been determined to produce an effect has necessarily been determined in this way by God; and one which has not been determined by God cannot determine itself to produce an effect.

IP28 says that

Every singular thing, or any thing which is finite and has a determinate existence, can neither exist nor be determined to produce an effect unless it is determined to exist and produce an effect by another cause, which is also finite and has a determinate existence; and again, this cause also can neither exist nor be determined to produce an effect unless it is determined to exist and produce an effect by another, which is also finite and has a determinate existence, and so on, to infinity.

On the face of it, these two propositions may seem inconsistent: one says that God is what determines a thing to produce an effect (with Spinoza adding, in the demonstration, that "God, from the necessity of his nature, is the efficient cause both of its essence and of its existence"), and the other says that another finite thing is what determines a thing to produce an effect. But because finite things just are modes of God, the second proposition is perfectly consistent with the first. What the two propositions together are saying is that every causal relationship among finite things is a function both of those finite things themselves and of the infinite things (natures and laws) that govern the behavior of those finite things. Every event in nature stands at the intersection of two causal nexuses: a "horizontal" nexus within which a thing is temporally and causally related to (infinitely many) prior and posterior things; and a "vertical" nexus within which a thing and its relationship to other things is causally related to eternal principles, culminating in Nature's attributes. IP28 refers to the first causal nexus and IP26 refers to the second one. As the finite thing is embedded in its horizontal relationship to infinitely many other finite things, the infinite series of causally related finite things (a mediate infinite mode) is in turn embedded in – and derives its necessity from – a vertical relationship to higher infinite modes and, ultimately, substance itself. The infinite chain of finite causes itself is brought into being by the infinite causes. Or, as one commentator so elegantly puts it, every finite mode is brought about by (or deducible from) an infinite series of other finite causes and a finite series of infinite causes.[18]

God thus determines finite things not directly, as God determines the immediate infinite modes, but indirectly, insofar as God is modified *both* by the infinite modes and by other finite modes. "[Every singular thing must] follow from, or be determined to exist and produce an effect by God or an attribute of God insofar as it is modified by a modification which is finite and has a determinate existence" (IP28d). In this way, everything depends on God or Nature: either immediately, as is the case with the immediate infinite modes (IP26), or mediately; and if mediately either through infinite things alone, as is the case with the mediate infinite modes (IP26), or through infinite things and finite things, as is the case with finite modes (IP28).[19] "All things that are, are in God, and so depend on God that they can neither be nor be conceived without him" (IP28sII). (This will prove to be an important point later in the *Ethics*, when Spinoza relates human virtue and well-being to a special kind of explanatory knowledge of nature, one that relates things to their eternal causes, and especially to God.)

Spinoza thus has an answer to one kind of question that can be asked of why the world is as it is, or why the infinite series of finite

---

[18] Curley 1988, p. 48.
[19] It is, admittedly, a bit misleading to speak of a finite thing *x* being determined *mediately* by God. What this cannot mean is that something distinct from God stands between God and *x*. In fact, since the other finite things through which God determines *x* are themselves God (as modified in particular ways), then perhaps it can still be said that it is God (albeit *qua* finite things) that is *immediately* the cause of *x*.

things constituting the mediate infinite mode, what he calls "the common order of nature," is such as we find it. He can say in general that those things have the specific order and connection they do because this is determined by higher, infinite, and eternal causes. And he can say that for any particular finite thing within that order, it is as it is because of both those infinite causes and other finite causes.

But there is another kind of question that may prove more difficult for Spinoza to answer: why is there a diversity of finite things in the first place? If the attribute is a singular, infinite, and eternal nature, then everything that follows necessarily from it should be singular, infinite, and eternal. But, then, whence the plurality of finite, temporal, and mutable things within the eternal and unchanging infinite modes of each attribute? How is one supposed to get deductively from infinite unchanging things to finite changing things?

This interesting and important question gets raised in one of the last extant letters we have from Spinoza's correspondence. Tschirnhaus insists that from the simple definition of any thing considered in itself, one is able to deduce only one property; to be able deduce more than one property, one must add to the definition to make it more complex and so able to generate more implications. But, Tschirnhaus, who had a copy of the manuscript of the *Ethics*, goes on to say, this principle "seems to be at variance to some extent with Proposition 16 of the *Ethics* . . . In this proposition [which states that "infinitely many things" follow from each of the attributes of God, each of which represents a simple essence] it is taken for granted that several properties can be deduced from the given definition of any thing." In short, Tschirnhaus is curious to know how "from an attribute considered only by itself, for example, Extension, an infinite variety of bodies can arise" (Letter 82).

This problem of how Spinoza can deduce that there is a plurality of finite things – even if they together constitute a single infinite world – from a unique and simple infinite starting point has long troubled commentators. Spinoza's reply to Tschirnhaus is not very illuminating. He denies that the principle cited by Tschirnhaus regarding what can be deduced from a definition applies to real things (such as God, from whose essence one can deduce that God is infinite, unique, immutable, etc.), as opposed to abstract entities.[20] And yet, he also concedes that "with regard to your question as to whether the variety of things can be demonstrated a priori solely from the conception of Extension, I think I have already made it quite clear that this is impossible" (Letter 83). But what he adds to this suggests that Spinoza nonetheless believes that he *can* deduce the variety of things from *his* conception of the attributes of God: "That is why Descartes is wrong in defining matter through Extension; it must necessarily be explicated through an attribute which expresses eternal and infinite essence." He does not say anything further, however, and tells Tschirnhaus that they will have to discuss this at some later time, "for as yet I have not had the opportunity to arrange in due order anything on this subject." The opportunity most likely never arose, as Spinoza died seven months after writing this letter.

I do think that Spinoza probably believed that from the attribute of Extension, together with motion (the immediate infinite mode, which expresses the power of *Natura naturans* through Extension), a plurality of (essences of) finite bodies necessarily follows. For what divides undifferentiated extended matter up into particular bodies for someone who is a Cartesian in his physics (as Spinoza is) just is motion. The essence of a body is nothing but a parcel of extension individuated from other parcels of extension only by a relatively stable ratio of motion and rest among its constituent parts.

I would also suggest that Spinoza is not troubled in the *Ethics* with the problem of how to derive a world consisting of a plurality of finite modes from starting points that are singular, uniform, and infinite because for him the universe of finite modes is simply a given. Experience tells us that there are finite things in the world around us. So the problem is not how to deduce that there is a plurality of finite things. Rather, the problem is to determine what exactly the ontological status of those finite things is. That is, given that (as we know from experience) there are finite things, and given that (as we know deductively from the propositions of *Ethics* I) there are infinite things, how can we connect the finite things up

---

[20] Tschirnhaus had used the example of the definition of the circumference of the circle, from which only one property can be deduced: "that it is everywhere alike or uniform."

with their infinite causes and "complete" the chain of explanation? The trouble with this approach, though, is that it leaves the existence of a plurality of finite things itself undetermined and unexplained, a kind of brute fact. And this would seem to run counter to Spinoza's causal rationalism.

## DETERMINISM AND NECESSITARIANISM

To put it all together, then, we have the following metaphysical picture.

First, there is God or Nature as a whole, the infinite, eternal, necessarily existing, active universe that includes absolutely everything. The first necessary and eternal effects of God or Nature – effects that are immanent since they, like everything, are in Nature – are (depending on which interpretation of the immediate infinite modes one adopts) either infinite series of atemporal essences of things or simply general natures and laws. (Perhaps they are both, since Spinoza nowhere says that under each attribute there is one and only one immediate infinite mode.)

The second necessary and eternal effect of God or Nature, one mediated by that first effect, is the world of actually existing things. This world, which (being infinite and eternal) itself stands outside of time or duration, is composed of the finite and mutable existents that are the instantiations in time of those essences and laws.

More particularly, from the eternal, absolutely necessary and most fundamental elements of Nature – God's attributes (i.e., Nature's most universal principles), taken together with the essential active power that is God or Nature itself – there follows, first of all, the eternal essences and laws of bodies (within the material aspect of Nature) and the eternal essences and laws of minds (within Thought). From these, in turn, there follow, respectively, an infinite series of actually existing bodies (again, within the material aspect of Nature) and an infinite series of actually existing minds (in Thought). (A correlative picture will, of course, describe as well the infinite and finite modes that follow from all of the other, infinitely many but unknown attributes or aspects of Nature.)

The cosmos that Spinoza describes is clearly a strictly deterministic one. Everything, without exception, is causally determined to be such as it is; and, given its causes, no thing could have been otherwise than as it is. Immediately after establishing (in IP26 and IP28) the two dimensions of causation, infinite and finite, Spinoza concludes, with IP29, that there is no contingency in the universe: not for the universe itself, and not for anything within it. "In nature there is nothing contingent, but all things have been determined from the necessity of the divine nature to exist and produce an effect in a certain way."

For Spinoza, the term 'contingent' is ambiguous. First, and especially in Part One, it can mean what is causally undetermined. But in Part Four, Spinoza will distinguish 'contingent' from 'possible.' Things are called "possible" when "while we attend to the causes from which they must be produced, we do not know whether these causes are determined to produce them" (IVD4); things are called "contingent," by contrast, when there is nothing within its essence "which necessarily posits [its] existence or which necessarily excludes it" (IVD3), that is, when it is neither necessary by reason of its essence (as God/substance is) nor impossible because its essence involves a contradiction. Something that is contingent in this second sense (which is our ordinary understanding of the term) will still be causally determined and therefore, for Spinoza, necessary, albeit "by reason of its cause."

Now there certainly *is* contingency in the universe in this second sense – namely, for everything that is not substance and its attributes. When Spinoza says that "there is absolutely nothing in things on account of which they can be called contingent" (IP33s1), he means that there is no contingency in the first sense (that is, the sense in which it turns out to be synonymous with 'possible'). Nothing escapes the determinations of Nature's causal processes. This is true of all physical events, but it is also true of all thinking events, including, as we shall soon see in more detail, all of the ideas and volitions that occur in the human mind. Any belief in contingency (in the first sense) is due only to ignorance, to an inadequate grasp of the order of Nature.

A thing is called contingent only because of a defect of our knowledge. For if we do not know that the thing's essence involves a contradiction, or if we do know very well that its essence does not involve a contradiction, and nevertheless can affirm nothing certainly about its existence, because the order of causes is hidden from us, it can never seem to us either necessary or impossible. So we call it contingent or possible. (IP33s1)

The import of the second clause of IA3, "If there is no determinate cause, it is impossible for an effect to follow," is now clear.

So Spinoza is a strong determinist. But is he also a necessitarian? Does he believe that not only is everything (whether it be infinite or finite) causally determined to exist as it is and to bring about the effects it does, but also that the causal order of nature could not possibly have been otherwise than it is? The conclusion that he does seems inescapable.[21]

Because of Spinoza's identification of causal with logical necessity, not only are the essences and laws of things an absolutely or logically necessary effect of Nature, but so too is the world of existing things. The natural world itself, the familiar empirical landscape of physical and mental items as a whole, is for Spinoza eternal, infinite, and necessary, just because it is the necessary effect of an eternal, infinite, and necessary being. Given its status as a mediate infinite mode, the series of finite things "must follow either from the absolute nature of some attribute of God, or from some attribute, modified by a modification which exists necessarily and is infinite" (IP23). And as Spinoza says (in IP21 and IP22), whatever follows from an eternal, necessary, and infinite being – whether it follows immediately or through the mediation of something that follows immediately – must itself be eternal, necessary, and infinite. Unlike the logical necessity of substance and its attributes (or *Natura naturans*), however, which is the necessity "by reason of its essence" characteristic of an uncaused being that "is in itself," the logical necessity that belongs to the infinite modes is a "necessity by reason of its cause." These things (including "the face of the whole universe") could not possibly have been otherwise, but that is because they have been necessarily determined by something that, in and of itself, could not possibly have been otherwise.

As for any individual finite mode, as a constituent part of a series that itself could not have been otherwise, it too is absolutely necessary. Moreover, each finite mode is causally (and therefore logically)

---

[21] For a debate over this question, see D. Garrett 1991 vs. Curley and Walski 1999.

necessitated by the relevant combination of infinite modes and other finite modes. Because the infinite modes (i.e., the laws of nature) are absolutely necessary, and because the series of prior finite events is infinite – from which it follows that there is no member of that series that is not necessitated by some prior causes and therefore could have been different – there is no particular thing or event in nature that could possibly have been otherwise. Everything that happens *had* to happen, in the strongest possible sense: not just because its causes happened (this would be mere determinism), but because its causes themselves *had* to happen.

In other words, for Spinoza there are no possible worlds other than the actual world. If it is absolutely impossible for God to exist but the particular infinite series of finite modes that makes up this world not to exist; and if God's existence is, as Spinoza argues, absolutely necessary in itself, then this world is the only possible world.[22] This extraordinary claim is something that Spinoza seems to embrace. IP33 says "Things could have been produced by God in no other way, and in no other order than they have been produced." Spinoza's first demonstration for this proposition seems unnecessarily complicated. In the scholium to the proposition, however, he argues for it more directly by relying on the fact that *Natura naturans*, God's power and God's attributes, the ultimate cause of everything, is necessary "by its own nature." "If things had been produced by God otherwise than they now are, God's intellect and his will, i.e., (as is conceded) his essence, would have to be different [from what it now is]. And this is absurd" (G II.76/C I.438). The only way there could be a different world, for "the order of nature" to be different, is if God's nature, from which that order necessarily follows, could be different. But since it has been established that God's nature is absolutely necessary in itself, and not simply by

---

[22] Some scholars are unhappy with reading Spinoza in this way, and they hope to rescue him from necessitarianism. See Curley and Walski 1999. They are responding to D. Garrett 1991, who argues for a necessitarian reading. The fear is that with necessitarianism comes the loss of a number of crucial distinctions – between necessary and contingent truths, between essential and accidental properties of things – and an inability to account for such important conceptual tools as counterfactuals; see Bennett 1984, pp. 111–24. Bennett grants, though, that it is hard to avoid the conclusion that Spinoza's considered position ("what Spinoza consciously, explicitly held") was the necessitarian one (p. 123).

reason of its cause, God's nature could not possibly have been different. Therefore, the world of things, no less than the universal features of the cosmos, has to be what it is and could not have been otherwise.

It should be clear from all this, as well, that Spinoza denies that there is any such thing as the *creation* of the world, if what is meant by that is that God exists before willfully bringing the world into being *ex nihilo*, from a prior state of nonbeing, and that God could also have *not* brought the world into being. The world of existing things is a necessary and co-eternal effect of God's (Nature's) being. Thus, it is absolutely impossible for God to exist but the world not to exist. Spinoza thereby rejects the opening chapters of the Bible as an imaginative fiction.

For Spinoza, the necessity that governs the universe – in its origins and in its inner workings, and whether that necessity derives from essences or from a causal order – is nothing less than the absolute necessity found among the truths of mathematics. This is a conclusion that Spinoza is not shy about publicly proclaiming. In the "Metaphysical Thoughts" appended to his exposition of Descartes's *Principles of Philosophy*, the only work published under his name during his lifetime, he asserts that "if men understood clearly the whole order of Nature, they would find all things just as necessary as are all those treated in Mathematics" (CM, G I.266/C I.332).

### DIVINE FREEDOM

By denying even the logical possibility of there being other worlds, Spinoza forecloses a crucial and (in the seventeenth century) popular way of conceiving of God's freedom. To get a sense of Spinoza's radical originality here, it is useful to contrast him with the two other most important philosophers of the period: Descartes and Leibniz.

Descartes believed that God was free with what philosophers today would call libertarian freedom. For Descartes, God's freedom consists in the fact that God's will or choice is absolutely undetermined. Nothing whatsoever compels or even guides God to do what he does: no force outside of God, of course, but not even any features intrinsic to the divine nature (such as goodness or wisdom). God created the world, but, all things being the same, he could just as well have not created it or created some different world. In fact, God is the free and "indifferent" cause not only of existing things, but also of all essences and truths. The laws of physics, the principles of metaphysics, even the so-called eternal truths of logic and mathematics are all ultimately dependent on an arbitrary act of God. There are no standards of truth or goodness before God wills them. But that means that there are no standards of truth or goodness to determine God in his choices. To insist otherwise and claim that there are objective truths independent of God that he follows, Descartes says, "is to talk of him as if he were Jupiter or Saturn and to subject him to the Styx and the Fates."[23] God made $1 + 1 = 2$, but could just as well have made it *not* be the case that $1 + 1 = 2$, without violating any absolute canons of rationality.

Leibniz, by contrast, believes that God's freedom manifests itself in the rational decisions that God makes. Unlike the libertarian freedom of Descartes's God, the choices that Leibniz's God makes are determined. God acts on the basis of objective and universal reasons, reasons that are independent of God's will and that lead God to prefer one thing rather than another. God, for example, chooses to create this world rather than any other of the infinitely many possible worlds in his understanding because God perceives that this world is, objectively speaking, the best. The actual world holds the greatest appeal to his goodness and rationality, and this "morally" (but not absolutely or metaphysically) determines him to create it.[24] If Descartes's account of divine freedom gives priority to God's omnipotence, Leibniz's account gives priority to God's rationality, wisdom, and beneficence.

Spinoza explicitly rejects both of these ways of conceiving God's freedom. In fact, he rejects the whole notion of God even choosing anything. Spinoza's God is not free by way of having freedom of choice or volition. "God does not produce any effect by freedom

---

[23] Letter to Mersenne, 15 April 1630, AT I.145/CSM III.23.
[24] The fullest picture of Leibniz's conception of God's freedom is in the only book he published in his lifetime, *Theodicy*.

of the will" (IP32C1). God is not some rational, volitional agent who deliberates over possibilities and then chooses to realize one of them.

Spinoza agrees with Descartes that God is the cause of all truths and all essences, as well as all existents. But this is because he agrees that all things depend causally on God, and that thus there is nothing outside of God (or Nature).

I confess that this opinion, which subjects all things to a certain indifferent will of God, and makes all things depend on his good pleasure, is nearer the truth than that of those who maintain that God does all things for the sake of the good. For [the latter] seem to place something outside of God, which does not depend on God, to which God attends, as a model, in what he does, and at which he aims, as at a certain goal.

Nonetheless, Spinoza insists, Descartes is, like Leibniz, wrong to think that God – acting like a human agent – makes some choice, arbitrary or not, or that he can do otherwise than as he has done.

Others think that God is a free cause because he can (so they think) bring it about that the things which we have said follow from his nature (i.e., which are in his power) do not happen or are not produced by him. But this is the same as if they were to say that God can bring it about that it would not follow from the nature of a triangle that its three angles are equal to two right angles; or that from a given cause the effect would not follow – which is absurd. (IP17s1)

For Spinoza, God is still a free cause. But this is because nothing compels or constrains God to produce the effects that naturally and necessarily follow from its attributes. IP17 states that "God acts from the laws of his nature alone, and is compelled by no one." Because there is nothing outside of God or Nature, there is "nothing outside [of God] by which he is determined or compelled to act." It follows from this, Spinoza adds in a corollary, that "God alone is a free cause. For God alone exists only from the necessity of his nature and acts from the necessity of his nature." All of *Natura naturata* is a spontaneous effect of God's being. The infinite and finite modes may all be necessitated by God or Nature, but because the necessity derives from God's nature itself, there is no threat to God's freedom. As Spinoza says to Schuller, "although God exists necessarily, he nevertheless exists freely because he exists solely from the necessity of his own nature . . . So you see that I place freedom not in free decision, but in free necessity" (Letter 58). To this we can add what Spinoza wrote in the *Short Treatise*: "True freedom is nothing but [being] the first cause, which is not in any way constrained or necessitated by anything else, and only through its perfection is the cause of all perfection" (KV I.4, G I.37–8/C I.82). It will follow from Spinoza's conception of freedom, however, that ultimately *only* God is an absolutely free cause, because all other things – including human beings – are determined by causes outside themselves.

### MIRACLES

The question of divine freedom is intimately bound up with the issue of miracles, since these are ordinarily taken to be free acts of God that interrupt the course of nature and that represent an immediate manifestation of God's power. But for Spinoza there are no exceptions to the natural causal determinism that governs things. There are no spontaneous or undetermined states of affairs within nature, and there are no events that are violations of the laws of nature (i.e., that are contrary to the causal principles of *Natura naturans* and the infinite modes).

Miracles, therefore, understood as supernatural happenings that do violate the laws of nature are, for Spinoza, impossible. There may be (or may have been in the Biblical past) miracles in the epistemic sense of events whose natural explanations happen to escape human understanding in a purely de facto way, but not in the sense of events for which there is no natural explanation or which in principle cannot be understood by us. Spinoza makes this point quite directly in the *Theological-Political Treatise*:

Nothing . . . can happen in Nature to contravene her own universal laws, nor yet anything that is not in agreement with these laws or that does not follow from them. For whatever occurs does so through God's will and eternal decree; that is, . . . all that happens does so in accordance with laws and rules which involve eternal necessity and truth. Nature, then, always observes laws and rules involving eternal necessity and truth although these are not all known to us, and thus it also observes a fixed and immutable order.

From this, he continues, it follows "most clearly"

that the word miracle can be understood only with respect to men's beliefs, and means simply an event whose natural cause we – or at any rate the writer or narrator of the miracle – cannot explain by comparison with any other normal event. (TTP, Chapter 6, G III.83–4/S 73)

For Spinoza, there can be no greater manifestation of God's (Nature's) power than the law-like and necessary course of nature itself. God's providence is not revealed by ad hoc interventions or interruptions of nature's ways. Rather, it appears in the ordinary causal order of things. And God's "decrees" are nothing other than the laws of nature themselves. Again, the *Theological-Political Treatise* offers a fine gloss of this aspect of the *Ethics*:

God's decrees and commandments, and consequently God's providence, are in truth nothing but Nature's order; that is to say, when Scripture tells us that this or that was accomplished by God or by God's will, nothing more is intended than that it came about by accordance with Nature's law and order, and not, as the common people believe, that Nature for that time suspended her action, or that her order was temporarily interrupted. (TTP, Chapter 6, G III.89/S 78)

### PANTHEIST OR ATHEIST?

Spinoza was often called an "atheist" by his contemporaries. Bayle, for one, described Spinoza as "a Jew by birth, and afterwards a deserter from Judaism, and lastly an atheist."[25] It was a charge that Spinoza deeply resented. When another one of his critics, Lambert van Velthuysen, accused him of "teaching sheer atheism," Spinoza responded by saying that Van Velthuysen "perversely misinterpreted my meaning," and protested that he should be ashamed of leveling such a charge against him (Letters 42 and 43). Still, the label stuck – perhaps not without good reason – and in the latter half of the seventeenth century and throughout the eighteenth century, "Spinozism" became synonymous with atheism. It was an epithet that one hurled at one's opponents in order to discredit them and their ideas.

The term 'atheist' is certainly ambiguous, and it often serves as an all-purpose charge. But the meaning of the word becomes especially

---

[25] Bayle 1965, p. 288.

hazy when viewed in the context of the volatile religious and political environment of late seventeenth-century Holland. To many of Spinoza's Dutch contemporaries, 'atheist' meant someone who simply showed disrespect for religion, and the Reformed religion in particular. Spinoza did not, to be sure, have a very high opinion of most organized religions, especially as they existed in his day. But he did believe in what he called the "true religion," a kind of non-sectarian moral piety that his nonconfessional friends probably practiced. Thus, he was taken aback by the claim that he had "renounced all religion." "Does that man, pray, renounce all religion, who declares that God must be acknowledged as the highest good, and that he must be loved as such in a free spirit? And that in this alone does our supreme happiness and our highest freedom consist?" (Letter 43, G IV.220/SL 238).

Of course, Spinoza's rejection of the label is just as ambiguous as the label itself. If by 'atheist' is meant someone who rejects religion per se, Spinoza is saying to Van Velthausen, then he denies that he is an atheist. At another point in the same correspondence, however, he seems to take the charge to refer not to his religious beliefs but to his mode of living: "If he [Van Velthuysen] had known [what manner of life I pursue], he would not have been so readily convinced that I teach atheism. For atheists are usually inordinately fond of honors and riches, which I have always despised, as is known to all who are acquainted with me" (Letter 43, G IV.219/SL 237).

Ultimately, as one might expect, the issue of Spinoza's alleged atheism is not to be decided on the basis of his values and lifestyle – even Bayle admitted that Spinoza was of an exemplary character – nor on the basis of his attitude toward religion, nor even on the basis of whether the concept of 'God' plays a role in his philosophy. There can be no question that the concept of God is an integral part of the *Ethics*, but this does not settle the matter. The real question is, what does Spinoza mean by 'God'?

He certainly does *not* mean by 'God' what the Judeo-Christian religious tradition means by 'God'. In the first place, the God of Judaism and Christianity is a transcendent being, ontologically distinct from the world it creates; Spinoza's God, as we have seen, is not transcendent but immanent. God, for Spinoza, is not a supernatural being that stands outside of the world; God *is* Nature (however one wants to interpret that phrase).

Second, the Judeo-Christian God is an all-wise, all-knowing, all-powerful, beneficent but occasionally wrathful divinity who stands in judgment over us, both in this lifetime and in the hereafter. This is the providential God of Abraham, Isaac, and Jacob – a God who commands and expects certain modes of behavior from creatures, a higher being who conceives and carries out a plan for creation. This God cares about humanity, and rewards those who follow its will and punishes those who disobey it. It is a God endowed with psychological characteristics (intelligence, will, desire, even emotion) and moral characteristics (benevolence, a sense of right vs. wrong and good vs. bad).

It is just this traditional religious picture of God that Spinoza rejects as foolish anthropomorphism. Immediately after establishing, in IP1–15, that "whatever is, is in God," Spinoza adds the following brief remark, in the scholium to IP15: "There are those who feign a God, like man, consisting of a body and a mind, and subject to passions. But how far they wander from the true knowledge of God, is sufficiently established by what has already been demonstrated." The theme is taken up at greater length in the fascinating and all-important appendix that appears at the end of Part One.

Spinoza's fundamental insight in Part One is that Nature is an indivisible, infinite, uncaused, substantial whole – in fact, it is the *only* substantial whole. Outside of Nature there is nothing, and everything that exists is a part of Nature and is brought into being *by* and within Nature with a deterministic necessity through Nature's laws. This substantial, unique, unified, active, infinitely powerful, necessary being just *is* what is meant by 'God.'

The appendix of Part One now draws out the religious and theological implications of the metaphysics that has been demonstrated in the foregoing propositions. Because of the necessity inherent in Nature, there is no teleology for or within the universe, outside of the projects that human beings may set for themselves. Nature itself does not have any purpose or act for any ends, and things within nature do not exist for the sake of anything. To put it in terms of Aristotle's philosophy, with which Spinoza was familiar, there are no "final causes"; everything is brought about solely through the operation of efficient causation. God or Nature does not "do" things to achieve any goals. The order of things just follows from God's attributes with necessity. All talk of God's purposes, intentions, goals, preferences or aims is just an anthropomorphizing fiction.

All the prejudices I here undertake to expose depend on this one: that men commonly suppose that all natural things act, as men do, on account of an end; indeed, they maintain as certain that God himself directs all things to some certain end, for they say that God has made all things for man, and man that he might worship God. (I, Appendix, G II.78/C I.439–40)

God is not some goal-oriented planner who then judges things by how well they conform to his purposes. Things happen only because of Nature and its laws. "Nature has no end set before it . . . All things proceed by a certain eternal necessity of nature." To believe otherwise is to fall prey to the same superstitions that lie at the heart of the organized religions.

[People] find – both in themselves and outside themselves – many means that are very helpful in seeking their own advantage, e.g., eyes for seeing, teeth for chewing, plants and animals for food, the sun for light, the sea for supporting fish . . . Hence, they consider all natural things as means to their own advantage. And knowing that they had found these means, not provided them for themselves, they had reason to believe that there was someone else who had prepared those means for their use. For after they considered things as means, they could not believe that the things had made themselves; but from the means they were accustomed to prepare for themselves, they had to infer that there was a ruler, or a number of rulers of nature, endowed with human freedom, who had taken care of all things for them, and made all things for their use. And since they had never heard anything about the temperament of these rulers, they had to judge it from their own. Hence, they maintained that the Gods direct all things for the use of men in order to bind men to them and be held by men in the highest honor. So it has happened that each of them has thought up from his own temperament different ways of worshipping God, so that God might love them above all the rest, and direct the whole of Nature according to the needs of their blind desire and insatiable greed. Thus this prejudice was changed into superstition, and struck deep roots in their minds. (I, Appendix, G II.78–9/C I.440–41)

In a letter to one of his more troublesome correspondents, the Dutch merchant Willem van Blijenburgh, Spinoza emphasizes the absurdity of conceiving God in this way. The language of traditional theology, he says, represents God "as a perfect man" and claims that "God desires something, that God is displeased with the deeds of the impious and pleased with those of the pious." In all philosophical rigor, however, "we clearly understand that to ascribe to God those attributes which make a man perfect would be as wrong as to ascribe to a man the attributes that make perfect an elephant or an ass" (Letter 23, G IV.148/SL 166). Some years later, in another letter, this time to Hugo Boxel, Spinoza turns to sarcasm to make his point:

When you say that you do not see what sort of God I have if I deny him the actions of seeing, hearing, attending, willing, etc. and that he possesses those faculties in an eminent degree, I suspect that you believe that there is no greater perfection than can be explicated by the aforementioned attributes. I am not surprised, for I believe that a triangle, if it could speak, would likewise say that God is eminently triangular, and a circle that God's nature is eminently circular. (Letter 56, G IV.260/SL 277)

A judging God who has plans and acts purposively is a God to be obeyed and placated. Opportunistic preachers are then able to play on our hopes and fears in the face of such a God. They prescribe ways of acting that are calculated to avoid being punished by that God and earn his rewards. But, Spinoza insists, to see God or Nature as acting for the sake of ends – to find purpose in Nature – is to misconstrue Nature and "turn it upside down" by putting the effect (the end result) before the true cause. In Spinoza's view, the traditional religious conception of God leads only to superstition, not enlightenment.

Like the belief in miracles, the projection of purposiveness onto God or Nature is due only to ignorance of the true causes of phenomena.

If a stone has fallen from a room onto someone's head and killed him, they will show, in the following way, that the stone fell in order to kill the man. For if it did not fall to that end, God willing it, how could so many circumstances have concurred by chance (for often many circumstances do concur at once)? Perhaps you will answer that it happened because the wind was blowing hard and the man was walking that way. But they will persist: why was the wind blowing hard at that time? Why was the man walking that way at that time? If you answer again that the wind arose then because on the preceding day, while the weather was still calm, the sea began to toss, and that the man had been invited by a friend, they will press on – for there is no end to the questions which can be asked: but why was the sea tossing? Why was the man invited at just that time? And so they will not stop asking for the causes of causes until you take refuge in the will of God, i.e., the sanctuary of ignorance. (I, Appendix, G II.80–1/C I.443)

This is strong language, and Spinoza is clearly not unaware of the risks of his position. The same preachers who take advantage of our credulity will fulminate against anyone who tries to pull aside the curtain and reveal the truths of Nature. "One who seeks the true causes of miracles, and is eager, like an educated man, to understand natural things, not to wonder at them, like a fool, is generally considered and denounced as an impious heretic by those whom the people honor as interpreters of nature and the Gods. For they know that if ignorance is taken away, then foolish wonder, the only means they have of arguing and defending their authority, is also taken away."

At the very least, then, Spinoza eliminates the anthropomorphic fantasies that, he insists, have endowed God with psychological and moral characteristics that are unworthy of the kind of being God is. "This doctrine [which would have God act as humans act] takes away God's perfection" (I, Appendix, G II.80/C I.442). But this alone does not make Spinoza an atheist. It just means that his conception of God departs from the traditional religious picture. One of the rumors circulating at the time of Spinoza's banishment from the Amsterdam Portuguese-Jewish community was that he believed that "God exists only philosophically." This is a vague charge, but could possibly mean only that Spinoza had a minimal, overly rationalistic conception of God, perhaps a rather impersonal God that bears certain metaphysical and causal functions but that, without the psychological and moral features of the Judeo-Christian God, is of little comfort to us suffering but hopeful creatures. But one could also argue that Descartes's God, who plays mainly a metaphysical and epistemological role in Descartes's system, can be seen merely as a "philosophical God" as well without intending to impute atheism to Descartes.

The more difficult feature of Spinoza's conception of God, the one that makes a true theism problematic, is the identification of God with Nature and the elimination of God's transcendence. It has often been said, over the centuries, that Spinoza is a pantheist. Now what is distinctive about all forms of pantheism is the denial of the transcendence of God. So far, the label seems to fit. But 'pantheism' can be taken in at least two senses. First, pantheism can be understood as (a) the claim that God is ontologically distinct from the world and its contents but nonetheless ubiquitously "contained" or "immanent" within them, perhaps in the way in which water is contained in a soaked sponge or juices are contained within a fruit. This might be called "immanentist pantheism." Second, pantheism can be understood as (b) the assertion that God is in fact identical with everything that exists. "God is everything and everything is God," as the position has been expressed. On this view, God is the world and all its contents, and nothing distinct from them. This would be "reductive pantheism."

Despite the fact that Spinoza explicitly tells us that God is "immanent" in Nature, he clearly is not a pantheist in the first, immanentist sense. The phrase 'God or Nature' is intended to assert a strict numerical identity between God and Nature, not a containment relationship. God is not "in" Nature in such a way that nature contains, in addition to its natural contents, a distinct divine and supernatural content. There is no supernatural divine spark or spirit or juice either in natural things or in or under Nature as a whole.

But neither, I would insist, is Spinoza a pantheist in the second, reductive sense, and it is important to see why.

On the face of it, it might seem that the debate over whether God is to be identified with the *whole* of Nature or only a *part* of Nature (i.e., *Natura naturans*), examined in the previous chapter, is crucial to the question of Spinoza's alleged pantheism. After all, if pantheism is the view that God is everything, then Spinoza is a pantheist only if he identifies God with *all* of Nature – that is, only if we adopt the inherence interpretation of the relationship between substance and modes in his metaphysics. Indeed, this is exactly how the issue is framed in the recent literature (which, unlike the debates over Spinoza's view of God in the seventeenth and eighteenth centuries, involves less religious and political passion and more clear-eyed analysis). Both those who believe that Spinoza *is* a pantheist and those who believe that he is *not* a pantheist focus on the question of whether God is to be identified with the whole of

Nature, including finite modes, or only with substance and attributes but not modes.[26]

I would like to suggest, however, that this debate about the *extent* of Spinoza's identification of God with Nature is not really to the point. To be sure, if by 'pantheism' is meant the idea that God is everything, and if one reads Spinoza as saying that God is only *Natura naturans*, then Spinoza's God is not everything and consequently he is not a pantheist. Finite things, on this reading, while caused by the eternal, necessary, and active aspects of Nature, are not identical with God or substance, but rather are its effects. But this is not the interesting sense in which Spinoza is not a pantheist. For even if Spinoza does indeed identify God with the whole of Nature, it does not follow that Spinoza *is* a pantheist. The real issue is not what is the proper reading of the metaphysics of Spinoza's conception of God. On either interpretation, Spinoza's move is a naturalistic and reductive one. God is identical either with all of Nature or with only a part of Nature; for this reason, Spinoza shares something with the pantheist (on the reductive version). But – and this is the important point – even the atheist can, without too much difficulty, admit that God is nothing but Nature. Reductive pantheism and atheism are, in ontological terms, extensionally equivalent, since neither recognizes anything above and beyond what is natural.

Rather, the question of Spinoza's pantheism is really going to be answered on the psychological side of things, with regard to the proper attitude to take toward *Deus sive Natura*. I would insist that, whichever of the two readings of the substance/mode relationship that one adopts, it is a mistake to call Spinoza a "pantheist" in so far as pantheism is still a kind of theism. What really distinguishes the pantheist from the atheist is that the pantheist does not reject as inappropriate the religious psychological attitudes demanded by theism. Rather, the pantheist simply asserts that God – a being

---

[26] Thus, on one side Bennett argues that Spinoza is a pantheist because God is identical to the whole of nature (1984, p. 58); Yovel takes a similar line (1989, p. 76). On the other side, Donagan argues that "Spinoza is not a pantheist" since he denies that "the totality of finite things is God" (1988, p. 90); agreeing with him, and for the same reasons, are Curley (1991), and Sylvain Zac (1991, p. 238).

before which one is to adopt an attitude of worshipful awe – is or is extended throughout Nature. And nothing could be further from the spirit of Spinoza's philosophy. As we have seen to some degree already, and as we shall examine in more detail in later chapters, Spinoza does not believe that worshipful awe is an appropriate attitude to take before God or Nature.[27] There is nothing holy or sacred about Nature. It is certainly not the object of a religious experience – with its concomitant emotions of hope and fear – and there is no place in Spinoza's system for a sense of mystery in the face of Nature. Instead, one should strive to understand God or Nature, with the kind of adequate or clear and distinct intellectual knowledge that reveals Nature's most important truths and shows how everything depends essentially and existentially on higher natural causes. The key to discovering and experiencing God, for Spinoza, is philosophy and science, not religious awe and worshipful submission. The latter give rise only to superstitious behavior and subservience to ecclesiastic authorities; the former lead to enlightenment, freedom, and true blessedness (i.e., peace of mind).

To be sure, Spinoza is at times capable of language that seems deeply religious. He says that "we feel and know by experience that we are eternal" (VP23s), and that virtue and perfection are accompanied by a "love of God [*amor Dei*]" (VP15, VP32s, VP33). But, as we shall see, such phrases are not to be given their traditional religious meaning. Spinoza's naturalist and rationalist project demands that we provide these notions with a proper intellectualist interpretation. Thus, the love of God will turn out to be simply an awareness of the ultimate natural cause of the joy that accompanies the improvement in one's condition that the third kind of knowledge (*intuitus*) brings; to love God is nothing but to understand Nature. And the eternity in which one participates is represented

---

[27] Bennett dissents from this reading. He rightly sees that a major part of the question of Spinoza's pantheism is about the appropriate attitude to take toward God or Nature. However, he insists that Spinoza is indeed a theist (pantheist) for just this reason: "Spinoza had another reason for using the name 'God' for Nature as a whole – namely his view of Nature as a fit object for reverence, awe, and humble love . . . He could thus regard Nature not only as the best subject for the metaphysical *descriptions* applied to God in the Judaeo-Christian tradition, but also as the best object of the *attitudes* which in that tradition are adopted toward God alone." "Spinoza," he concludes, "did accept pantheism as a kind of religion" (1984, pp. 34–5).

solely by the knowledge of eternal truths that makes up a part of one's mind.

There was a great debate in the eighteenth century between the German philosophers Friedrich Jacobi and Moses Mendelssohn called the *Pantheismusstreit*. Among the issues was whether or not pantheists are atheists, and in particular whether Spinoza was a pantheist; and if so, whether he was also an atheist. This seems to me more a debate about epithets and intellectual categorization than about philosophical substance. By definition, I would argue, pantheism is not atheism. And it is absolutely clear, to me at least, that Spinoza is, in substance, an atheist. The Romantic thinker Novalis got it wrong when, impressed by what he saw as Spinoza's pantheism, he called Spinoza "the God-intoxicated man." Spinoza did not elevate nature into the divine. On the contrary, he reduced the divine to nature – he naturalized God – in the hopes of diminishing the power of the passions and superstitious beliefs to which the traditional conceptions of God gave rise. If there is a theism in Spinoza, it is only a nominal one. He uses the word 'God' to refer to 'Nature', but only because the basic characteristics of Nature or Substance – eternity, necessity, infinity – are those traditionally attributed to God. It was a way of illuminating his view of Nature and Substance, not of introducing a divine dimension to the world.

# CHAPTER 5

# The human being

By the end of Part One, Spinoza has laid out the broad metaphysical picture of his universe. Everything that is belongs to a single, necessarily existing, infinite substance, a unique and all-encompasing system outside of which there is nothing and whose own internal power and principles immanently bring about all things with an absolute or mathematical necessity. This substance can be called 'God' or it can be called 'Nature'. Either way, it leaves no room for the kind of psychologically and morally endowed deity that the Judeo-Christian tradition posits as the creator of things and which Spinoza rejects as an anthropomorphic fiction that encourages superstition.

In Part Two, Spinoza turns his attention to the world of actually existing finite modes, and in particular to one of the "singular things" that make up this durational realm: the human being. Because Spinoza's ultimate goal is an explanation of human happiness in a deterministic universe, he needs first of all to investigate what exactly a human being is and how it fits into the metaphysical scheme of things. The striking feature of Spinoza's anthropology will be his opposition to any conception of human nature that makes it a kind of "dominion within a dominion" that is exempt from the laws of nature that govern everything else. Ontologically speaking, there is nothing whatsoever that distinguishes a human being from any other particular and determinate mode in nature. It is just one of the infinitely many finite things that follow from the attributes and infinite modes.

I pass now to explaining those things which must necessarily follow from the essence of God, or the infinite and eternal Being – not, indeed, all of them, for we have demonstrated that infinitely many things must follow from it in infinitely many modes, but only those that can lead us, by the hand, as it were, to the knowledge of the human Mind and its highest blessedness. (II, Preface, G II.84/C I.446)

At a certain point early in Part Two of the *Ethics*, Spinoza momentarily suspends the march of propositions and addresses the reader with uncharacteristic informality. He seems aware of the extraordinary nature of the claims he is making, and begs the reader's patience. "Here, no doubt, my readers will come to a halt, and think of many things which will give them pause. For this reason I ask them to continue on with me slowly, step by step, and to make no judgment on these matters until they have read them through" (IIP11s).

There are quite a few things in the first eleven propositions of Part Two, after which this aside occurs, as well as the three propositions that follow immediately, that might (to put it mildly) give one pause. There are the general and important claims that Spinoza makes about the relationship between the finite modes of the attributes, his so-called parallelism; and there are the specific claims about the human being that he subsequently deduces from them. Spinoza is going to argue that the human being is not a substance in its own right (IIP10); but by now this should come as no surprise. What is remarkable, however, is the notion that the human mind is nothing but the "idea" of the human body, and the way in which this gives Spinoza an idiosyncratic solution to a number of philosophical problems about mind-body relations, personhood, and freedom.

## PARALLELISM

As we have seen, and as Spinoza reminds us in the first two propositions of Part Two, Thought and Extension are two of God's attributes, or two of the most general natures of things in the universe. There are, in fact, infinitely many such attributes, but these are the only two of which we have any knowledge. A natural question, of course, is why this is the case. If there are infinitely many aspects to Nature, why is it that we know only two of them?

While the existence of infinitely many unknown attributes is indeed one of the more mysterious aspects of Spinoza's system, Spinoza actually does have an answer to this question; we will shortly be able to consider it, once we have looked more closely at the nature of the human mind itself and its powers.

Everything that exists – and now we must limit ourselves to the realm of physical things and the realm of mental things, ignoring those mysterious unknown realms – falls under one or the other of the two known attributes. In fact, everything that exists turns out to be one and the same substance manifesting its power under each of the attributes; this is why these things are but modes of that substance.

The modes of Thought are what Spinoza calls "singular thoughts"; he also calls them "ideas" and "minds." He defines an idea as "a concept of the Mind that the Mind forms because it is a thinking thing" (IID3). These ideas in Thought are not necessarily the familiar psychological contents of our own mental lives. Not all ideas belong to human minds, and not all ideas are like human ideas. Rather, as we have seen in our discussion of the immediate infinite mode of Thought – i.e., God's infinite intellect – the ideas that "express" the attribute of Thought, "an attribute whose concept all singular thoughts involve and through which they are also conceived," are, first and foremost, God's ideas or God's singular thoughts of things. They are not so much psychological entities as conceptual ones, and they constitute the absolute and adequate knowledge of their objects existing in Nature.

One thing that these ideas do have in common with human psychological states is that they are *of* things. Spinoza recognizes that there is something special about Thought that distinguishes its modes from the modes of other attributes. Thought is unique, since thinking is always thinking *of* something – it has what philosophers call 'intentionality.' Spinoza says that "whatever follows formally from God's infinite nature follows objectively in God from his idea in the same order and with the same connection" (IIP7c). In the seventeenth century, to exist "formally" is to have real or actual being; to exist "objectively" is (contrary to the way we use the word today) to exist in the mind as something thought about, as an object of thinking – that is, as the *content* of an idea. The sun has formal existence in the sky; when I think about the sun, it also thereby has objective existence in my mind as the content of my idea (of the sun). Thus, the modes of Thought (or particular ideas) – like all finite modes – have their own formal reality as modes. But they (unlike the finite modes of other attributes) are also *of* things; they are *of* just those things that are contained objectively in them.

More particularly, what these ideas or thoughts are *of* or about are all of the finite modes of all the attributes, as well as of the attributes themselves. (To put it in the same technical language used above, in all the attributes, things exist formally as finite modes; but those same modes exist objectively in modes of Thought, in ideas.) The finite modes of Extension are singular bodies. But all of the attributes, not only Thought and Extension but also the infinitely many unknown attributes, have their own proper modes. And *of* each mode of each attribute there is a corresponding singular idea in God under the attribute Thought.

IIP3: In God there is necessarily an idea, both of his essence and of everything that necessarily follows from his essence.

DEM.: For God (by IIP1) can think infinitely many things in infinitely many modes, or (what is the same, by IP16) can form the idea of his essence and of all the things which necessarily follow from it. But whatever is in God's power necessarily exists (by IP35); therefore, there is necessarily such an idea, and (by IP15) it is only in God, q.e.d.

The modes in the other attributes are mirrored in modes of Thought (ideas) that have them as their objects.

Now Spinoza is not saying simply that there is a one-to-one correspondence of modes across the attributes – that for every mode of Extension, there is a corresponding mode of unknown attribute X, a corresponding mode of unknown attribute Y, and so on, ad infinitum, including a corresponding mode of Thought. We might diagram this reading as follows, with 'body $a$' representing a mode $a$ of Extension, $X(a)$ representing the corresponding mode $a$ in unknown attribute X, and $Y(a)$ representing the corresponding mode in unknown attribute Y:

| Attribute: | Thought | Extension | X | Y |
|---|---|---|---|---|
| Mode: | Idea of *a* | body *a* | X(*a*) | Y(*a*) |

We will see below why this is an unacceptable reading; it is related to the answer to the question of why we have knowledge of only two of the attributes. For now, let me suggest that Spinoza is saying, rather, that for each individual mode *m* of each attribute – for "every singular thing that follows from God's essence" – there is an exclusive corresponding individual mode of Thought, a correlative idea in God's infinite intellect, that has *m* as its object. This means that the attribute of Thought has a special status relative to the other attributes in Spinoza's system, a status reflecting the intentionality of thinking. There are infinitely more modes in Thought than in any other attribute, since each of the infinitely many modes in each of the infinitely many attributes is replicated by a discrete individual mode in Thought. There is an idea in Thought of body *a* (a mode of Extension); another, distinct idea in Thought of the mode in attribute X that corresponds in X to body *a* in Extension; and so on:

| Attribute: | Thought | Extension | X | Y |
|---|---|---|---|---|
| Mode: | Idea of body *a* | body *a* | X(*a*) | Y(*a*) |
| | Idea of X(*a*) | | | |
| | Idea of Y(*a*) | | | |

There is, thus, a one-to-one correspondence between the modes of Thought (ideas), on the one hand, and, on the other hand, the modes of every attribute.[1] (It should be noted, as well, that this

---

[1] That this is Spinoza's view is confirmed by his letter to Tschirnhaus of 18 August 1675 (Letter 66). Tschirnhaus had wondered (in Letter 65) why the mind does not have knowledge of the attributes other than Extension, since presumably what expresses itself as modes through all the other attributes is identical to that which is expressed in the attribute of Thought as a single mode/idea, and thus that single idea's relationship to the mode in Extension should be duplicated by that idea's relationship to the modes of the other attributes. "Hence there now arises the question as to why the mind, which represents a particular modification – which same modification is expressed not only by extension but by infinite other attributes – why, I ask, does the mind perceive only the particular modification expressed through extension, that is, the human body, and not any other expression through other attributes?" Spinoza's answer is basically to deny that there is only one mode of Thought corresponding to all the modes of the other attributes; rather, he says, "although each thing is expressed in infinite modes in the infinite intellect of God, the infinite ideas in

schema applies within the attribute of Thought, since there is a corresponding mode of Thought for every mode of every attribute, including the modes of the attribute of Thought. For every mode of Thought, there is a corresponding mode of Thought that has that first mode as its object; that is, there are ideas of ideas, and then ideas of ideas of ideas, and so on. Thus, under 'Thought' in the chart above, there should also be the Idea of the Idea of body $a$, the Idea of the Idea of X($a$), etc.) And, more importantly for our purposes, since we are ignoring the unknown attributes, there is a one-to-one correspondence between the modes in Thought that are ideas of extended bodies and the modes in Extension that are extended bodies themselves.

But Spinoza goes well beyond the thesis that there is a one-to-one correspondence between the modes of Thought, on the one hand, and the modes of all the attributes, on the other hand. This is made clear by IIP7: "The order and connection of ideas is the same as the order and connection of things." Spinoza is making the stronger claim that there are ordered series of ideas in Thought each of which corresponds in its order to the ordering of modes in one of the other attributes. More particularly, the order and connection of the modes in Thought that are ideas of extended bodies is the same as the order and connection of the modes in Extension that are those bodies. Just as body $a$ is causally related to body $b$, which in turn is causally related to body $c$, and so on, so the idea of body $a$ is causally and (since we are in the realm of ideas here) logically related to the idea of body of body $b$, which in turn is causally and logically related to the idea of body $c$, etc. In God or Nature, the causal order of things is the same as the causal/logical order of ideas.

This is Spinoza's famous doctrine of parallelism. His explicit argument for IIP7 is very brief, although its meaning is relatively straightforward. He says that the proposition "is clear from IA4. For the idea of each thing caused depends on the knowledge of the cause of which it is the effect." IA4 says that "the knowledge of an effect depends on and involves the knowledge of its cause." If body $b$ is

which it is expressed cannot constitute one and the same mind of a particular thing, but an infinite of minds. For each of these ideas has no connection with the others."

the cause of body *a*, then since the (adequate) idea of body *a* represents the knowledge of *a*, it will have to "depend on" or include the idea or knowledge of body *b*. Therefore, speaking in terms of the absolute adequate knowledge of things represented by the ideas in God's infinite intellect, the epistemic relationship between the idea of *a* and the idea of *b* will mirror the causal relationship between *a* and *b*. Similarly, the idea or knowledge of body *b* will refer to the idea or knowledge of body *c*, when *c* is the cause of *b*. Because each idea belongs to an infinite series of finite modes of Thought, and each body belongs to an infinite series of finite modes in Extension, the "involving" relationship among ideas goes on infinitely, just as the causal relationship among bodies extends infinitely. Thus, the infinite series of ideas is a mirroring in Thought of the order and connection in the infinite series of bodies.

In addition to this epistemological argument for the parallelism, Spinoza also provides it with a metaphysical grounding. Because ultimately everything is an expression of the power of one and the same substance, a substance from which "there must follow infinitely many things in infinitely many modes," there is, he is saying, really only one order of things. This order of things that has its source in substance must express itself within each of the substance's attributes. Ideas of bodies and the bodies themselves are thus not merely extrinsically related series that happen to correlate with each other. Rather, each idea of a body is, at the most fundamental onto-logical level, identical with the body of which it is an idea – they are one and the same thing (the substance in one of its determinate expressions) manifesting itself in two different ways.

[W]hatever can be perceived by an infinite intellect as constituting an essence of substance pertains to one substance only, and consequently . . . the thinking substance and the extended substance are one and the same substance, which is now comprehended under this attribute, now under that. So also a mode of extension and the idea of that mode are one and the same thing, but expressed in two ways. (IIP7s)

Just as Thought and Extension are two different natures of the one substance, so an idea of a body (a mode of Thought) and the body itself (a mode of Extension) are simply more particular and deter-minate expressions of that one substance through the two attributes.

"For example, a circle existing in nature and the idea of the existing circle, which is also in God, are one and the same thing, which is explained through different attributes" (IIP7s). As an illustration of this identity across attributes, consider that whether I express a certain proposition in English or in French, while the expressions of that proposition will differ linguistically – 'You are beautiful' and 'Tu es belle' – it is still the same underlying proposition that is being expressed in each language.

It follows from this, Spinoza insists, that the series of ideas in the attribute of Thought and the series of bodies in the attribute of Extension are, in the deepest metaphysical way, one and the same series of things expressing itself in two different ways. And this implies that the order and connection in one expression will necessarily be identical to the order and connection in the other expression. "Therefore, whether we conceive nature under the attribute of Extension, or under the attribute of Thought, or under any other attribute, we shall find one and the same order, or one and the same connection of causes, i.e., that the same things follow one another."

Spinoza's use of the words 'conceive' and 'comprehended' in these texts to describe how a mode of substance is situated within an attribute has given rise to the view that the attributes for Spinoza are not real features of Nature but simply ways in which Nature is perceived. Thought and Extension would therefore be nothing more than perspectives that we take upon things, but not real essences of things in the universe. This "subjective" reading of what the attributes are seems to be reinforced by Spinoza's original definition of an attribute as "what the intellect perceives of a substance, as constituting its essence" (ID4), as well as his explanation to his friend Simon deVries that "attribute is . . . called attribute in relation to the intellect, which attributes such and such a definite nature to substance" (Letter 9, G IV.46/C I.195). One prominent scholar who adopts this reading insists, as well, that God's simplicity and indivisibility precludes there being a real diversity of essential attributes in God, and thus concludes that the attributes are only a perceived diversity, existing merely *in intellectu.*[2]

---

[2] Wolfson 1934, I.146–57.

This interpretation of the ontological status of the attributes has been well refuted in the literature.[3] There is no indication, for example, that Spinoza, who does argue for the unity and absolute indivisibility of God, is also committed to anything like a strong doctrine of the *simplicity* of God that requires God to be free of any diversity of natures. And Spinoza's reply to De Vries's question as to how one substance can have several attributes – namely, that it is the same as when we call one person by different names ('Jacob' and 'Israel') – does not imply that the attributes are merely denominations that we project onto substance or Nature. Rather, the plurality of attribute-names indicates real and distinct aspects of the substance. Finally, as Spinoza clearly says in IP9–P11, the more reality a thing has, the more attributes belong to it; and an infinite substance must have infinite attributes, each of which expresses an eternal and infinite essence. There is no reason to think that 'belong' carries here only a subjective meaning. Suffice it to say that Spinoza regards the attributes as real and essential features of Nature. They represent objective kinds or categories of things, and not merely phenomenal or subjective ways of regarding things.

It is important to note that there is one kind of argument for the parallism between the modes of Thought and the modes of other attributes that Spinoza does not give. One could imagine a Spinozistically inclined philosopher arguing that there is a one-to-one correspondence and a correlation in the ordering between ideas and bodies and other modes because there is a *causal* relationship between them. That is, perhaps there is an idea of body *a* corresponding to body *a* just because body *a* causes the idea of itself in Thought. This would make the correspondence of modes across attributes a matter of the ordinary correspondence that obtains between causes and their effects. However – and this is a crucial aspect of his metaphysics – Spinoza explicitly rules out any kind of causal relationship across the attributes. While there is a causal series among the modes of any one attribute, there is not and cannot be any causal activity between one attribute and another nor between

---

[3] See especially Gueroult 1968, I.428–61; and Donagan 1979.

the modes of one attribute and the modes of another attribute. The modes within any attribute follow only from that attribute and its other modes. Thus, bodies causally interact with other bodies within the extended realm, and ideas causally intereact with other ideas within the realm of Thought, but a bodily event cannot cause a thought event, nor a thought event cause a bodily event.

The formal being of the idea of the circle can be perceived only through another mode of thinking, as its proximate cause, and those modes again through another, and so on, to infinity. Hence, so long as things are considered as modes of thinking, we must explain the order of the whole of nature, or the connection of causes, through the attribute of Thought alone. And insofar as they are considered as modes of Extension, the order of the whole of nature must be explained through the attribute of Extension alone. (IIP7s)

What this scholium is saying is that any mode of an attribute is to be explained solely by the general principles of that attribute (the infinite modes) and other finite modes within it. A body is causally explained only by the principles of extension and motion and the movement or rest of other bodies; an idea or mind is to be explained only by the principles of thinking and its relationship to other ideas or minds. Each attribute therefore represents a causally closed and exclusive system. This is the upshot of IIP5 and IIP6. IIP5 initially makes the point about ideas:

The formal being of ideas admits God as a cause only insofar as he is considered as a thinking thing, and not insofar as he is explained by any other attribute. I.e., ideas, both of God's attributes and of singular things, admit not the objects themselves, or the things perceived, as their efficient cause, but God himself, insofar as he is a thinking thing.

IIP6 then generalizes this notion to the modes of any attribute:

The modes of each attribute have God for their cause only insofar as he is considered under the attribute of which they are modes, and not insofar as he is considered under any other attribute.

Spinoza's argument for this denial of trans-attribute causality relies on what he has established about the epistemology of causation. When one thing is the cause of another, the latter cannot be conceived without the former (IA4: "The knowledge of an effect depends on, and involves, the knowledge of its cause."). Now the mode of any attribute is conceived only through the attribute of which it is a mode and not through any other attribute. And each attribute is conceived only through itself and not through any other. But if a mode *were* caused by the mode of an attribute other than the attribute of which it is itself a mode, then its conception would require the conception of an attribute other than the attribute of which it is a mode. And Spinoza's principles rule this out.

This is why Spinoza can say, in his short digression on physics in Part Two, that "a body which moves or is at rest must be determined to motion or rest by another body, which has also been determined to motion or rest by another, and that again by another, and so on, to infinity" (IIIL3). Bodily events are never caused by thought events, and vice versa. This causal closure of the realm of physics and of the realm of thought will play an important role in Spinoza's account of the relationship between mind and body in a human being.

## MIND AND BODY

There is nothing surprising about Spinoza's initial definition of a human being: "Man consists of a mind and a body" (IIP13c). Anyone, with the exception of the most eliminative of materialists, can accept this general statement. It does not specify what exactly the mind consists in, nor how it is supposed to relate to the body. The claim seems to capture something we all intuitively believe about what we are, whether or not we can say much more about the mind and the body.

To get a sense of the originality – and, one might say, the singularity – of Spinoza's conception of the human being, it is useful to contrast him with Descartes. Descartes not only had an enormous influence (both positive and negative) on Spinoza in this matter, but his own conception of a human being as consisting in a mind and a body is perhaps the most important in the history of philosophy.

Descartes believed that the human mind and the human body is each a substance in its own right. He also believed that these two substances have absolutely nothing in common besides their substantiality. This is his doctrine of the "real distinction" between mind (or soul) and body. The mind is an unextended thinking substance, and the body is an extended or material substance devoid of thought. As he argues at length in the *Meditations*, each can be clearly and distinctly understood without the other. I can know what it is to be a thinking thing without importing any terms from the world of body (such as shape or motion); and I can know what it is to be an extended thing without appealing to any mentalistic or spiritual notions (such as belief or volition). Moreover, this conceptual independence reflects an ontological independence. Each substance is perfectly well capable of existing without the other. After death, Descartes insists, the soul can exist disembodied while the corpse is left to decay on its own. Finally, the basic functioning of each does not require the other. While there are indeed some mental states that result only from the mind's union with the body (for example, sensations), there are also purely intellectual thoughts in the mind that do not depend at all on the body; likewise, there are many (involuntary) motions in the body that bear no relation to anything that is happening in the mind.

Descartes is thus what contemporary philosophers call a substance dualist. There are two kinds of substance in the universe, mental and material, and everything that exists is either a mental substance or a property of a mental substance, or a material substance or a property of a material substance.

Nonetheless, Descartes insists, these two really distinct substances are united in a human being. In fact, the human being is itself a kind of composite substance, constituted by the union of the mind and the body. He says that "the mind is united in a real and substantial manner to the body," and not just by "position or disposition" or what might be called an "accidental" union.[4] There is a kind of "mingling" of the two, such that we might even think of the mind as, in a sense, extended throughout the body. This is something that we discover through ordinary experience.

---

[4] Letter to Regius, AT III.493/CSMK III.206.

Nature also teaches me, by these sensations of pain, hunger, thirst, and so on, that I am not merely present in my body as a sailor is present in a ship, but that I am very closely joined and, as it were, intermingled with it, so that I and the body form a unit. If this were not so, I, who am nothing but a thinking thing, would not feel pain when the body was hurt, but would perceive the damage purely by the intellect, just as a sailor perceives by sight if anything in his ship is broken. Similarly, when the body needed food or drink, I should have an explicit understanding of the fact, instead of having confused sensations of hunger and thirst. For these sensations of hunger, thirst, pain and so on are nothing but confused modes of thinking which arise from the union and, as it were, intermingling of the mind with the body.[5]

Within the union of mind and body in a human being, there is also a great deal of causal intercourse. Mental states cause physical states, and physical states cause mental states. When I will to raise my arm, my volition is, Descartes believes, the cause of my arm rising. And when I sit on a thumbtack, the damage to my body (or, more precisely, the motions communicated by the nerves from the damaged part to the brain) is a cause of the pain I feel on that occasion.

While this account is notoriously fraught with problems, as we shall see below, it remained, at least in its generalities, the dominant paradigm in the early modern period for thinking philosophically about what a human being is. Some philosophers adopted it whole-sale; others accepted its fundamental dualist premise but rejected one particular component or another (for example, Malebranche denied there was genuine causal interaction between mind and body in a human being); and others rejected even its most basic assumptions (for example, Leibniz or Berkeley). But I think it is safe to say that every major philosophical account of mind and body in the seventeenth and eighteenth centuries represents a response in some way to Descartes's metaphysics of the human being.

Spinoza, of course, is not a substance dualist. Not only is the human being not a substance (or a "substantial union") in its own right, but its constituent parts – the mind and the body – are not substances either. There is only one substance, God or Nature, and

---

[5] *Meditations*, VI, AT VII.81/CSM II.56.

thus the human mind and the human body must, like all "ideas" and all bodies, be only modes of the attributes of this substance. "The essence of man is constituted by certain modes of God's attributes" (IIP10d). But his rejection of Cartesian dualism goes well beyond denying substantiality to the human mind and the human body. He rejects Descartes's whole conception of a human being as some kind of joining together of two elements that are themselves disparate to the end of forming a unity. For Spinoza, there is a fundamental identity between mind and body – and thus a fundamental unity to the human being – that goes much deeper than any differences there may be between them.

Spinoza defines the human mind as the idea of a particular body. That is, the mind is one of those finite modes of Thought that have as their objects finite modes of Extension (as opposed to those modes of Thought that have as their objects the modes of unknown attributes). And the particular mode of Extension of which the mind is an idea or thought-correlate is the human body. In IIP11 he says that "The first thing that constitutes the actual being of a human Mind is nothing but the idea of a singular thing which actually exists"; and in IIP13 he specifies what that "singular thing" is: "The object of the idea constituting the human Mind is the Body, or a certain mode of Extension which actually exists, and nothing else." Thus, a human mind is just one of the infinitely many ideas – all corresponding to the modes of the attributes – that make up the infinite intellect of God, which (as we have seen) is itself the immediate infinite mode under the attribute Thought. "The human mind is a part of the infinite intellect of God" (IIP11c). And (as IIP11 tells us) when the body of which a human mind is the idea actually exists, the human mind actually exists – that is, the person enjoys a durational life.

In this respect, the human mind is absolutely no different from any other finite mode of Thought (or, more precisely, from any other mode of Thought that has as its object a mode of Extension). All bodies with any basic integrity have corresponding modes in Thought, correlative ideas, as the parallelism doctrine implies. The human mind is therefore, ontologically speaking, just like the "ideas" of other extended bodies, all of which together – along with all the ideas of all the modes of the unknown attributes – constitute

God's infinite intellect. "Our mind . . . is an eternal mode of thought, which is determined by another eternal mode of thought, and this again by another, and so on *ad infinitum*, so that all taken together form the eternal and infinite intellect of God" (VP40). Put another way, every extended body has, in some sense, a "mind." Spinoza does not hesitate to proclaim this, since it goes right to the heart of his project to show that the human being is as much a part of Nature as anything else.

The things we have shown so far are completely general and do not pertain more to man than to other Individuals, all of which, though in different degrees, are nevertheless animate. For of each thing there is necessarily an idea in God, of which God is the cause in the same way as he is of the idea of the human body [i.e., the human mind]. (IIP13s)

This might seem a remarkable thing for Spinoza to say, and can be interpreted in very different ways. Some have taken his account of the human mind together with the universal parallelism to imply that Spinoza was a kind of animist or panpsychist about nature, believing that all things are living and thinking beings with minds or souls like the human mind. But this, again, is to psychologize what an idea is for Spinoza, which, as I have suggested, is a mistake. Other commentators, adopting a more measured approach, suggest that what Spinoza means is not that all things have souls in some strong sense, but only that all things, to varying degrees (depending upon their animateness), have something to them besides their matter; this something might, for example, be like an Aristotelian form which gives unity, activity, and, in some cases, life to a material body.[6] An even more nominalist, less metaphysically bold reading would insist that, because the modes in Thought corresponding to the modes of Extension, whatever bodies these may be, just are ideas in God's infinite intellect, all Spinoza means is that God has (or there is in Nature) an adequate idea of every body, a true knowledge of every singular thing in Extension.[7] In this way, Spinoza can be

---

[6] See Wolfson 1934, II.58–9.

[7] For an even more reductive reading, whereby what Spinoza is saying is merely that for every "fact" in Extension there is a proposition corresponding to that bodily mode, see Curley 1969, pp. 119–27.

read as saying that human beings, animals, plants, and, presumably, even inanimate objects all have some level of thought that corresponds to their bodily component. This does not necessarily mean that, in each case, its "mind" or "soul" involves conscious thinking, or even sensation or animation; it means only that there is a thought or idea (in God or in Nature) for every body and that constitutes adequate knowledge of that body. (In the *Short Treatise*, Spinoza actually refers to the "soul" as the "Idea, knowledge, etc. of our body in the thinking thing" (II, G I.51/C I.95).) Spinoza's point in IIP13s, in other words, is not to extend the specialness of the human mind to all beings. On the contrary, his point is to show that, at least ontologically speaking, there is nothing so special about the human mind that distinguishes it from what corresponds to all bodies.

When we move beyond general ontology, however, there is, of course, something special about the thought or idea in God or Nature that is the human mind. Unlike all those other ideas or "minds" that have extended bodies as their objects, the idea that has the human body as its object and that is the human mind does indeed have real thinking and consciousness. What does distinguish the human mind from all other minds or ideas is that it has greater and more complex functions and capacities. Among these capacities are memory, imagination, and self-awareness. And what explains the superiority of the human mind over all other minds is simply the superior capacities of its object, that is, the human body.

Immediately after claiming that whatever has been said about the human mind must also be said about the idea of any thing, Spinoza concedes that

> However, we also cannot deny that ideas differ among themselves, as the objects do, and that one [idea] is more excellent than the other and contains more reality, just as the object of the one is more excellent than the object of the other and contains more reality.

The object of the idea that is the mind is the human body, and thus the complexity and excellence of the mind is a function of the complexity and excellence of the human body.

> And so to determine what is the difference between the human Mind and the others, and how it surpasses them, it is necessary for us . . . to know the nature of its object, i.e., of the human body . . . I say this in general, that in

proportion as a Body is more capable than others of doing many things at once, or being acted on in many ways at once, so its Mind is more capable than others of perceiving many things at once. And in proportion as the actions of a body depend more on itself alone, and as other bodies concur with it less in acting, so its mind is more capable of understanding distinctly. And from these [truths] we can know the excellence of one mind over the others. (IP13s)

As Spinoza succinctly puts it in the *Short Treatise*, "as the body is, so is the soul" (G I.53/C I.96). And, as the scholium from IIP13 indicates, he means this not only with respect to the appetitive and sensory functions of the soul, which we would naturally expect to depend in some way on the body, but its cognitive and intellectual functions as well!

It follows from this that any investigation into the human mind and its capacities must begin with an investigation into the human body and its makeup and capacities. This is why, immediately after establishing the general nature of the human mind in IIP11–13, Spinoza offers a brief discourse on the nature of body and physics. The axioms and lemmas that come between IIP13 and IIP14 establish a number of important facts and principles about bodies and the way they behave. Perhaps the most important claim to be found in this section is Spinoza's account of what makes a particular body the individual body that it is and distinguishes it from other bodies.

All bodies necessarily share a number of features, simply by virtue of all being modes of Extension. Among those features are shape, size, divisibility and, of course, "motion and rest." Spinoza also delivers a principle of inertia with respect to the motion and rest of bodies: "A body in motion moves until it is determined by another body to rest; and . . . at body at rest also remains at rest until it is determined to motion by another" (IIL3c).

As to the individuation of particular bodies, because all bodies are essentially extension, and extension itself is uniform throughout all bodies – they are all modes of one and the same attribute – what distinguishes one parcel of extension from another can be only the relative motive differences between the two parcels. "Bodies are distinguished from one another by reason of motion and rest, speed and slowness, and not by reason of substance" (IIL1). Like Descartes, Spinoza believes that the individuation of composite bodies – that is, those that are collections of what Spinoza calls "the simplest bodies," and collections of those collections, and so on – is purely relational.[8] This body is different from that body only because the parts of this collection of matter are contiguous and together moving differently from the contiguous parts of that collection of matter. This does not mean that the parts of a body are necessarily at rest relative to each other.

When a number of bodies, whether of the same or of different size, are so constrained by other bodies that they lie upon one another, or if they so move, whether with the same degree or different degrees of speed, that they communicate their motions to each other in a certain fixed manner, we shall say that those bodies are united with one another and that they all together compose one body or Individual, which is distinguished from the others by this union of bodies. (IIA3″, definition)

This "certain fixed manner" in which the bodies in a collection "communicate their motions to each other" is what Spinoza calls "the ratio of motion and rest" in a body. It is not the case that all the parts of a body need to be moving together in exactly the same direction with exactly the same speed. Rather, they constitute a relatively stable collection of body-parts because they maintain among themselves either the same relative positions or the same changes of position and differences in degrees of motion and rest. Just because one part of my body is moving forward – say, my arm – it does not follow that every other part of my body is moving forward. My foot can be, relative to my hand, at rest. But the hand and the foot are both parts of one and the same body because they maintain among themselves, and among the other parts of my body, the same ratio of motion and rest, which is something they presumably do not maintain in any consistent way relative to external bodies. The hand as a whole may move forward while the foot stays still, but the parts composing the hand maintain among themselves and relative to the parts composing the foot and all the other parts

---

[8] Descartes, however, would argue that only inanimate bodies are individuated by relative differences in motion. Animate bodies – i.e., human bodies – are individuated by the souls that animate them; see the letter to Mesland, 1645 or 1646, AT IV.346/CSMK III.278–9.

composing the other parts of the body the same "internal" kinetic relationships.

IIIL5: If the parts composing an Individual become greater or less, but in such a proportion that they all keep the same ratio of motion and rest to each other as before, then the Individual will likewise retain its nature, as before, without any change of form.

IIIL7: Furthermore, the Individual so composed retains its nature, whether it as a whole moves or is at rest, or whether it moves in this or that direction, so long as each part retains its motion, and communicates it, as before, to the others.

Basically, a body gets its integrity and individuality from the fact that its parts all continue to relate to each other in the same general way; something is external to that body, by contrast, because it does not share in that relatively stable relationship.

The human body has an extraordinarily large number of parts and is thus extremely complex, much more complex than any other kind of body. It can act on other bodies and be acted upon by them in countless ways. To put this in more familiar terms, the human body – with respect to its nervous system, sensory apparatus, brain functions, creative adaptability, etc. – can do and experience more things in a greater variety of ways than other bodies. And this means that the human mind enjoys greater thought-capacities than the idea of any other extended body. "The human Mind is capable of perceiving a great many things, and is the more capable, the more its body can be disposed in a great many ways" (IIP14). The reason why this is so is that the constitution of the human mind is an expression (in Thought) of the constitution of the body (in Extension). Because of the parallelism between modes of Extension and modes of Thought – indeed, because of the fundamental identity between the modes of Extension and the modes of Thought – there is a one-to-one correspondence not only between what we might call the macro-modes of Extension (things like human bodies, trees, etc.) and the macro-modes of Thought (the human mind, the idea of the tree, etc.), but also between the smaller bodies that make up these macro-bodies and the "smaller" ideas that compose the correlative macro-ideas. The human mind, for Spinoza, is, when looked at on a grand scale, the idea of the whole body. But because its object (the body) is a composite of smaller parts, the mind is itself a composite of smaller parts.

IIP15: The idea that constitutes the formal being of the human mind is not simple, but composed of a great many ideas.
DEM.: The idea that constitutes the formal being of the human Mind is the idea of a body (by IIP13), which is composed of a great many highly composite Individuals. But of each Individual composing the body, there is necessarily (by IIP8c) an idea in God. Therefore (by IIP7), the idea of the human Body is composed of these many ideas of the parts composing the human Body, q.e.d.

Like God's infinite intellect, the infinite mode of Thought that is a collection of infinitely many ideas (many of which are human minds), the human mind is made up of a collection of ideas, viz., all of the ideas that have as their objects the different parts of the human body. Just as the human mind as the idea of the body is a member of the infinite set of ideas composing God's infinite intellect, so it is itself a set of ideas.

The greater the number of parts in a body and the more complex their relationships, the greater the number of ideas in that body's corresponding idea (or mind) and the more varied, responsive, and complex their associations and connections. For every part of the body, in fact, for everything that happens in a body, there is a corresponding idea in the mind. "Whatever happens in the object of the idea constituting the human mind . . . there will necessarily be an idea of that thing in the mind" (IIP12). Whether this means that the mind literally perceives and knows everything that takes place in the body is a question we will have to defer until the next chapter.

With this understanding of the nature of the human mind and its constituent ideas in hand, we can now return to a question that we had earlier put aside but that has been lurking in the wings: why is it that we have knowledge of only two of the infinitely many attributes in Nature? Tschirnhaus asks just this question of Spinoza (Letter 63). Spinoza's answer to Tschirnhaus is that it is just a necessary fact of our nature, given the kind of being we are, that we have knowledge only of Thought and Extension. We are ourselves modes of Thought and Extension. Our bodies are modes of Extension, and our minds are the ideas (in Thought) of our extended bodies. But if the mind is nothing but a mode of Thought that is an idea of an extended thing, then it can contain knowledge or ideas only of those two attributes – namely, the attribute to which it belongs and the attribute of whose mode it is an idea.

The human mind can acquire knowledge only of those things which the idea of an actually existing body involves, or what can be inferred from this idea. For the power of any thing is defined solely by its essence . . . and the essence of mind consists . . . solely in its being the idea of an actually existing body. Therefore, the mind's power of understanding extends only as far as that which this idea of the body contains within itself, or which follows therefrom. Now this idea of the body involves and expresses no other attributes of God than extension and thought. (Letter 64)

According to the universal parallelism, it is metaphysically necessary that the same thing that expresses itself as a human body in Extension also expresses itself as modes in all of the infinitely many other but unknown attributes of substance; and correlatively, that there are ideas in Thought corresponding to all those unknown modal expressions under the other attributes, in addition to the idea that corresponds to the body in Extension (i.e., the human mind). But because the human mind is that idea that is of the human body, it thus has knowledge only of the attributes of Thought and Extension.

We can now understand, too, *why* the proper interpretation of Spinoza's parallelism between the attributes cannot be that there is a one-to-one correspondence of modes across all the attributes (including Thought), but rather that there must be one discrete idea in Thought for each mode of every other attribute, and thus a kind of duplication in Thought for each of the other attributes' series of modes (one series of ideas for Extension, another series of ideas for attribute X, etc.). For *if* our mind, the idea of the extended body, were also the idea in Thought of the mode in attribute X corresponding to the human body in Extension, and the idea of the corresponding mode in Y, etc., then the mind, as an idea of those modes, would have to involve knowledge of the X-mode and of the Y-mode (and of the attributes X and Y themselves) in addition to knowledge of the body (and of Extension). But then Spinoza would not be able to defend the non-negotiable claim that those other attributes are unknown, and the particular explanation that he offers in reply to Tschirnhaus would simply not make sense.

## MONISM

From the foregoing, it is clear that Spinoza rejects the most basic elements of Descartes's dualism. Mind and body are not distinct substances. Indeed, not only are they not substances at all, but we might also say that they are not really distinct.

To be sure, in a metaphysically important sense, ideas and bodies are different from each other. Modes of Thought and modes of Extension have absolutely nothing in common, since they belong to different attributes and thus are expressions of entirely different natures. Thus, we can say that Spinoza is a kind of dualist – perhaps what philosophers call a "property dualist," since there are two kinds of things (even if those things are themselves not substantial).[9] There is just one substance, but that substance has mental modes (ideas) and physical modes (bodies). Similarly, in a human being, there is a mental or thinking aspect and a material or bodily aspect.

We might even say that Spinoza's dualism is, in one sense, more extreme than Descartes's, since Spinoza insists (as we have seen) that there can be no causal interaction between the mental and the physical. Any mode of Thought – whether it be the human mind itself or any of its constituent ideas – has in its causal history only other modes of Thought, other ideas, and the most general principles of Thought; and any mode of Extension – the human body and any motions therein – has as its cause only other bodily modes and their motions, along with the principles of extension and the laws of physics. Thus, in a human being, no mental state has a bodily state as its cause and no bodily state has a mental state as its cause. "The body cannot determine the mind to thinking, and the mind cannot determine the body to motion, to rest, or to anything else (if there is anything else)" (IIIP2). My volition to raise my arm is not the cause of my arm rising; that bodily event is determined

---

[9] Of course, for Spinoza there are *infinitely* many different kinds of things, since there are an infinite number of attributes in Nature. But within our limited experience, at least, Nature is dualistic.

only by antecedent bodily events, along with the principles of matter and motion. And my cutting my finger is not the cause of the pain I feel on that occasion; that unpleasant mental event follows only from prior states of the mind, in conjunction with the principles of Thought. At one point, Spinoza says that, even independently of his own metaphysical reasons for denying mind-body interaction, he finds the whole notion of such intercourse inconceivable:

No one knows how, or by what means, the mind moves the body, nor how many degrees of motion it can give the body, nor with what speed it can move it. So it follows that when men say that this or that action of the body arises from the mind, which has dominion over the body, they do not know what they are saying, and they do nothing but confess, in fine-sounding words, that they are ignorant of the true cause of that action, and that they do not wonder at it. (IIIP2s, G II.142/C I.495)

Thus, it may seem as if there is a dualist divide in Spinoza's universe even more radical than what we find in Descartes.

But when we recall that Spinoza's parallelism doctrine has a deep grounding in the metaphysical unity of all things in one substance, and the consequent claim that a mode of Thought and a mode of Extension are but one and the same thing expressed in two ways, we see that the veneer of dualism in the world of attributes and their modes serves only to mask that more fundamental monism about things. Thus, the human mind and the human body are not two ontologically distinct things. They are two different expressions – incommensurable and independent expressions, to be sure – of one and the same thing. "The mind and the body are one and the same individual, which is conceived now under the attribute of thought, now under the attribute of extension" (IIP21s). I think a good way to understand what that thing is, and to grasp Spinoza's point here, is to refer to the more primary notion of "a human being" or, alternately, "a person." The human body is the expression of the human being (or the person) under the attribute of Extension; it is what that human being is in his material aspect. The human mind, or the idea of the human body, is the expression of that same human being under the attribute of Thought; it is what that person is in his mental or thinking aspect. Similarly, to take the analysis down to a finer level, the cutting of my finger and the pain I feel are two different expressions of one and the same event in a human being (myself). This event in me expresses itself in the extended realm as the cutting of my finger, and expresses itself in the realm of thinking as a pain. The pain is the idea in my mind that corresponds to the state of my body "finger-being-cut" – or, better, to use Spinoza's terms, it is the idea *of* that state of my body.[10]

Notice that this metaphysical monism provides Spinoza with an answer to a question naturally generated by his denial of causal interaction: why *is* there a correlation between the states of my mind and the condition of my body? Why do I have a pain at just that moment when I cut my finger? And why does my arm rise just when I will it to?

Descartes had used the causal interaction between the mind and the body to explain that correspondence: the pain occurs just when the finger is cut because the cut is the cause of the pain. Occasionalists like Malebranche, who denied any causal powers whatsoever to finite creatures, mental or physical, used God's continuous causal activity to account for the regularity. Neither of these options is acceptable to Spinoza. But neither does he need them. The strong parallelism doctrine, with its thesis of the fundamental identity of the modes of the attributes, suffices to account for the correlation between states of the mind and states of the body in a human being without causal interaction or divine intervention. There is a correlation between cut and pain (or volition and arm-rising) just because they are one and the same event – one and the same substance – expressing itself in two different natures. An analogy might be the correlation between what is seen by two people wearing different colored glasses but looking at the same thing. There are differences in what appears to each of them, because they are perceiving the thing through different aspects (colors). But because of the identity of the object they are looking at, there will necessarily be correlations in the respective appearances.

---

[10] This still leaves Spinoza's talk of these "things" of which the modes are expressions somewhat mysterious. For an important and creative approach to this issue, see Bennett 1984, pp. 139–49.

This means that it is, in an important sense, misleading to label Spinoza's account of mind-body relations in a human being a "parallelism."[11] Parallelism suggests a correlation or matching between two external series that run independently but in the same way, much like the two clocks in Leibniz's preestablished harmony that, having been set at the same starting time and wound up, will chime together on the same hours. But for Spinoza the correlations in a human being between the states of his mind and the states of his body are not an external relationship between two independent series. They are one and the same series unfolding in two different ways. It is true, however, that the result of this underlying and prior unity is that the sequence that represents the unfolding of that series under one attribute (i.e., the sequence of ideas in the mind) runs parallel to the sequence that represents the unfolding of that series under the other attribute (i.e., the sequence of states of the body). When the body chimes "cut," the mind chimes "pain"; and when the mind chimes "move that arm," the body chimes "arm moving."

### DUALISM AND ITS DISCONTENTS

So Spinoza is not a Cartesian (substance) dualist. He appears, at best, to be a property dualist, or what is sometimes called a dual aspect theorist (there are two aspects to reality).

And yet, it is hard to overlook Spinoza's strikingly strong claims about the relationship between mind and body, and especially his view that the capacities of the mind are a function of the capacities of the body, and that to understand the mind requires one first to understand the body. An idea is best understood through its object, what the idea is *of*; and the object that the mind is the idea *of* is the body. This apparent asymmetry, with the powers of the mind grounded in the powers of the body, has led one scholar to suggest that Spinoza is, in fact, a kind of materialist about the mind. This commentator, who is fully sensitive to the distinctness and irreducibility of the mental and the material aspects of reality in Spinoza,

---

[11] See, for example, Bennett 1996, p. 78.

suggests that if we "follow out the consequences" of Spinoza's identification of mind and body

> we would see that its fundamental thrust is materialistic rather than dualistic . . . If we follow out the details of Spinoza's treatment of the mind, as it develops in the course of Part II, I do not see how we can characterize it as anything but a materialistic program.[12]

It is not just the general powers of the mind that appear to be a function of the powers of the body, but its actual episodic functioning as well. Consider the following strongly materialist-seeming statement from Part Three:

> Does not experience also teach that if . . . the body is inactive, the mind is at the same time incapable of thinking? For when the body is at rest in sleep, the mind at the same time remains senseless with it, nor does it have the power of thinking, as it does when awake. And then I believe everyone has found by experience that the mind is not always equally capable of thinking of the same object, but that as the body is more susceptible to having the image of this or that object aroused in it, so the mind is more capable of regarding this or that object. (IIIP2s, G II.142/C I.495)

Spinoza never suggests that the direction of understanding can go from mind to body; it is always from body to mind. And unlike Descartes's view, in which there are pure intellectual ideas that have no basis in the body, for Spinoza there are no states of the mind that are not correlated with – indeed, identical to! – some aspect of our physical existence.

It would certainly not be an eliminative materialism, of course, since Spinoza nowhere suggests that the category of the mental is illusory or dispensable. In fact, this category is absolutely required to describe an entire aspect of the universe – namely, that aspect represented by the attribute Thought. And despite the fact that much about mental items, the modes of Thought, is explained by their extended objects, mentalistic terms and descriptions are not reducible to physical terms and descriptions (this is guaranteed by the real differences between the attributes). One might think that Spinoza's theory resembles central state materialism (e.g., the mind-brain identity thesis), according to which every mental state is identical with a

---

[12] Curley 1988, pp. 74–8.

state of the body (e.g., a pain is identical with a particular chemical and neurological state of the brain), and in a superficial sense it does: Spinoza explicitly says that the thinking-mode and the extended-mode are ultimately one and the same thing.[13] However, according to central state materialism, the mental terms refer only to physical states (of the brain or the central nervous system), and this is something that Spinoza could not countenance. The mind and the body may ultimately, at the deepest metaphysical level, be one and the same thing, but the expressions of this thing in the different attributes – the body and the idea of the body – are distinct and irreducible modes; to refer to one of them is not to refer to the other.

Perhaps Spinoza's account of the human being could best be called an "explanatory materialism," one which presupposes the categorical or property dualism that really breaks Nature (as we know it) up into two distinct and irreducible ways of being but which does not rule out the functioning of one side of the divide being explained or understood by the functioning of the other side.

In the end, however, even this weak brand of materialism leaves the reader with a rather nagging question. If the functioning of the mind can be explained by the functioning of the body, then why is this not a breach of IA5: "Things that have nothing in common with one another also cannot be understood through one another"? The modes of one attribute have nothing in common with the modes of another attribute, and thus the modes of one attribute cannot be explained in terms of the modes of another attribute (IIP7s). As soon as Spinoza says that in order to "know the excellence of one mind over the others" he needs first "to premise a few things concerning the nature of bodies," he seems to have violated this important principle. Even if nothing from the realm of extension enters into the specific explanation of any particular event or act of the mind, still, understanding the nature of the human mind itself, including its rich capacities, requires going beyond the attribute of Thought and its infinite and finite modes.[14]

---

[13] See, for example, Allison 1987, p. 86.
[14] Della Rocca (1996b, chapter 8) and Bennett (1996, pp. 143–9) wrestle with various forms of this problem.

And this appears to be inconsistent with the causal and explanatory gap that Spinoza places between the attributes.

Spinoza could respond to this problem by saying that the excellence of the idea of the human body (the mind) is not the *causal result* of the excellence of the human body – which would certainly violate not only the spirit but also the letter of the law – but rather is a function of the excellence of only the content of that idea. Because the mind is the idea *of* the human body, and because both the mind and the human body are expressions of one and the same thing but in different attributes, the content of that idea, something that is intrinsic to the idea itself, has the same degree of excellence as the body. We can also therefore get a sense of that excellence of the idea by looking at the excellence of the body. But the excellence of the idea itself is something that the idea wears on its own; and it is certainly not caused by the excellence of the body.[15]

Be that as it may, one of the interesting questions about Spinoza's conception of mind and body in a human being concerns the motivation for his rejection of what we might call the "standard model", that is, Cartesian dualism (whether the interactionist or occasionalist variety).

According to the traditional story, often told in both textbooks and the scholarly literature, Spinoza abandoned the standard model for his own idiosyncratic account because of the philosophical problems that plagued Descartes's dualism and its commitment to interaction.[16] Given the radical difference in nature between extended bodily substance and unextended thinking substance, the argument goes, there is no way of explaining how these two constituents of a human being might causally engage each other and thus no way of explaining the evident correlation between states of the mind and states of the body through interaction. This problem was succinctly raised for Descartes by Princess Elizabeth:

How can the soul of man, being only a thinking substance, determine the spirits of the body in order to bring about voluntary actions? For it seems that every determination of motion takes place by an impulse on the thing

---

[15] This suggestion was made to me by Don Garrett.
[16] See Bennett 1996, pp. 62–3; Watson 1987, p. 117.

moved, by it being pushed by that which moves it, or better, by the qualification and figure of the superficies of that latter. And contact is required for the first two conditions, and extension for the third.[17]

Although Descartes tries to help Elizabeth to conceive better how the mind moves the body, he generally appears not to have had any worries about the *possibility* of such interaction. In reply to the philosopher Pierre Gassendi, who had expressed a concern similar to that of Elizabeth, Descartes says simply that "the whole problem contained in such questions arises simply from a supposition that is false and cannot in any way be proved, namely that, if the soul and the body are two substances whose nature is different, this prevents them from being able to act on each other."[18] But other philosophers, then and now, were not so dismissive of the difficulty.

Spinoza, the story goes, does an end-run around the problem by making the mind and the body not two distinct substances, but rather two modes of one and the same substance; and by ruling out causal interaction between them and offering instead a theory of correlation that relies on mutual expression – a mental state being nothing other than the expression in Thought of exactly the same thing that expresses itself as a bodily state in Extension. Spinoza's retreat to his own conception of the human mind and its relationship to the body, in other words, is taken to be a response to the classic mind-body problem.

A variant on this narrative in the historiography of modern philosophy focuses on a slightly different but related problem and thus also has Spinoza responding to a tension generated by Cartesian dualism. This time, however, the tension is not between the doctrine of dualism and the question of causal interaction, but rather between dualism and the question of the unity of the human being. Spinoza, on this account, rejects substance dualism and Descartes's concomitant conception of the mind because if the mind is indeed a distinct substance from the body, then it is hard to see how they can together form a true union that is a human being.[19]

---

[17] Letter of May 1643, AT III.661.
[18] AT IXa.213/CSM II.275.
[19] Thus, Curley (1988) insists that Spinoza "is responding to the tension . . . between the Cartesian doctrine of real distinction and the Cartesian doctrine of substantial union." On

Descartes, his critics say, is just as badly in need of an explanation of how there can be a "substantial union" between two things as radically different as mind and body as he is of an explanation of their causal engagement. Mind and body cannot be united in the clear and distinct way that bodies are united, by local proximity, since the mind is not a spatial entity and so cannot literally be in contact with the body. But then what kind of union is it and what is "substantial" about it? It is Gassendi who first makes this objection, in the objections he composed to Descartes's *Meditations*:

You still have to explain how that 'joining and, as it were, intermingling' or 'confusion' can apply to you if you are incorporeal, unextended and indivisible . . . Must not every union occur by means of close contact? And . . . how can contact occur without a body? How can something corporeal take hold of something incorporeal so as to keep it joined to itself? And how can the incorporeal grasp the corporeal to keep it reciprocally bound to itself, if it has nothing at all to enable it to grasp or be grasped?[20]

Spinoza, by making the mind the idea of the body, has again short-circuited the problem. No longer is it a matter of bringing together into a union two distinct substances to form a new, composite substance, the human being. Rather, the unity is what is metaphysically prior. Mind and body are simply two distinct expressions, under different attributes, Thought and Extension, of one and the same thing (the human being).

Is the mind-body problem, either in its causal version or its "substantial union" version, the motivation for Spinoza's abandonment of Cartesian dualism? Spinoza does explicitly deny that two things that have nothing in common can causally interact; this is one of the

the one hand, Descartes says that the mind (and, thus, consciousness) is an ontologically distinct substance from the body. On the other hand, as Curley puts it, "I take a very personal interest in my body . . . I and my body are one. That is why I have the concern for it that I do and why I have the awareness of it that I have." How is an intimate relationship between mind and body possible? This is, according to Curley, "the question that lies at the heart of Spinoza's theory of identity." It is, he insists, "more important in the genesis of the Spinozistic position than any concerns about the intelligibility of interaction between distinct substances" (pp. 59–62).

[20] Fifth Objections, AT VII.343–4/CSM II.238–9.

first propositions of the *Ethics* (IP3). So there is an important sense in which Spinoza would not be satisfied by Descartes's casual response to Gassendi. And, as we have seen, interpreting Spinoza as giving priority to the unity of the human being (and, indeed, of any thing) underneath the bifurcation into distinct modes through the two attributes of Thought and Extension is a good way to make sense of much of what he says in IIP1–14.

I would like to suggest, however, that there is an even more important issue in Spinoza's mind, one that, above any metaphysical problems internal to dualism, strongly moves Spinoza to abandon the Cartesian picture of mind and body.

Descartes prided himself on the felicitous consequences of his philosophy for religion. In particular, he believed that by so separating the mind from the corruptible body, his radical dualism offered the best possible defense of and explanation for the immortality of the soul. In the Letter to the Sorbonne that accompanies the *Meditations*, Descartes explicitly says that one of his aims in the book is to combat those who would deny the immortality of the soul and to take up the call to arms to demonstratively establish the truth of that doctrine. Disappointingly, Descartes does not explicitly offer any full demonstration for the immortality of the soul in the *Meditations* themselves. The Synopsis that prefaces the work indicates that Descartes believes that the immortality of the soul follows immediately from the real distinction between mind and body. But he says that while these arguments "are enough to show that the decay of the body does not imply the destruction of the mind, and are hence enough to give mortals the hope of an after-life," nonetheless a full demonstration of the fact that "the mind is immortal by its very nature" would require "an account of the whole of physics." We need to know that substances are, by their nature, incorruptible and cannot ever cease to exist unless they are reduced to nothingness by an act of God; and that while body is a substance, and thus just as imperishable as a soul, any particular human body, being nothing but a collection of material parts, lacks the integrity of a true substance and is subject to decay.[21] In the Replies to the

---

[21] AT VII.13–14/CSM II.9–10.

Second Set of Objections to the *Meditations*, he claims that "Our natural knowledge tells us that the mind is distinct from the body, and that it is a substance . . . And this entitles us to conclude that the mind, insofar as it can be known by natural philosophy, is immortal."[22] Though he cannot with certainty rule out the possibility that God has miraculously endowed the soul with "such a nature that its duration will come to an end simultaneously with the end of the body," nonetheless, because the soul is a substance in its own right, and is not subject to the kind of decomposition to which the body is subject, it is by its nature immortal. When the body dies, the soul – which was only temporarily united with it – is to enjoy a separate existence.

It is exactly this kind of robust doctrine of personal immortality that Spinoza rejects. And he rejects it on both metaphysical grounds and, more importantly, moral and political grounds. For reasons that will become clear in the following chapters, Spinoza thinks that the belief in immortality, like the belief in an anthropomorphic God, fosters only superstition. In his eyes, it is a pernicious doctrine that leads to a life in bondage to irrational passions. In Part Five of the *Ethics*, Spinoza will expressly address the question of immortality when he discusses the eternity of the mind. But if I may be allowed to read those later sections of the work back into what is happening in Part Two, I think that there can be no question that one of the reasons why Spinoza felt compelled to abandon Descartes's conception of the mind and its relationship to the body is because of the support the Cartesian account lends to the doctrine of immortality. Exactly the same extra-philosophical reasons that Descartes uses to promote his "real distinction" between mind and body – the contribution it makes to a traditional religious doctrine – lead Spinoza to another metaphysical point of view.

[22] AT VII.153/CSM II.108–9.

CHAPTER 6

# Knowledge and will

Writing in November of 1665, just as he was probably nearing completion of a first draft of the *Ethics*, Spinoza tells Oldenburg,

The human body is a part of Nature. As regards the human mind, I maintain that it, too, is a part of Nature; for I hold that in Nature there also exists an infinite power of thinking which, in so far as it is infinite, contains within itself the whole of Nature ideally, and whose thoughts proceed in the same manner as does Nature, which is in fact the object of its thought.

This "infinite power of thinking which . . . contains within itself the whole of Nature ideally" is clearly a reference to substance and its attribute Thought and to infinite intellect, the immediate infinite mode of Thought which is the infinite collection of adequate ideas of all things. Spinoza then continues,

Further, I maintain that the human mind is that same power of thinking, not in so far as that power is infinite and apprehends the whole of Nature, but in so far as it is finite, apprehending the human body only. The human mind, I maintain, is in this way part of an infinite intellect. (Letter 32)

The infinite intellect "apprehends the whole of Nature" just because it is composed of infinite ideas, each of which is *of* some object in one or another of the attributes and which together are of all objects in all the attributes. Human minds, as we have seen, constitute a subset of those ideas composing the infinite intellect – namely, just those ideas that have human bodies as their immediate objects. Furthermore, as modes of substance under the attribute Thought, all human minds are expressions of one and the same power of thinking. It is the same power of thinking that manifests itself in

Thought in an infinite manner as (God's) infinite intellect, only with human minds this power manifests itself in finite ways.

This is why Spinoza says that when the human mind has an idea or perceives something, it is actually God (or Nature) itself having the idea or perceiving the thing – not, however, as infinite intellect but as modified by a finite mode, viz., the human mind itself.

> The human mind is a part of the infinite intellect of God. Therefore, when we say that the human mind perceives this or that, we are saying nothing but that God, not insofar as he is infinite, but insofar as he constitutes the essence of the human mind, or insofar as he is explained through the nature of the human mind, has this or that idea. (IIP11c)

When the human mind thinks or perceives $x$, it is God (or Nature) thinking or perceiving $x$, not absolutely but through the refraction of that human mind.

But just how does the human mind know or perceive things? What kind of knowledge can it have of the world and of itself? And how do the ideas possessed by human minds relate to the ideas possessed by infinite intellect, by God or Nature itself? Spinoza believes that knowledge and adequate understanding are the key to human happiness, freedom and well-being, and so addressing these epistemological questions constitutes a major step in his overall moral project.

### IDEAS

Descartes was certainly aware that his use of the term 'idea' in the *Meditations* and other writings to refer to contents of the human mind was idiosyncratic and might be confusing to many of his early modern readers. Previously, the word had been used primarily (but not exclusively) to refer not to psychological items but to metaphysical and logical ones. For Plato, of course, Ideas are eternal, immutable essences, the so-called Forms of things that exist in an intelligible realm of Being distinct from this ever-changing world of Becoming. For medieval thinkers in the Platonic tradition, such as St. Augustine, *Ideae*, while still eternal and immutable, are the contents of God's understanding; they are revealed to human beings only through a process of divine illumination. Descartes, by contrast, self-consciously took these contents of the divine mind and moved them into the human mind and made them its own proper modifications. Thus, as he says to the English philosopher Thomas Hobbes in reply to the latter's objections to the *Meditations*, "I am taking the word 'idea' to refer to whatever is immediately perceived by the mind . . . I used the word 'idea' because it was the standard philosophical term used to refer to the forms of perception belonging to the divine mind."[1] Descartes, for better or for worse, thereby set the stage for a good deal of epistemological wrangling in the seventeenth and eighteenth centuries, as philosophers – including Locke, Arnauld, Malebranche, Leibniz, Berkeley, and Hume – struggled to make sense of what ideas were and how they allowed for human knowledge.[2]

Spinoza was less troubled by many of the ontological and epistemological questions about ideas that exercised some of his contemporaries. Unlike Descartes in the *Meditations*, for example, Spinoza evinces few serious skeptical worries in the *Ethics* about knowing how ideas in the mind might or might not match up with things in the world. But he is certainly interested in showing how ideas mediate knowledge of the body, of external things, of the mind, and ultimately of God or Nature itself, and in examining the differences between the adequate, rationally acquired ideas that provide us with true understanding and the mutilated inadequate ideas that come from our haphazard encounters with the world around us and that lead us into error.

As we have seen, there is a kind of nesting of ideas in Spinoza's system. The infinite intellect is constituted by ideas of things; and those ideas are themselves collections of ideas of smaller things, and so on. Thus, any human mind is the idea of a human body, an idea that is itself, in turn, a collection of ideas of the parts of that body. "The idea that constitutes the formal being of the human Mind is not simple, but composed of a great many ideas" (IIP15). Thus, unlike Descartes, for whom the human mind is a simple substance and its ideas the modes of that substance, for Spinoza the human

[1] AT VII.180/CSM II.127.
[2] For surveys of the use of the term 'idea' in seventeenth-century philosophy, see McRae 1965 and Yolton 1975.

mind (the macro-idea of the body) is nothing but a complex idea that is made up of other ideas (the sub-ideas that are of the parts of that body).

The ideas making up the human mind are still, in important ways, like the psychological items of Descartes's conception of the mind.[3] First, as discussed above, they, like Cartesian ideas, have intentionality. The ideas of the human mind are *of* things. Primarily, they are ideas *of* parts of the human body, just as the immediate and primary object of the mind itself is the whole body. A feeling of pain as a state in the mind is really the idea *of* the injured body part. Unlike Descartes's ideas, however, the relationship between the idea and its object is not an external relationship between two distinct things. The idea of a part of the human body is the idea *of* that part of the body not because it resembles or otherwise represents an independent reality. Rather, as we now know, the idea and the bodily state of which it is the idea are ultimately identical – they are one and the same thing being expressed through two different attributes. The pain is the expression in Thought of the same thing that is expressed in Extension as an injured body part. This ontological identity, and not what we ordinarily think of as a representational relationship, is what makes an idea the idea *of* a bodily state. (On the other hand, and somewhat confusedly, Spinoza continues also to think of ideas in representational terms, especially with respect to *external* bodies, such that an idea is *both* the ontological correlate under the attribute of Thought of a state of the body and a representation of some extended state of affairs.[4])

Now the parallelism doctrine implies that for *whatever* state the human body is in, there will be a corresponding state in the human mind. But any state of the human mind is an idea. Thus, for every state of the human body, there is a corresponding idea in the human mind. This is really just the application of IIP9c – "Whatever

---

[3] For a contrasting view, according to which Spinoza's ideas are logical, not psychological items, see Curley 1969, pp. 119–30.

[4] See, for example, IIP17c, where he says that ideas "present [*repraesentant*] external bodies" to us (G II.106/C I.465). There has been a good deal of discussion trying to make sense of the relationship between the correspondence relation and the representational relation; see Bennett 1984, pp. 153–61; Della Rocca 1996b, pp. 49–64; Radner 1971; and Wilson 1999b, pp. 131–3.

happens in the singular object of any idea, there is knowledge of it in God, only insofar as he has the idea of the same object" – to the particular case of the idea of the human body: "Whatever happens in the object of the idea constituting the human Mind must be perceived by the human Mind, or there will necessarily be an idea of that thing in the Mind; i.e., if the object of the idea constituting a human Mind is a body, nothing can happen in that body which is not perceived by the Mind" (IIP12). Fortunately for Spinoza, this need not have the counter-intuitive ramification that one consciously perceives and knows everything that happens in the body. He does not think that every idea in the mind is necessarily a conscious idea, attended with awareness. Not only would such a claim be patently false – there is obviously much that happens in my body of which I am not consciously aware, such as the circulation of the blood and the stomach's breaking down of food – but it would also imply, by way of the universal scope of the parallelism thesis, that all things in nature, and not just human beings, are consciously aware. Spinoza will have other means of accounting for conscious awareness, as we shall see.

The immediate object of the mind and its ideas, then, is the body and its states. But through its body, the human mind can also achieve a connection or directedness to external bodies.

IIP16: The idea of any mode in which the human Body is affected by external bodies must involve the nature of the human Body and at the same time the nature of the external body.

DEM.: For all the modes in which a body is affected follow from the nature of the affected body (by IIA″). So the idea of them (by IA4) will necessarily involve the nature of each body. And so the idea of each mode in which the human body is affected by an external body involves the nature of the human Body and of the external body.

When an idea of external object *x* occurs in the mind, it is only because *x* has causally brought about some effect in the human body, which state of the body is explained through and reflects both the nature of the human body and the nature of *x*. But this means that the idea in the mind that is the expression in Thought of the affected part of the body also captures something about the external body that has impinged upon that part. Strictly speaking, the idea is only *of* the state of the human body. But because that state of the human body *qua* effect bears reference to its cause, so too the idea of that state will bear some reference to that cause.

It follows from this, Spinoza concludes, that the mind's ideas achieve intentionality not only toward that mind's body, but toward external bodies as well: "From this it follows, first, that the human Mind perceives the nature of a great many bodies together with the nature of its own body" (IIP16c1). However, the information thereby conveyed about the external body is rather limited, and really tells one more about one's own body – that it is in such and such a state, brought about by some other thing – than about the external body. "It follows, second, that the ideas which we have of external bodies indicate the condition of our own body more than the nature of the external bodies" (IIP16c2). In fact, in ordinary experience, all of our ideas of external objects are mediated by the human body, and thus cannot provide anything more than partial and relative information about those objects, viz., that they cause certain states in our own body. We will return to this point below, when considering Spinoza's classification of the varieties of knowledge.

Among the questions debated among early modern philosophers, especially in the Cartesian tradition, is whether the mind's ideas are objects or acts. Are ideas like mental pictures that the mind apprehends, or are they mental acts of apprehending? Are they things directly and immediately perceived (with external objects perceived only indirectly and mediately, through representational ideas) or perceptions of things?[5] Descartes himself seems to treat them in both ways. On the one hand, he frequently speaks of ideas as things that the mind immediately perceives.[6] On the other hand, he also describes an idea as an "operation of the intellect,"[7] and denies that an idea is "different from the action itself."[8]

---

[5] This was one of the subjects of the philosophical side of the great debate between Arnauld and Malebranche; see Nadler 1989.
[6] See, for example, *Principles of Philosophy* I.13–14.
[7] Fourth Replies, AT VII.232/CSM II.163.
[8] Letter to Mersenne, 28 January 1641, AT III.295.

Spinoza, while he seems to have little patience for this debate, puts himself firmly on the side of those who view ideas as mental activities. He appears unwilling to concede that ideas are, as Descartes says in the *Meditations*, "like images of things [*tanquam rerum imagines*]."[9] He says that "an idea consists neither in the image of anything, nor in words" (IIP49s2). He absolutely rejects the notion that ideas are like "pictures," dead and inert mental objects that are there for the mind to apprehend.

To have a true idea means nothing other than knowing a thing perfectly, or in the best way. And of course no one can doubt this unless he thinks that an idea is something mute, like a picture on a tablet, and not a mode of thinking, viz. the very [act of] understanding. (IIP43s)

Part of what motivates Spinoza to take this stand is his view that every idea essentially involves mental activity. When he first defines 'idea,' he says that it is "a concept of the Mind that the Mind forms because it is a thinking thing" (IID3). In the explanation of that definition, he notes that "I say concept rather than perception, because the word perception seems to indicate that the Mind is acted on by the object. But concept seems to express an action of the Mind." The reason why every idea involves activity is because every idea includes some kind of affirmation or negation. To have an idea of a red ball is not just casually to entertain some thought without making any positive or negative assertions. To have an idea of a red ball is actively to affirm in the mind that the ball is red. Similarly, to have an idea of a unicorn is to affirm in the mind that a white horse has a horn on its forehead, although it is not necessarily also to assert that such a thing really exists outside the mind. There are thus no inactive ideas for Spinoza; every thought involves an attitude of some kind toward its content – a content which, itself, appears to be propositional rather than imagistic. "What is perceiving a winged horse other than affirming wings of the horse?" (IIP49s3b2). He cautions us not to allow our conception of ideas to "fall into pictures" (IIP48s) or image-objects. Speaking of those who "think that ideas consist in images which are formed in us from encounters with external bodies," he says that "they look on ideas . . . as mute

---

[9] AT VII.37/CSM II.25.

pictures on a panel. And preoccupied with this prejudice, do not see that an idea, insofar as it is an idea, involves an affirmation or negation" (IIP49s2). This inclusion of affirmation and negation within the content of the idea itself will have an important role to play in Spinoza's concept of the will.

## TRUTH AND ADEQUACY

According to Spinoza, a person's ultimate well-being is contingent upon his level of knowledge and understanding. In particular, it is dependent upon his increasing the number of true and adequate ideas in his mind and thus moving closer to having an intellect that more closely resembles the infinite intellect, that is, God's (Nature's) infinite and eternal collection of adequate ideas of things.

The truth of an idea is an extrinsic relationship in which the idea stands to its object. An idea is true if the object is as the idea represents it as being. This is what Spinoza calls "the agreement of the idea with its object" (IID4), and clearly amounts to a correspondence theory of truth. A false idea, on the other hand, is an idea that does not agree with its purported object. The difference between a true and a false idea, then, lies not at all in the content or nature of the idea itself but only in this "extrinsic denomination." "A true idea has no more reality or perfection than a false one" (IIP43s). Considered simply as a mode of the mind, an idea is what it is. "There is nothing positive in ideas on account of which they are called false" (IIP33).

Given Spinoza's parallelism between Thought and Extension, the question naturally arises as to how an idea can possibly be false? Does not every mode in Thought, every idea, have a corresponding mode of Extension with which it agrees, since both modes are essentially one and the same thing expressing itself in different attributes? The answer to this question is that, in a sense, all ideas are indeed necessarily true. In so far as an idea belongs to the infinite intellect, it cannot but agree with its object in Extension.

IIP32: All ideas, insofar as they are related to God, are true.
DEM.: For all ideas which are in God agree entirely with their objects (by IIP7c), and so (by IA6) they are all true.

God's idea of an extended object will necessarily agree with the essence of the object itself because both are expressions of one and the same thing but under different attributes. It is not the case, however, that every idea possessed by a human mind will necessarily be true. Just because one has the idea of a unicorn, for example, it does not follow that a unicorn really exists. In the human mind, an idea can fail to agree properly with its object in a number of ways. First, every idea in the mind will indeed necessarily have a corresponding extended mode – the parallelism guarantees this much – but that does not mean that the extended mode that corresponds to the idea will be the object that the idea purports to represent. Thus, there is a mode in Extension that corresponds to my idea of a unicorn, but it is not a real unicorn; rather, it is a state of my body, viz., the motions in my brain that correlate to the imaginative idea in my mind. Second, my idea of an object may not be properly related to ideas of other objects, and thus may not provide the proper causal information about that object; in this way, my idea of an extended object will be false through its incompleteness. As we shall see below, this privative feature of an idea is what Spinoza calls 'inadequacy.'

How does one know that one has a true idea? Or, alternatively, how can one be sure that the ideas that one believes to be true are in fact true and correspond with the way things are outside the mind? This is the skeptical question that Descartes takes so seriously in the *Meditations.* Why should one's subjective certainty about the veridicality of one's ideas be an indicator of their objective truth? Descartes identified the clarity and distinctness of an idea as the candidate criterion of its truth – "all clear and distinct ideas are true" is the principle he formulated. But he also believed that unless he could further establish that his faculty of thinking was created by an omnipotent and non-deceiving God, then he would have no warrant for any lasting confidence that the clear and distinct ideas that that faculty produces, when it is used properly, really do agree with their objects. We need some such demonstration of the inherent and systematic reliability of our rational faculty, Descartes insisted; otherwise, for all we know, that faculty might have been given to us by an evil deceiver, such that even when we use it perfectly well the clear and distinct ideas to which it gives rise are false.

Spinoza, by contrast, feels no need to appeal to a divine guarantee in order to validate or justify the confidence to which true ideas give rise. (Not the least, presumably, because any appeals to God's benevolence reek of teleological anthropomorphism.) He believes that the truth of a true idea is something that it wears on its sleeve. A true idea is self-evidently true to the person who has it, and in the face of a true idea there can be no room for either ordinary doubt or even the kind of metaphysical doubts that Descartes entertains. "He who has a true idea at the same time knows that he has a true idea, and cannot doubt the truth of the thing" (IIP43). "How can a man know that he has an idea that agrees with its object? . . . [T]his arises solely from his having an idea that does agree with its object – truth is its own standard" (IIP43s). For Spinoza, it seems, the skeptical gap between certainty and truth can arise only if one does not understand the true nature of ideas (IIP43s). We must be careful here, however, lest we attribute to Spinoza too strong a view. All that he commits himself to in these propositions is a claim about the *transparency* of truth: if one has a true idea, then one knows with certainty that one has a true idea. I do not see any reason for thinking that he is also making a statement about the *incorrigibility* of truth claims: that if one believes that an idea is true, then it must be true. The problem, of course, is just how is one to distinguish the reliable certainty to which a true idea gives rise from the unreliable but perhaps equally strong certainty that so often leads one into error. Does he believe there is a phenomenological difference between the certainty brought about by a true idea and the certainty that accompanies false ideas, such that a sufficiently careful person can always distinguish the two?

Spinoza would reply that there is such a reliable mark of truth, and it lies in the idea's adequacy. This, at least, is suggested by his initial definition of an adequate idea: "By adequate idea I understand an idea which, insofar as it is considered in itself, without relation to an object, has all the properties, or intrinsic denominations of a true idea" (IID4).

An idea is adequate in the strict sense of the term when it encompasses perfect and complete knowledge of its object. An adequate idea contains "all the properties" of a thing, and for each such property allows one to "deduce" that it belongs to the object.[10] The adequate idea of a circle enables one to see what properties necessarily characterize a circle (for example, that all the radii drawn from the center to the circumference are equal). Moreover, Spinoza insists, such knowledge is intimately bound up with causal understanding. As we know from IA3 and IA4, to know a thing is to know its causes and to see how it necessarily follows from them. This connection between adequacy, deduction of properties, and cause is summed up well in a letter to Tschirnhaus, where Spinoza says that

in order that I may know which out of many ideas of a thing will enable all the properties of the object to be deduced, I follow this one rule, that the idea or definition of the thing should express its efficient cause. (Letter 60)

Thus, an adequate idea of $x$ is an idea that makes possible a full explanation of $x$. It shows how $x$ is related to its total causal and logical grounds and reveals the absolute necessity of $x$ and everything about $x$. Inadequate ideas, by contrast, are "mutilated and confused." There is something lacking in an inadequate idea, namely, just that relevant causal information that renders the concept of the thing determinate and complete. Inadequacy is thus a matter of ignorance or a "privation of knowledge." This is why Spinoza says that inadequate ideas are "like conclusions without premises" (IIP27). One knows something about the thing, but not enough to be able to state truly why it is such. Inadequate ideas often lead us to regard things not as necessary but as contingent, since, lacking a sufficient and coherent causal story for them, we simply do not see them as necessitated by causes (IIP44).

All true ideas are also adequate ideas, and vice versa. "Between a true and an adequate idea," Spinoza writes to Tschirnhaus, "I recognize no difference but this, that the word 'true' has regard only to the agreement of the idea with its object, whereas the word 'adequate' has regard to the nature of the idea in itself. Thus there is no real difference between a true and an adequate idea except for this extrinsic relation" (Letter 60). Similarly, false ideas are inadequate ideas. To speak of their truth or falsehood is to consider the

---

[10] See, for example, Letter 60.

question of their agreement with their objects; to speak of their adequacy is to consider only the intrinsic features of the ideas themselves.

Strictly speaking, only God has perfectly adequate knowledge of anything. This is because only God, in the infinite intellect, can encompass in its ideas the infinite number of conditions that causally determine anything. Every singular thing, as we have seen, stands in two causal nexuses: the finite series of infinite and eternal causes (the attributes and their infinite modes) and the infinite series of finite causes (other singular things). "Adequate knowledge of how things are constituted is in God, insofar as he has the ideas of all of them" (IIP30d). Indeed, all of God's ideas are necessarily adequate and true, since (as the parallelism doctrine demands) the infinite intellect contains the infinite series of ideas in the same order and connection as the infinite series of things. "God's [actual] power of thinking is equal to his actual power of acting. I.e., whatever follows formally from God's infinite nature follows objectively in God from his idea in the same order and with the same connection" (IIP7c). "All ideas," Spinoza says, "insofar as they are related to God, are true" (IIP32).

The human mind, as a finite mode of Thought, cannot possibly encompass an infinite series of ideas and causes. However, this does not mean that the human mind is doomed to a lifetime of only inadequate knowledge. Adequate knowledge of an abbreviated sort is available to human beings. It is all a matter of how ideas are ordered in a person's mind. One's partial knowledge of a thing can still be adequate, as long as the idea of the thing is properly situated in its causal/logical nexuses, however incomplete our grasp of those nexuses may be. I may not know every causal antecedent for a particular event, since there are an infinite number (according to Spinoza's metaphysics). But I can certainly have at least a partial knowledge of the finite and infinite causes that have determined it to be as it is. To have that partial knowledge is, in fact, to have the ideas in my mind represent a properly ordered subset of the ideas in the infinite intellect. The following diagram captures what such abbreviated but (in terms of Spinoza's moral-psychological project) sufficient adequacy amounts to:

Causal series in Extension:

. . . ->body A->body B->body C->**body D**->body E->body F-> . . .

Adequate knowledge of D in infinite intellect:

. . . ->idea of A->idea of B->idea of C->**idea of D**->idea of E->idea of
  F -> . . .

Adequate knowledge of D in finite intellect:

[idea of B->idea of C->**idea of D**->idea of E]

Inadequate knowledge of D in finite intellect:

[idea of B->idea of C] **[idea of D**-> idea of E] *or* [idea of A->**idea of
  D**->idea of F]

The example that Spinoza provides to illustrate the contrast between adequate and inadequate knowledge concerns a question that, for him, is of the utmost importance. To conceive adequately the nature of the human will is to see *that* all of our volitions are, like all events in the mind, determined by antecedent causes and to see to some extent what those causes are. The false belief in a spontaneous human freedom, with volitions undetermined by any conditions, has its source in the fact that one is missing an important part of the picture; the error is grounded in inadequate ideas (IIP35s).

IIP35: Falsity consists in the privation of knowledge which inadequate, or mutilated and confused ideas involve.

SCHOLIUM: In IIP17s, I explained how error consists in the privation of knowledge. But to explain the matter more fully . . .: men are deceived in that they think themselves free [NS: i.e., they think that, of their own free will, they can either do a thing or forbear doing it], an opinion which consists only in this, that they are conscious of their actions and ignorant of the causes by which they are determined.

The human mind, then, has an adequate idea of a thing when that idea and its logical and causal relations to other ideas in the mind (all corresponding to the causal relations among the objects of these ideas) mirror the logical and causal relations among ideas in God or Nature, in the infinite intellect. "Our mind, insofar as it perceives things truly, is part of the infinite intellect of God (by IIP11c); hence, it is as necessary that the mind's clear and distinct ideas are true as that God's ideas are" (IIP43s). In perceiving things adequately, we achieve a kind of cognitive identity with God's mind. The order and connection of our ideas is identical to the way those same ideas are ordered and connected in the infinite intellect. In short, for a human mind, to conceive something adequately is to conceive it as God or Nature conceives it. Conversely, when a human mind has an adequate idea of a thing, God perceives that thing adequately, "not insofar as he is infinite, but insofar as he is explained through the nature of the human mind, or insofar as he constitutes the essence of the human mind, has this or that idea" (IIP11c). "An idea true in us is that which is adequate in God insofar as he is explained through the nature of the human mind" (IIP43d).

Another way to look at the distinction between the adequacy and inadequacy of ideas is to consider the issue in terms of the causes of an idea in the mind. An idea is adequate if its causal antecedents lie in other adequate ideas possessed by the mind. My idea of an object (say, a right triangle) is an adequate idea if it follows from other knowledge that I possess (in this case, geometric knowledge) – if the mind itself, in other words, is the cause of the idea. I know the thing adequately under these conditions because *my* conception of the thing is properly situated causally and logically among *my* ideas. On the other hand, if my idea of an external body is generated in me not by other ideas in my intellect but by my sensory experiences – that is, by the interaction of the idea of my body (i.e., my mind) with the idea of that external body, which ideal interaction is simply the reflection in Thought of the interaction of my body with another body – then the idea of the external body essentially comes disconnected from true and adequate understanding. This is the meaning of the corollary to IIP11:

When we say that God has this or that idea, not only insofar as he constitutes the nature of the human mind, but insofar as he also has the idea of another thing together with the human mind, then we say that the human mind perceives the thing only partially or inadequately.

To say that God has a particular idea (e.g., an idea of a part of the human body) only insofar as he constitutes the nature of the human mind – that is, only insofar as God has the idea of the human body – is to say that that particular idea derives from the mind's own intellectual resources. To say that God has the particular idea not only insofar as God has the idea that is the human mind but also because God has the idea of something else is to say that the idea does not derive from the mind/idea of the body alone, but is a mental reflection of the interaction of the human body with another body.

The necessary adequacy of God's ideas, then, is a function of the fact that the infinite intellect contains all ideas, and thus any idea in the infinite intellect necessarily must follow from other ideas in that same intellect. For human minds, however, our ideas often derive not from adequate knowledge but from our haphazard encounters with things in the world and the way they impinge on our bodies. In such a case, the idea in the mind follows not from the mind itself but is caused by the conjunction of the idea of the external thing with the idea of the body (since only ideas can cause other ideas).

We can clarify all this by considering the various things that we generally come to know. In fact, there are very few things in this life that ordinarily we know adequately. Spinoza considers in Part Two the mind's knowledge of external bodies, of its own body, and of itself. In all three cases, our usual cognitive acquaintance is through experience, not the intellect, with the result that our ideas of external bodies, of our own bodies and even of our own minds are mostly inadequate.

External bodies, as we have seen, are experienced primarily through our own body. This is just how sense experience works. Our ideas of things in the world around us are mediated by the body. The immediate object of any idea in the mind is a state of the body. When the state of the body is brought about by some external body, the idea in the mind of that bodily state is in fact the idea of a complex extended mode that is explained by both the human body and the external body, just as the nature of a seal is explained by both the wax and the stamp whose imprint it bears. But this means that such ideas reflect our own bodies as much as they do external bodies (IIP16). The information that they convey about those external things is therefore highly limited and perspectival. These ideas give us only a relative knowledge of such objects – how they appear from one particular point of view and how they affect us through our bodies. We know the objects only insofar as they are reflected in the mode of the human body that results from their causal impingement upon the body. Therefore, such sensory based or perceptual ideas do not provide adequate knowledge of external things. "The idea of any affection of the human body does not involve adequate knowledge of an external body" (IIP25). This is really just an "imagistic" apprehension of a thing, Spinoza says, because it is mediated by images in the body caused by external things. He adds that "insofar as the human mind imagines an external body, it does not have adequate knowledge of it" (IIP26c).

Nor does ordinary experience provide one with an adequate idea of one's own body. We essentially know the body in experience only through its interactions with other bodies, and this cannot provide us with anything but a partial and "mutilated" knowledge of what the body is and how it persists. "The human mind does not know the human body itself, nor does it know that it exists, except through ideas of affections by which the body is affected" (IIP19). What Spinoza means is that it is mainly through the sensory correlates of the body's causal interactions with other bodies that the mind is stimulated and knows its body and its condition. But then all that we really have is relative knowledge of the body – a knowledge of how it is affected by other bodies – and not an adequate knowledge of what the body is in itself. Even this relative knowledge of the body is highly limited. To the extent that the mind's attention is focused only on a particular affection of the body – through the idea of that affection – it must remain ignorant of or inattentive to the many other ways in which the body is or can be affected. This is why, as Spinoza says in IIP27, "the idea of any affection of the human body does not involve adequate knowledge of the human body itself." Indeed, Spinoza asserts, we do not even have adequate knowledge of any particular affection of the body.

For the ideas of the affections of the human body involve the nature of external bodies as much as that of the human body (by IIP16), and must involve the nature not only of the human body [NS: as a whole], but also of its parts. But (by IIP24 and IIP25) adequate knowledge of external bodies is in God not insofar as he is considered to be affected with the human mind, but insofar as he is considered to be affected with other ideas. (IIP28d)

Since the mind, taken by itself, is the idea only of the human body and not of any external bodies; and since any externally caused affection of the human body also involves the nature of the (inadequately known) external body, the mind by itself does not involve an adequate knowledge of the affection. "These ideas of the affections," Spinoza concludes, "insofar as they are related only to the human mind, are like conclusions without premises" (IIP28d). We know only the effects in our own bodies, not their causes, and therefore our ideas of the effects are "confused."

Spinoza's general point here is that any body, human or otherwise, is a part of Nature and thus exists only through a network of causal relations with other bodies. "The human body, to be preserved, requires a great many other bodies, by which it is, as it were, continually regenerated" (IIPost.4). If the human body so essentially depends causally on other bodies, and if we can know those other bodies only inadequately, then our knowledge of the human body can be only inadequate. Moreover, the mind's attention is often most immediately focused (through its ideas) on the effects in the human body of its interactions with other bodies, and not on those other bodies themselves and their law-governed, causally necessary relationships with the human body. I attend primarily to the pleasure I feel when drinking a cool glass of water, and not to the relations and principles through which my consumption of the water sustains my body's existence. There is a good explanation for this. To the extent that the human mind is the idea of the human body, and not of the other bodies that are causally responsible for regenerating the human body, its perspective on things is necessarily limited. Its ideas will generally lack the broad causal content that adequate ideas involve. Thus, on the one hand, while it may be the case that "God has the idea of the human body, or knows the human body, insofar as he is affected by a great many other ideas" – in particular, the ideas of other bodies – and not simply "insofar as he constitutes the nature of the human mind," and therefore has adequate knowledge of the human body, on the other hand, the human mind, insofar as it is only the idea of the human body and possesses only inadequate ideas of other bodies, does not have adequate knowledge of the human body (IIP24).

Finally, our knowledge of the human mind itself is no more adequate than our knowledge of the body – necessarily so, since the mind is only the idea of the body and we do not know the body adequately. Just as there is in God an idea of the human body (i.e., the mind), so, too, is there in God an idea of the human mind itself, since there is an idea in God (under the attribute Thought) of every attribute and of every mode of every attribute (IIP20). And this idea of the human mind is united with the human mind in the same way that the human mind is united with the human body. They are one and the same thing being expressed in two different ways, except in this case the two expressions fall under one attribute, Thought. The idea of the human mind is, therefore, an idea of an idea and constitutes a part of the idea that is its object. In other words, the idea or knowledge of the human mind, as well as the ideas or knowledge of its own affections, belong to the human mind itself (IIP21). However, the idea that the human mind has of itself is no more adequate than its object. And its object – which is the idea of the body – is, we know, not itself an adequate idea of *its* object. Spinoza's conclusion is that to the extent that the human mind's knowledge of itself is a function of the mind's knowledge of the body, "the human mind does not know itself" (IIP23). That is, insofar as the mind's knowledge of itself is stimulated and determined by ordinary experience, insofar as it is nothing but the mind's reflection upon its own sensory awareness of the body, it is only a knowledge of the various ways in which the mind is being affected, just as the same experience provides the mind only with a knowledge of the various ways in which the body is affected. "The idea of the idea of any affection of the human body does not involve adequate knowledge of the human mind" (IIP29).

It is tempting to take Spinoza's talk of "ideas of ideas" – the claim that every mode of thinking, whether it be the idea that is the human mind itself or one of the sub-ideas that make up the mind, is itself the object of a second-order mode of thinking – to be his way of describing the nature of consciousness. After all, it would be natural to suppose that to have an idea of an idea is to be *aware* of the mind and its activity.[11] And yet, if this is Spinoza's account of conscious awareness, then he must once again confront some

---

[11] See, for example, Curley 1969, pp. 126–9.

seriously counterintuitive ramifications of his philosophy of mind. We saw above that the universal scope of Spinoza's parallelism between ideas in Thought and bodies in Extension should not be read as implying that every extended thing also has a human-like mind. But the parallelism does imply that there is a mode of Thought for every single mode of every attribute (including the modes of the attribute Thought). Thus, just as every body in Extension has a corresponding idea in Thought, so every idea in Thought corresponding to every body also has a corresponding idea. For every idea, there is an idea of the idea, and an idea of that idea, and so on. Now if this notion of an "idea of an idea" is Spinoza's way of explaining consciousness, then it follows that every idea corresponding to every body involves consciousnesss. This is a conclusion that I am certain Spinoza does not accept.

The solution is not to think of the "idea of idea" doctrine as Spinoza's explanation of consciousness. What *does* explain consciousness, however, remains something of a mystery for Spinoza. I believe the best approach is to think of consciousness and self-awareness as the distinctive complexity in the human mind that corresponds (via the parallelism) to the distinctive complexity of the human body. Recall that what distinguishes the human body from other bodies are its greater capacities to act and be acted upon, the fact that – through its more complex nervous system, brain, and sensory apparatus – it is "more capable than others of doing many thing at once, or being acted on in many ways at once." This dimension of the body is necessarily reflected in the way that the human mind "surpasses" all other ideas corresponding to extended bodies; it, too, has greater capacities. "From these [truths] we can know that excellence of one mind over the others" (IIP13s). A passage from later in the *Ethics* more explicitly connects these greater capacities with consciousness:

Because human bodies are capable of a great many things, there is no doubt but what they can be of such a nature that they are related to minds which have a great knowledge of themselves . . .

He continues with a concrete illustration:

He who, like an infant or child, has a body capable of very few things . . . has a mind which considered solely in itself is conscious of almost nothing of itself . . . On the other hand, he who has a body capable of a great many things, has a mind which considered only in itself is very much conscious of itself. (VP39s)

What the greater complexity in the mind amounts to, on this reading, just is consciousness itself.[12]

WAYS OF KNOWING

The upshot of all this is that in ordinary experience there is practically nothing that the mind knows adequately. The ideas that we acquire through the senses and the imagination are connected not as they are in the infinite intellect, according to God or Nature's absolute knowledge of things, but according to the random and relative ways in which we happen to be affected by the objects around us. The ideas that we have of external bodies, our own bodies, and our minds are ordered by the manner in which we experience the world as durational beings occupying a particular place in space and time. A person will know these things according to their relationships to his body and the ways in which that body interacts with other bodies in time. This is what Spinoza's calls knowing things "from the common order of nature."

So long as the human mind perceives things from the common order of nature, it does not have an adequate but only a confused and mutilated knowledge of itself, of its own body, and of external bodies. For the mind does not know itself except insofar as it perceives ideas of the affections of the body (by IIP23). But it does not perceive its own body (by IIP19) except through the very ideas themselves of the affections [of the body], and it is also through them alone that it perceives external bodies (by IIP26). (IIP29c)

Just because A follows B in my own experience, which is a function of where my body C is spatially and temporally with respect to A and B, it does not follow that A and B are, absolutely speaking, related in that particular way.

The contrast is with knowing things as they are truly – i.e., logically and causally – ordered from a non-temporal perspective

---

[12] Wilson (1999b, pp. 126–40), however, denies that this can work as Spinoza's account of conscious awareness.

and thereby coming to have a mind whose ideas represent a proper finite subset of the infinite ideas in the infinite intellect.

I say expressly that the mind has, not an adequate, but only a confused [NS: a mutilated] knowledge of itself, of its own body, and of external bodies, so long as its perceives things from the common order of nature, i.e., so long as it is determined externally, from fortuitous encounters with things, to regard this or that, and not so long as it is determined internally, from the fact that it regards a number of things at once, to understand their agreements, differences, and oppositions. For so often as it is disposed internally, in this or another way, then it regards things clearly and distinctly. (IIP29s)

Ideas so determined "internally" have their ordering principle not in the vicissitudes of sensory experience, or how things happen to impinge upon us in the course of our everyday lives, but in the logical principles of Thought, which mirror the absolute physical and causal principles of Extension. Ideas will then follow other ideas inferentially through connections established by the intellect, not temporally through connections established by the senses, imagination, and memory. (The difference is between believing that the sum of the three interior angles of a triangle is equal to 180 degrees because of a mathematical demonstration, and, to use Spinoza's example in IIP19s, thinking of an apple when one hears the word 'apple' only because one has often heard the word while looking at the fruit.) Through the intellect, I come to know things not from a relative, durational perspective, according to how they may be related in time to my existence, but from an absolute, atemporal perspective. This is what Spinoza calls knowing a thing *sub specie aeternitatis* – "under the form of eternity." It is to know the thing as God or Nature itself knows it. The human mind thereby achieves a "connection of ideas" that, in contrast to the "connection [that] happens according to the order and connection of the affections of the body . . . happens according to the order of the intellect, by which the mind perceives things through their first causes, and which is the same in all men" (IIP18s).

In the middle of Part Two of the *Ethics*, however, such intellectual understanding, not to mention the ethical rewards it brings, seems a long way off. The human mind appears irredeemably lost amidst its inadequate ideas, unable to know anything – not even itself – with any real certainty. And yet, with IIP38, hope appears on the horizon in the form of what Spinoza calls "common notions." These are elements that every human mind knows, and knows adequately, simply by virtue of being the kind of thing it is, viz., the idea of the body.

There are certain things that are common to all bodies, necessarily, just because they are all modes of Extension and therefore share the same basic nature and undergo the same kinds of modifications. Although Spinoza does not go into specifics, presumably these things are shape (not any particular shape, but having shape), size, divisibility, and mobility, as well as the principles of geometry and laws of motion and rest – basically, whatever is involved in the attribute of Extension and its infinite modes. But this means that such common features will be expressed in every idea corresponding to every body. Regardless of the many aspects of a body that can be conceived only inadequately by its corresponding mind because they depend on that body's particular interactions with other bodies, these common things in bodies will have as their correlates adequate ideas. "Those things which are common to all, and which are equally in the part and in the whole, can only be conceived adequately" (IIP38). They are conceived adequately by the body's mind because their possession by the body is due not to that body's having any particular modifications but simply to its being a body.

Thus, there are certain general features of the human body and of external bodies that the human mind will conceive adequately (IIP39). This is because these features of the human body follow from the nature of the human body itself as a parcel of extension and not because of its determinate causal relationship to any external body. As Spinoza says, the ideas of these features "will necessarily be adequate in God insofar as he constitutes the human mind, or insofar as he has ideas that are in the human mind" (IIP38d). It would seem to follow, as well, that there are common notions under the attribute of Thought, and that the mind has adequate knowledge of those features common to all minds simply by virtue of being modes of Thought, including the nature of thought itself and its most general principles.

Common notions are therefore somewhat like the innate ideas that other seventeenth-century thinkers, such as Descartes and

Leibniz, employ to explain how we can have knowledge (mathematical, moral, and metaphysical) that is independent of what we learn from sense experience. Of course, Spinoza is not entitled to a distinction between those ideas that are innate and those that are caused by external things in sense experience, since (as we know from Part One) no ideas (no modes of Thought) are caused by external things (modes of Extension). And it may be that for Spinoza, as for innate ideas theorists, sensory input is needed to stimulate the mind actually to think of these ideas of the common features of things. But he denies that the common notions are derived from experience in the sense of being mental correlates of affections of the body that are caused by other bodies, that is, by the human body's interaction with the world; rather, they follow from the nature of the mind (the idea of the body) itself.

Common notions are not to be confused with universals, Spinoza warns us. Universals are abstract concepts that are ordinarily derived from attending to certain aspects common to a number of ideas of things and ignoring others (namely, those wherein the ideas differ from one another), and thereby forming a distinct but not necessarily clear idea of only those common features.

Those notions they call *Universal*, like man, horse, dog, etc., have arisen . . . because so many images (e.g., of men) are formed at one time in the human body that they surpass the power of imagining – not entirely, of course, but still to the point where the mind can imagine neither slight differences of the singular [men] (such as the color and size of each one, etc.), nor their determinate number, and imagines distinctly only what they all agree in, insofar as they affect the body. For the body has been affected most [NS: forcefully] by [what is common], since each singular has affected it [by this property]. And [NS: the mind] expresses this by the word *man*, and predicates it of infinitely many singulars. (IIP40s1)

Universals are formed by different people in different ways, since we are all affected in different ways by things and may take notice of different commonalities among them. Universals thus suffer from the same contingency and relativity that infects concrete ideas drawn from the common order of nature. The ideas of common natures, by contrast, are not abstracted from particulars; they are known directly. And they are the same in all people and are present in all minds.

From this it follows that there are certain ideas, or notions, common to all men. For (by IIL2) all bodies agree in certain things, which (by IIP38) must be perceived adequately, or clearly and distinctly, by all. (IIP38c)

Common notions thus represent an important step in the epistemological part of Spinoza's project. For they stand as the first instance of the mind coming to have certain ideas through being "determined internally," from its own resources rather than from the common order of nature. They are the most accessible and prominent adequate ideas available to the mind. From them, moreover, it is possible to deduce other adequate ideas, since "whatever ideas follow in the mind from ideas that are adequate in the mind are also adequate" (IIP40). In this way, a knowledge of things can be had through ideas that follow the order of the intellect rather than "the order and connection of the affections of the human body." Ultimately, one will be able to achieve an adequate knowledge of the essences of particular things, an understanding of them *sub specie aeternitatis* and in relation to their infinite and eternal causes rather than in the context of their temporal determinations.

In IIP40s2, Spinoza offers a threefold classification of ways of knowing, hierarchically ordered, that is supposed to reflect the differences between the sensory acquisition of inadequate ideas, the rational discovery of common notions and of the adequate ideas that can be derived from them, and, finally, the intuitive apprehension of the essences of particular things.

The first kind of knowledge, or way in which "we perceive many things," is "from singular things which have been represented to us through the senses in a way that is mutilated, confused, and without order for the intellect . . . for that reason I have been accustomed to call such perceptions knowledge from random experience." In the *Short Treatise*, where Spinoza offers an earlier version of the division, he includes in his first category both those ideas derived from sense experience and those derived "from report," that is, opinions based on the testimony of others or indirect evidence (G I.54/C I.97). In the *Treatise on the Emendation of the Intellect*, it is a four-part division, with the first two categories involving, respectively, "the perception we have from report or from some conventional sign" and "the perception we have from random experience, that is, from experience that is not determined by the intellect" (G II.10/ C I.12). Examples of that which is known "by report" are the date of one's birth and the identity of one's parents. On the other hand, my belief that I shall die is known by random experience if it is based only on the fact that "I have seen others like me die" (G II.10/C I.13). Knowledge of the first kind (and, in the *Treatise*, of the first and second kinds) is, Spinoza insists, "the only cause of falsity [*unica falsitatis causa*]" (IIP41). By itself, it is not a source of adequate ideas.

Knowledge of the second kind, which Spinoza calls "reason [*ratio*]," is described in the *Ethics* as the way in which "we perceive many things . . . from the fact that we have common notions and adequate ideas of the properties of things." Knowledge of the third kind, which he calls "intuitive knowledge [*scientia intuitiva*]," is described as proceeding "from an adequate idea of the formal essence of certain attributes of God to the adequate knowledge of the [NS: formal] essence of things." Both of these definitions are frustratingly spare, and Spinoza does little to spell out in detail what exactly each of these two kinds of knowledge involves. Knowledge of the third kind, in particular, seems rather mysterious, and has often given rise to the suggestion that Spinoza is ultimately a kind of mystic. As I hope to show, nothing could be further from the truth; Spinoza is a rationalist, through and through.

Both knowledge of the second kind and knowledge of the third kind are "necessarily true" (IIP41) and consist in adequate ideas. They also involve a true perception of the necessity of things. It is not very clear, however, what exactly the difference is between them, and especially what Spinoza intends to include under knowledge of the second kind. At the very least, he wants to put in that category the mind's knowledge of common notions, as well as of any general principles that follow deductively from them. But there is some debate among scholars as to whether or not and in what way Spinoza also thinks that knowledge of the second kind reaches individuals and includes adequate ideas of particular things.

One interpretation is that the *Ethics* definition of knowledge of the second kind refers *only* to the mind's apprehension of common notions and of the properties of things in general (e.g., what it is to be square) but not to any knowledge of particular things that instantiate such properties.[13] If knowledge of the second kind does extend to particulars, on a slightly more liberal version of this reading, it is only insofar as it subsumes them in a broad manner under the common notions and thus includes the general recognition that all individual things are modes that depend on substance and are governed by the general principles of their respective attributes.[14] To know a particular by the second kind of knowledge, on this view, is simply to know *that* it (like all finite modes) is necessitated by infinite and finite causes, but not to know how.

A more generous (and, I believe, more plausible) reading of the doctrine is that both the second and third kinds of knowledge involve adequate knowledge of individuals and thus lead to an idea of a thing that situates it in its proper causal context. Both ways of knowing, that is, consider a particular thing independently of its durational and changing relationships to other things and place it explicitly in relation to an attribute and to the eternal principles that govern all the modes of that attribute, such that one sees not only that the thing is necessitated, but how.

Consider, for example, knowledge of the human body. In the first kind of knowledge, we know the body only inadequately, by way of the affections that it may happen to undergo over time. The second kind of knowledge, by contrast, shows how and why the body is what it is by reference to the nature of Extension and the principles of physical science (or, more specifically, the principles of biology, physiology, chemistry, etc.). Since we know that "the human body requires a great many bodies by which it is, as it were, regenerated" (IIP19d), adequate knowledge of the human body must also make reference to other modes of Extension (other bodies); but it does so by showing the ways in which the human body is necessarily and essentially related to other bodies by the laws derivable from Extension and its infinite modes, not by looking at the temporal (and temporary) modifications any particular human body may experience in the course of nature. To draw a fairly loose analogy, it is one

---

[13] Allison (1987), for example, argues that "the province of reason is general truths – for example, axioms – which hold universally and do not pertain to any individuals in particular" (117). For the contrasting view, see Yovel 1989, chapter 6.

[14] This is the reading suggested by Lloyd 1986, pp. 227–8.

thing to know about the body's nutritional needs because one experiences hunger, thirst, and weakness; it is an entirely different thing to know those aspects of the body by scientifically understanding the role of proteins, carbohydrates, and fluids in sustaining the body.

Knowledge of the second kind provides, in other words, a true and adequate explanation for the body's nature and properties; in the knower's mind, the idea of the body is related to the ideas of other bodies (the horizontal dimension of causality) through the laws of nature (the vertical dimension of causality), mirroring the way things and their ideas are eternally related in a law-like way in the infinite intellect. "Our mind, insofar as it perceives things truly, is part of the infinite intellect of God" (IIP43s). Unlike knowledge of the first kind, in which things appear to be connected with each other haphazardly – thus giving rise to the belief in contingency – reason sees them as they truly are because it places them under their covering laws and thus introduces necessity. "It is of the nature of reason to regard things as necessary, not as contingent" (IIP44). At the same time, it abstracts from the particular affections that the body may be undergoing because of its causal interactions in time with other bodies. The second kind of knowledge thereby provides one with an understanding *sub specie aeternitatis* of an object.

It is of the nature of reason to regard things as necessary and not as contingent (by IIP44). And it perceives this necessity of things truly (by IIP41), i.e. (by IA6), as it is in itself. But (by IP16) this necessity of things is the very necessity of God's eternal nature. Therefore, it is of the nature of reason to regard things under this species of eternity. (IIP44c2d)

In his discussion of knowledge of the second kind, Spinoza refers often to ideas of singular things (e.g., IIP45), thus strongly suggesting that this species of knowledge is not just a knowledge of common notions or of the general fact that particular things are determined by laws of nature but also a knowledge of the particular things that it individually subsumes under those "foundations of reason." As Spinoza says, the common notions, because they are common to many things, "do not explain the essence of any singular thing" (IIP44c2d). They do, however, provide the conceptual and explanatory framework within which the truth of singular things can be apprehended.

Knowledge of the third kind also provides one with a view of the necessity of things and a perspective *sub specie aeternitatis* on each one of them. To know something by way of the second and third kinds of knowledge is to know it as eternal. The difference between the two kinds of knowledge, then, is to be framed not really in terms of content or information but in terms of their respective forms. Reason, or knowledge of the second kind, is discursive and involves inferring the effect from its causes – and especially the higher, eternal causes – much as a conclusion is logically derived from premises. Intuition, or knowledge of the third kind, by contrast, seems to be an immediate perception of the connection between causes and effect, resulting in a singular conception of the essence of a thing (which, as Spinoza has told us, must include knowledge of the thing's cause). Intuition represents a kind of epistemic compression of information. It involves a direct apprehension of the causal and logical relationship between its terms, such that the information is united into something grasped in a single act of the mind.[15] The distinction between the second and third kinds of knowledge is thus not unlike the distinction that Descartes draws, in his *Rules for the Direction of the Mind*, between deduction and intuition.[16] Both deduction and intuition involve the mind clearly and distinctly perceiving necessary connections between things. But whereas intuition is a simple and indubitable "conception of a clear and attentive mind" as it grasps either a single thing or a single connection between two things, a deduction involves a series of intuitions in an extended chain of reasoning.

We are distinguishing mental intuition from certain deduction on the grounds that we are aware of a movement or a sort of sequence in the latter but not in the former, and also because immediate self-evidence is not required for deduction, as it is for intuition.[17]

---

[15] See Yovel 1989 (pp. 154–65), who speaks of a "flash of intuition" that "internalizes" content that was previously only "externally" related.

[16] The *Rules* (*Regulae ad directionem ingenii*) were not published until after Spinoza's death, but it is possible that he saw one of the manuscript copies that circulated during his lifetime within some Cartesian circles. Leibniz may have shown Spinoza his own manuscript copy of the *Rules*, which he purchased in Amsterdam in 1670, when he paid a visit to Spinoza in The Hague in 1676. This would, however, have been too late to have had any real influence on the *Ethics*.

[17] AT X.370/CSM I.15.

In Spinoza's knowledge of the second kind, the knower infers one thing from another, thus producing an explanation of the thing that relates it to its cause(s). This may involve a number of steps, depending upon how causally remote the thing is from its conditions or how many causes are involved. In knowledge of the third kind, all of this causal information is synthesized and built into an adequate idea of the thing itself, thus producing what Spinoza calls the "essence" of the thing. In the *Treatise on the Emendation of the Intellect*, Spinoza defines the third kind of knowledge as "the perception we have when a thing is perceived through its essence alone, or through knowledge of its proximate cause" (G II.10/C I.13). Knowledge of the second kind is thus a necessary condition for knowledge of the third kind, since it provides the material that the mind may eventually perceive through intuition (much as Descartes says that a deduction can be transformed into an intuition by running through it often enough for it all to be held before the mind at one time[18]).

The mathematical example of the fourth proportional that Spinoza uses to illustrate the three kinds of knowledge brings out well these differences in form between them. The problem is to discover a fourth number that bears to a third number the same ratio that a second number bears to a first – in other words, to solve the following equation for $x$: $12:16::75:x$. In knowledge of the first kind, one merely relies on a practical method that one has been shown by others without really understanding the matter through mathematical principles; thus, for example, "merchants do not hesitate to multiply the second by the third, and divide the product by the first," not because they know something more basic about the numerical relationships, but because "they have not yet forgotten what they heard from their teacher." In knowledge of the second kind, one knows the solution to the problem because one has seen and understood the relevant demonstration in Euclid (Book VII, Proposition 7) concerning the relationship among certain quantities. In knowledge of the third kind, one has an immediate insight into the solution, without any demonstration

---

[18] AT X.387–8/CSM I.25.

required, such as occurs when the problem involves very simple numbers.

> Given the numbers 1, 2, and 3, no one fails to see that the fourth proportional number is 6 – and we see this much more clearly because we infer the fourth number from the ratio which, in one glance, we see the first number to have to the second. (IIP40s2)[19]

There is one other consideration that supports the interpretation of the difference between the second and third kinds of knowledge that I am proposing. If adequate ideas of singular things were limited to knowledge of the third kind, which (as Spinoza insists) is exceedingly difficult and rare to achieve – "a matter for the happy few," in Yovel's words[20] – then the most that the majority of humankind can really hope for, beyond the mutilated ideas of knowledge of the first kind, would be common notions and a vague recognition of the necessity of everything in nature. It is certainly possible that this is what Spinoza has in mind, but I doubt it. It does not seem likely that the only kind of adequate knowledge of particular things available is the intuitive understanding of the third kind of knowledge. Such a gap in content between reason and intuition would indeed make Spinoza out to be something of a mystic, since there would be a certain domain of substantive information – the adequate understanding of particulars – that can be achieved only by a kind of "leap" beyond what rational demonstration can access.

On the other hand, the interpretation of the three kinds of knowledge being offered here does leave us with the following question: How specific, detailed and complete must knowledge of the second kind (and, ultimately, knowledge of the third kind) be? Even if it is more than the general knowledge *that* particular things, as modes of substance, fit within a necessitating framework of laws, must it be so detailed and precise that it turns out that it is possessed only by a scientist, who sees exactly *how* a particular thing of a certain type is determined by the nature of the attribute, the principles derivable from it and other finite modes?

---

[19] The same mathematical example appears in the TIE (G II.11–12/C I.13–14) and the KV (G I.54–5/C I.97–8).
[20] Yovel 1989, p. 154.

It is worth noting that Spinoza's conception in the *Ethics* of ultimate knowledge being one of essences, including the very special kind of causal content they involve, is present early in his *oeuvre*. Thus, in the *Treatise on the Emendation of the Intellect*, we find him saying that

[t]he essences of singular, changeable things are not to be drawn from their series, or order of existing, since it offers us nothing but extrinsic denominations, relations, or at most, circumstances, all of which are far from the inmost essence of things. That essence is to be sought only from the fixed and eternal things, and at the same time from the laws inscribed in these things, as in their true codes, according to which all singular things come to be, and are ordered. Indeed these singular changeable things depend so intimately, and (so to speak) essentially, on the fixed things that they can neither be nor be conceived without them. (G II.36–37/C I.41)

Ultimately, both of the superior varieties of knowledge – knowledge of the second and third kinds – involve a knowledge of God or Nature itself. To know a thing adequately is to relate it conceptually to its highest causes, that is, to substance and to the specific attribute of which the particular thing is an expression. "All things are in God and are conceived through God." Thus, the adequate idea of anything must include an idea of one of God's attributes. If it is an adequate idea of a body, it includes the concept of Extension; if it is an adequate idea of a mind or idea, it includes the concept of Thought.

IIP45: Each idea of each body, or of each singular thing which actually exists, necessarily involves an eternal and infinite essence of God.

DEM.: The idea of a singular thing which actually exists necessarily involves both the essence of the thing and its existence (by IIP8c). But singular things (by IP15) cannot be conceived without God – on the contrary, because (by IIP6) they have God for a cause insofar as he is considered under the attribute of which the things are modes, their ideas must involve the concept of their attribute (by IA4), i.e. (by ID6), must involve an eternal and infinite essence of God.

There is a particularly fine expression of this conception of the role that knowledge of God plays in the understanding of things in the *Theological-Political Treatise*:

Since all our knowledge, and the certainty that banishes every possible doubt, depend solely on the knowledge of God – because, firstly, without

God nothing can be or be conceived, and secondly, everything can be called into doubt as long as we have no clear and distinct idea of God – it follows that our supreme good and perfection depends solely on the knowledge of God. Again, since nothing can be or be conceived without God, it is clear that everything in Nature involves and expresses the conception of God in proportion to its essence and perfection; and therefore we acquire a greater and more perfect knowledge of God as we gain more knowledge of natural phenomena. To put it another way, since the knowledge of an effect through its cause is nothing other than the knowledge of a property of that cause, the greater our knowledge of natural phenomena, the more perfect is our knowledge of God's essence, which is the cause of all things. (G III.59–60/S 51)

This leads Spinoza to make a pair of extraordinary claims, ones that must have left his critics gasping for air: "The knowledge of God's eternal and infinite essence which each idea involves is adequate and perfect" (IIP46) and "The human mind has an adequate knowledge of God's eternal and infinite essence" (IIP47). Spinoza is not saying, of course, that we have a complete and adequate knowledge of God, period. Because God has infinite attributes, an infinite number of which are necessarily unknown to our finite minds, he could not possibly mean this. Rather, he is saying that the knowledge that we do have by way of adequate ideas of bodies and of minds provides us with an adequate knowledge of the two infinite attributes that these finite modes express, viz., Thought and Extension. Indeed, he suggests that such an adequate knowledge of God's essence, like our adequate knowledge of common notions, is latent in *all* of our ideas, adequate and inadequate, and thus concludes that "God's infinite essence and his eternity are known to all" (IIP47s). Most people are not aware of this for the obvious reason that so much of our attention is devoted to the senses and the imagination. Making this knowledge explicit, in such a way that we achieve at least the second kind of knowledge and, ideally, the third kind of knowledge (IIP47s), is of the utmost importance for our well-being and happiness.

FREEDOM AND THE WILL

In the final two propositions of Part Two – IIP48 and IIP49, with its long scholium – Spinoza turns to the freedom of the human will, an issue for which he has already been preparing the ground, both with his discussion of divine freedom and with his account of the nature of the human mind. Spinoza finds it remarkable that the mind is so often regarded as a "dominion" unto itself. No one thinks that the body, subject as it is to the deterministic laws of nature, has any freedom in regard to what happens to it. And yet it is commonly supposed – by those who are unaware that the mind and the body are one and the same thing expressed under different attributes – that the mind is not subject to such laws in all that it does and has an absolute freedom, at least with regard to its volitions. "Men think themselves free" in their choices, affirmations, and other voluntary acts, and they do so according to what philosophers call a "libertarian" conception of freedom. On this view, a person's will is free when it is undetermined, such that having made a choice, all things being the same he could have made a different choice. At the ice-cream store, I order a vanilla sundae, but my choice, although made on the background of my beliefs (e.g., that vanilla is the best flavor) and my desires (e.g., for a satisfying ice-cream experience), is not so strictly determined by those background conditions that it could not have been otherwise; I could also have chosen chocolate.

This conception of our freedom is, Spinoza insists, false and grounded in the privation of knowledge that characterizes inadequate ideas.

Men are deceived in that they think themselves free [NS: i.e., they think that, of their own free will, they can either do a thing or forbear doing it], an opinion which consists only in this, that they are conscious of their actions and ignorant of the causes by which they are determined. This, then, is their idea of freedom – that they do not known any cause of their actions. (IIP35s)

Spinoza insists in the *Short Treatise* that "true freedom" does not consist in "being able to do or omit something," as if with a perfect spontaneity (KV I.4, G I.37–8/C I.82–3). In his deterministic universe, there are no spontaneous events, certainly not among extended bodies, but neither among things within the realm of Thought. This is necessarily the case, since the events within Thought must follow the same order and connection as the events within Extension. As we have seen, not even God's freedom consists in some capacity to will or not to will, in being able "both to do and not do something." Our acts of volition, like anything else in nature, are determined both by other finite modes (in fact, by an infinite number of them) and by the principles of nature.

IIP48: In the mind there is no absolute, or free, will, but the mind is determined to will this or that by a cause which is also determined by another, and this again by another, and so to infinity.

DEM.: The mind is a certain and determinate mode of thinking (by IIP11)., and so (by IP17c2) cannot be a free cause of its own actions, or cannot have an absolute faculty of willing and not willing. Rather, it must be determined to willing this or that (by IP28) by a cause which is also determined by another, and this cause again by another, etc.

In a letter intended for Tschirnhaus, Spinoza says that "that human freedom which all men boast of possessing . . . consists solely in this, that men are conscious of their desire and unaware of the causes by which they are determined." Freedom conceived as an absence of determination is "imaginary," not unlike when "a baby thinks that it freely desires milk . . . [or] a drunken man believes that it is from his free decision that he says what he later, when sober, would wish to be left unsaid" (Letter 58).

Spinoza begins his demolition of this false conception of human freedom by undermining the notion of volition on which it depends. He explicitly rejects Descartes's picture of the will and its relationship to the understanding. In the Fourth Meditation, Descartes distinguishes the will from the understanding as different and independent faculties of the mind. Volitions and ideas, though both mental modes, are separate from each other. In particular, ideas can be present to the mind without any volitional component; and while volitions are always directed at ideas, they are not internal to them. What happens in human judgment and choice is that the understanding presents ideas to the will for its consideration. The will can then assent to an idea, deny it, or suspend judgment. (Ideally, it will assent only to clear and distinct ideas; this is the way to avoid error.)

Spinoza denies that there is any such thing as a faculty (*facultas*) that can be called 'the will', any more than there is some faculty that can be called 'the understanding' (IIP48s). Such a faculty distinct from any actual idea or particular act of the mind is a pure abstraction, a "complete fiction." What there are in the mind are individual ideas. But ideas, as we have seen, always include an active element, either an affirmation or a negation. This active element that every idea involves, and not some bare faculty, is the locus of willing for Spinoza. "Volitions themselves," Spinoza insists, are not "anything beyond the very ideas of things" (IIP48s). He insists that "in the mind there is no volition, or affirmation and negation, except that which the idea involves insofar as it is an idea" (IIP49). Simply to have an idea of $x$ is to have a volitional attitude toward $x$ or some aspect of $x$, to make some kind of affirmation or negation about $x$. But if volitions are nothing beyond ideas, then they are subject to the same causal determinism to which ideas, as finite modes of substance, are subject (which is the same causal determinism, albeit through different laws, to which the objects of these ideas – bodies – are subject). In other words, there is no freedom of the will or freedom of choice. "Those . . . who believe that they either speak or are silent, or do anything from a free decision of the mind, dream with open eyes" (IIIP2s, G II.144/C I.497).

Spinoza does not deny that human beings can achieve freedom of a sort. In fact, the latter parts of the *Ethics* are devoted in large measure to showing what human freedom does consist in and how it can be attained. But Spinoza will have to show how freedom, in whatever way he conceives it, is compatible with determinism. He is clearly conscious of the challenge this poses. As he says in a letter to Hugo Boxel, "that 'necessary' and 'free' are contraries seems . . . absurd and opposed to reason"; rather, the relevant distinction is between "constraint or force, and necessity" (Letter 56, G IV.259/SL 276). Something is constrained or forced if its causal determinants lie outside it. To Tschirnhaus, he notes that

a stone receives from the impulsion of an external cause a fixed quantity of motion whereby it will necessarily continue to move when the impulsion of the external cause has ceased. The stone's continuance in motion is constrained, not because it is necessary, but because it must be defined by the impulsion received from the external cause. (Letter 58, G IV.266/SL 284)

Now, he reminds Tschirnhaus, echoing the claim of IP28, every finite mode is "necessarily determined by an external cause to exist and to act in a fixed and determinate way." Like the motion of the stone, all ideas in the human mind, as well as the idea that is the human mind itself, are determined by other ideas, other modes of Thought. Thus, strictly speaking, only God is going to be free in the sense of completely unconstrained. Human beings can never totally remove themselves from external causes. But even within this deterministic world there is a kind of freedom available to them. It will not consist in any freedom of will or of thought within the human mind. Rather, it is more appropriate to speak of the human being who is free. And what this freedom consists in is not an absence of determinism but activity. In so far as a person increases the extent to which what he does derives from within, from the knowledge that he possesses, he is active and free.

Before introducing the "free person" and the happiness he enjoys, however, Spinoza must first show us the life of "bondage." This is the way we ordinarily live, subject to a wide range of passionate responses to the world, with our desires moved in often contradictory ways and our happiness consequently at the mercy of the way things affect us. Only when confronted with such an image of ourselves, it seems, can we truly appreciate the difficult but extraordinary benefits of the life of reason and virtue.

# CHAPTER 7

# The Passions

In Part Three of the *Ethics*, Spinoza turns to human psychology. Having investigated the nature of the mind and of its contents and established what constitutes true and adequate knowledge, he now offers an analysis of the dynamics of the ways in which the mind moves, by association and by affect, among its various states. His focus is especially on our passionate responses to the world, that is, our emotions. The discussion as it proceeds in Part Three seems perfectly descriptive, although it will certainly have implications for the way we should lead our lives (to be brought out in Parts Four and Five). Moreover, while the propositions of this part, no less than the previous elements of the work, are presented in deductive terms (and not merely as the empirical result of introspection), much of what Spinoza says about the passions seems to capture some obvious and intuitive truths about the way we think and feel about things and regard other people. Unlike the alien territory of his metaphysics, the psychological analysis of Part Three, despite its rigorous Spinozistic terminology, seems remarkably (and uncomfortably) familiar.[1]

## PSYCHOLOGIA GEOMETRICA

Spinoza opens Part Three with an indictment of the way in which philosophers – perhaps merely making explicit the naive view of ordinary people – have generally treated the mind and its relationship to the rest of the world.

---

[1] For studies of Part Three, see Della Rocca 1996a and Yovel 1999. Damasio (2003) offers an approach to Spinoza's views on emotions and feelings in the context of recent neuroscientific work on them.

Most of those who have written about the affects, and men's way of living, seem to treat, not of natural things, which follow the common laws of nature, but of things which are outside nature. Indeed, they seem to conceive man in nature as a dominion within a dominion. For they believe that man disturbs, rather than follows, the order of nature, that he has absolute power over his actions, and that he is determined only by himself.

(III, Preface, G II.137/C I.491)

What Spinoza means by regarding the mind as a "dominion within a dominion" is treating it as an autonomous entity, one that is not governed by the same principles that legislate the behavior of other things. The mind, on this mistaken view, is not "natural" in the sense that it is not subject to the deterministic and law-like necessity to which all natural things are subject. Rather, it is supernatural – implanted (by God) in a body and surrounded by nature but endowed with the kind of freedom of will that leaves it undetermined in many of its operations.

Spinoza's main target here is Descartes, whom he cites as someone who "believed that the mind has absolute power over its own actions ... [and sought] to show the way by which the mind can have absolute dominion over its affects" (III, Preface, II.137–8/C I.491–2). To be sure, Descartes did attempt to explain both the way in which the will works in granting or withholding its assent as it considers ideas presented to it by the understanding, and provided an account of the passions that shows their causal connections to states of the body.[2] But Descartes also believed both that the will, standing outside the laws of nature (which, strictly understood, govern only bodies), is not causally determined in its volitions (although its assent is strongly influenced by clear and distinct ideas), and that the mind can achieve a total control over the emotions.[3]

As Spinoza has shown in Parts One and Two, the human mind, no less than anything else, is most certainly a part of Nature. Thus, we, too, in every dimension of our lives, are subject to the law-like determinism through which everything in Nature comes about. The thoughts we have and the things we feel are all, as much as the motions

---

[2] See the Fourth Meditation and *The Passions of the Soul*, respectively.
[3] See especially *The Passions of the Soul*, I.50. For a discussion of Descartes's conception of freedom of the will, see Chappell 1994.

of our bodies and the bodies around us, natural events that have their causes. Each of our states of mind – ideas, desires, passions, judgments, feelings, even willings – is a finite mode that, like all finite modes, "has a determinate existence [and] can neither exist nor be determined to produce an effect unless it is determined to exist and produce an effect by another cause" (IP28). Indeed, the laws that govern our states of mind are the same thing – the same power of Nature – as the laws that govern the motions of bodies, albeit conceived through the attribute of Thought rather than the attribute of Extension.

Nature is always the same, and its virtue and power of acting are every-where one and the same, i.e., the laws and rules of nature, according to which all things happen, and change from one form to another, are always and everywhere the same. So the way of understanding the nature of anything, of whatever kind, must also be the same, viz. through the universal laws and rules of nature. (III, Preface, G II.138/C I.492)

There are no exceptions to the laws of nature, neither in the realm of bodies nor in the realm of the mind.

Therefore, Spinoza proposes to treat human psychology in the same way in which the Cartesian scientist treats the physics of bodies. This is, indeed, demanded by the fact that any state of the mind is identical to the state of the body of which it is the expression.

All these things, indeed, show clearly that both the decision of the mind and the appetite and the determination of the body by nature exist together – or rather are one and the same thing, which we call a decision when it is considered under, or explained through, the attribute of Thought, and which we call a determination when it is considered under the attribute of Extension and deduced from the laws of motion and rest.
(IIIP2s, G II.144/C I. 497)

The result is a deterministic psychology – a psychology *more geome-trico* – in which states of the mind and the affective and associative transitions between them, all of which are reflections of the ways in which the body is affected by external things, are treated in precisely the same mathematically rigorous way in which the physicist calcu-lates transfers of motion between bodies and in which the geometer considers the properties of plane figures.

The affects, therefore, of hate, anger, envy, etc., considered in themselves, follow from the same necessity and force of nature as the other singular things. And therefore they acknowledge certain causes, through which they are understood, and have certain properties, as worthy of our knowledge as the properties of anything, by the mere contemplation of which we are pleased.[4]

Therefore, Spinoza concludes, in one of the more stunning statements of the *Ethics*, "I shall treat of the nature and power of the affects, and the power of the mind over them, by the same method by which, in the preceding parts, I treated God and the mind, and I shall consider human actions and appetites just as if it were a question of lines, planes and bodies" (III, Preface, G II.138/C I.492).

### ACTION AND PASSION

The most basic distinction within Spinoza's philosophical psychology is that between an action and a passion of the mind. It is not quite equivalent to the simple distinction between mental cause and mental effect, since even actions are caused and passions are causes. An active mind is no less a causally determined mind; this, I believe, is the point of the long scholium to IIIP2. Of course, action is connected to doing, while passions (like passivity itself) are related to suffering or undergoing. But the important difference between an action of the mind and a passion of the mind concerns the locus of the causal source of the mind's state. If the adequate or total cause of the state lies wholly within the mind itself – that is, if the nature and occurrence of the state can be adequately understood through the mind alone (IIID1), without reference to anything else – then it is a case of the mind being active. If, on the other hand, the mind is only a partial cause of the state, with the other causal contribution coming from outside the mind, then the state is a passion.

IIID2: I say that we act when something happens in us or outside us, of which we are the adequate cause, i.e., (by IIID1) when something in us or outside us follows from our nature, which can be clearly and distinctly understood through it alone. On the other hand, I say that we are acted on when something happens in us, or something follows from our nature, of which we are only a partial cause.

The mind is active when it is following its own nature and laws, when its condition follows from its own cognitive resources. And a

---

[4] See also TTP IV: "The fact that a man, in remembering one thing, forthwith calls to mind another like it, or which he has seen along with it, is a law that necessarily follows from the nature of man" (G III.58/S 48).

state of the mind follows from the mind's own cognitive resources when it follows from its adequate ideas. On the other hand, when a state of the mind follows not from adequate ideas in the mind but from an inadequate idea of the human body along with the inadequate idea of some external thing that is presently causing some effect in the human body, that mental state does not follow from the mind's own resources and is consequently a passion.

IIIP1: Our mind does certain things [acts] and undergoes other things, viz. insofar as it has adequate ideas, it necessarily does certain things, and insofar as it has inadequate ideas, it necessarily undergoes other things.

IIIP3: The actions of the mind arise from adequate ideas alone; the passions depend on inadequate ideas alone.

Passions come about not through the logical order of thought, but from the common order of nature. When the mind's condition is a reflection of the way in which the body is being affected by something else, then the mental state follows not only from the idea of the human body (i.e., the mind), but also from the idea of that external body bringing about the affection in the human body. Such a state is a passion of the mind. For example, my mind is active when my admiration of what a snowflake is follows from my adequate knowledge of the properties of water vapor, atmospheric conditions, and the principles of crystallization. My mind is passive, by contrast, when my admiration of what a snowflake is derives only from my sensory experience, from the way in which my body happens to be affected by seeing or feeling a snowflake. Increasing one's activity, then – which, as we will see, is closely related to increasing one's freedom and autonomy – will be a function of increasing one's store of adequate ideas. "The mind is more liable to passions the more it has inadequate ideas, and conversely, is more active the more it has adequate ideas" (IIIP1c).

## 'CONATUS'

The activity and passivity of the mind with which Spinoza is concerned in Part Three centers on changes in what he calls, alternately, "the power of acting [*potentia agendi*]" or "force of existing [*vis existendi*]." Every finite mode is, as we have seen, a partial and limited expression of one and the same infinite power of God/ Nature/substance, manifesting itself in the case of minds through the attribute of Thought and in the case of bodies through the attribute of Extension. Every particular mind, then, is a finite expression of God or Nature's infinite power through thinking; likewise, every particular body is a finite expression of God or Nature's infinite power in matter and motion. This finite quantum of power that constitutes each thing is what Spinoza calls *conatus*, a Latin word that can be variously translated as striving, tendency, or endeavor.

In any particular finite thing, this determination of power manifests itself as a striving to persevere as that thing.

IIIP6: Each thing, as far as it can by its own power, strives to persevere in its being.

DEM.: For singular things are modes by which God's attributes are expressed in a certain and determinate way (by IP25c), i.e. (by IP34), things that express, in a certain and determinate way, God's power, by which God is and acts. And no thing has anything in itself by which it can be destroyed, or which takes its existence away (by IIIP4). On the contrary, it is opposed to everything which can take its existence away (by IIIP5). Therefore, as far as it can, and it lies in itself, it strives to persevere in its being.

There is in all things – bodies and minds – a kind of existential inertia by which they resist any attempts to destroy them or change them for the worse. It is not a temporary or accidental feature of the thing, something that the thing can be without, but involves "an indefinite duration" and goes right to the heart of the thing's individuation (IIIP8). It provides a real metaphysical basis for distinguishing one thing from another, in so far as these parcels of power are distinct from each other (IIIP57d) and often strive against each other. Indeed, Spinoza insists, this *conatus* constitutes "the actual essence" of anything (IIIP7).[5] It is, he suggests, nothing

---

[5] Within the "physical digression" of Part Two, Spinoza had argued that the essence of any particular body consisted in a specific ratio of the communication of motion and rest among its parts (G II.99–100/C I.460). Now he says that it consists in a "striving to persevere." The inconsistency here may be only apparent, since one can say that the essence of any body consists in its striving to maintain that ratio of motion and rest.

different from the thing itself.[6] It also explains a good many of the dynamic features of the world. It accounts for why stones are hard to break, why a body at rest or in motion will remain at rest or in motion unless it encounters an outside force, why the human body fights disease, and why we desire many of the things we do.[7] The doctrine is much like what the ancient Stoics proclaimed, at least as this is reported by Cicero:

> Immediately upon birth . . . a living creature feels an attachment for itself, and an impulse to preserve itself and to feel affection for its own constitution and for those things which tend to preserve that constitution; while on the other hand it conceives an antipathy to destruction and to those things which appear to threaten destruction.[8]

Spinoza's argumentation for this important proposition about self-preservation has drawn some fire from commentators.[9] Spinoza begins by establishing that no thing considered by itself, on its own essential terms and without relation to anything else, can possibly contain within itself anything contrary to its being. This is because the definition or concept of any thing "affirms, and does not deny, the thing's essence." The essence of the thing only posits the thing's nature; it certainly can do nothing toward denying that nature. Thus, "while we attend only to the thing itself, and not to external causes, we shall not be able to find anything in it which can destroy it" (IIIP4d). Spinoza offers some elaboration in IIIP5, when he explains that there cannot be in any thing two elements that derive from the thing's nature and that are contrary to each other and therefore tend toward each other's destruction. This would be to admit into the essence of the thing an inconsistency, which would render the essence itself contradictory and the thing an impossible non-thing. No thing, then, can from its own resources be the source

---

[6] See CM, G I.248/C I.314.

[7] The doctrine also amounts to a rejection by Spinoza of a central element of Cartesian physics: that a body is nothing but extension and therefore completely passive, without any dynamic powers. For Spinoza, bodies, through their *conatus*, appear to have an innate principle of activity.

[8] *De finibus* III.5.

[9] Its most vociferous critic is probably Bennett, who accuses Spinoza of numerous fallacies; see Bennett 1984, pp. 231–46. For a response to Bennett's accusations, see D. Garrett 2002.

of its own destruction. All decay and destructive impulse must come from outside the thing itself.

Now one might think that, intuitively and empirically, this just seems false. Any living creature, even left to its own devices, will, as we all know so well, eventually age and break down, apparently from within. Spinoza could reply that this decay of the ageing process is really the effect of external forces, like gravity, working on the body over a long period of time. But then there is the phenomenon of suicide. Voluntarily taking one's own life would seem to be a prime counterexample to the claim of IIIP6. Spinoza, however, sticks to his guns and denies that suicide is a case of an individual "acting" in the robust sense, according to which what happens finds its total and adequate cause within the individual himself. Rather, suicide is the effect of external causes that compel a person to do something that, through adequate ideas alone, he would never do. In other words, one kills oneself as a result of the force of circumstances that are overwhelming and over which knowledge cannot prevail.

No one . . . unless he is defeated by causes external, and contrary to his nature, neglects to seek his own advantage, or to preserve his being. No one, I say, avoids food or kills himself from the necessity of his own nature. Those who do such things are compelled by external causes . . . That a man should, from the necessity of his own nature, strive not to exist, or to be changed into another form, is as impossible as that something should come from nothing. (IVP20s)

But even putting aside the empirical issues of ageing and suicide, there is a logical question that has troubled scholars. IIIP4 and IIIP5 are basically negative propositions that would seem to imply only that no thing can, from its own essential resources, be the source of its own destruction or non-existence. But how does it follow from these propositions that every thing thereby has an innate and apparently active striving to exist, which would seem to be a stronger and more positive claim?

One way to make sense of this is to see IIIP5 as implying that an individual would actively resist any external force which tries to introduce an element that is contrary to one of the essential and intrinsic features of the thing, that is, an element that would tend toward the thing's destruction. But all this would seem to entitle Spinoza to is a claim about the existential-inertial character of things – that they resist any efforts to terminate or even modify their being. But again, commentators ask, how does it follow from this that there is a teleological-like striving for self-preservation? As one critic has put it, it is one thing to say that if *a* does not aid the preservation of *s*, then *s* will not do *a* (or, equivalently, if *s* does *a*, then *a* is what will preserve *s*), but an entirely different thing to say that if *a* is something that will preserve *s*, then *s* will do *a*.[10]

Now part of the issue here is simply the validity of Spinoza's argument, that is, whether he is entitled to make any claims about active strivings simply on the basis of IIIP4 and IIIP5 as premises. But the larger, more interesting question is whether or not Spinoza, contrary to what would seem to be the lesson of the *Ethics* so far, is surreptitiously and (it has been argued) illegitimately introducing teleology into nature. To speak about individuals striving to do things because they are conducive to their self-preservation seems to introduce goal-oriented behavior. It could be argued that there is no problem here, however. That is, there is no reason to think that Spinoza intended to eliminate teleology in all natural things, and especially from the domain of human action; rather, his concern seems mainly to be with thinking of Nature (God) itself as acting teleologically. Human beings, unlike inanimate things and most animals, and certainly unlike Nature as a whole, set themselves goals and try to achieve them (without implying, of course, that any of this escapes the causal determinism that governs all things). Spinoza explicitly says as much: "Men act always on account of an end, namely, on account of their advantage, which they want" (I, Appendix, G II.78/C I.440).

The trouble with this approach, though, is that Spinoza may not be entitled to such a difference between how human beings behave and how inanimate things and animals behave. Given the universal parallelism, how can Spinoza justify attributing purposive action to human minds but not to other minds? This is similar to the challenge that he must face in according to human minds (but

---

[10] Again, the critic here is Bennett (1984, pp. 240–51). A partial defense of Spinoza appears in Manning 2002.

presumably no other minds) conscious awareness. On occasion, attributing purposiveness to non-human things appears to be something he wants to avoid, at least to judge from what he says in the appendix to Part One: "All the prejudices that I here undertake to expose depend on this one: that men commonly suppose that all natural things act, as men do, on account of an end" (G II.78/C I.439). On the other hand, he may indeed be perfectly willing to attribute to *all* things, human and otherwise, goal-oriented action, as long as this is properly understood in Spinozistic terms – i.e., without implying either freedom of choice or conscious endeavor[11] – and as long as it does not mean that God or Nature itself acts for the sake of ends.[12] Thus, *all* individuals have a basic kind of teleological behavior, in so far as they strive to do what best preserves their being. This need not involve beliefs and intentions, but only an individual's naturally tending to do certain things under its own power and left to its own resources. When conscious awareness is added to the mix, as it is in the case of human beings, then this basic teleological setup becomes something different: intentional behavior that involves setting goals for oneself and then striving to achieve them.

In Part Three, Spinoza confines himself mainly to the manifestations of *conatus* or striving in human beings. And within the human being, his focus is on mental phenomena, although each mental expression will (because of the parallelism) necessarily have its bodily correlate. In the mind, an individual's *conatus* manifests itself as will – not an abstract faculty of willing, as we have seen, but the particular affirmations or negations that make up much of our thinking life. When the human being is considered as a composite entity constituted by a mind and a body, its *conatus* consists in appetite. When a person is conscious of the striving of his mind and body together, when he is aware of an appetite, it becomes desire. In both cases, the mind and the mind-body composite, *conatus* is the motivational force that lies at the root of all a person's endeavors.

---

[11] Spinoza does say, however, that the human mind is necessarily "conscious of this striving it has" (IIIP9), and one thus wonders (as in the case of consciousness itself) what the source of this distinctive feature of human mentality is.

[12] See Curley 1990 and D. Garrett 1999 for a discussion of these issues.

When this striving is related only to the mind, it is called will; but when it is related to the mind and body together, it is called appetite. This appetite, therefore, is nothing but the very essence of man, from whose nature there necessarily follow those things that promote his preservation. And so man is determined to do those things. Between appetite and desire there is no difference, except that desire is generally related to men insofar as they are conscious of their appetites. So desire can be defined as appetite together with consciousness of the appetite. (IIIP9s)

In the human body, *conatus* presumably manifests itself as the body's physical resistance to any attempt to change the ratio of motion and rest among its parts to the point of dissolution. In the mind, it is the conscious striving after those things that (as far as it can tell) promote its well-being and the well-being of the body on which its existence depends.

### AFFECTS

The power or striving that constitutes the essence of any individual, while always "on" and steady, does not remain unmodified throughout a person's lifetime, but is constantly subject to change. In particular, the power can enjoy an increase or strengthening or it can suffer a decrease or diminution. (A complete extermination or even radical transformation of the power is, of course, death.) Any such change in an individual's power of acting, for better or for worse, is what Spinoza calls an 'affect.'

IIID3: By affect I understand affections of the body by which the body's power of acting is increased or diminished, aided or restrained, and at the same time the ideas of these affections [in the mind].

It is important to note – and Spinoza himself stresses this – that an affect (for example, an emotion) is not the *cause* of the change; rather, it is the transition itself from one condition to another. One experiences or undergoes an affect. It is, he says, "a passage [*transitio*]" (G II.191/C I.541). An affect is either the move from a better condition to a worse condition or the improvement to a better condition; it is not the end result of the move. In the case of the mind, it can move to a greater or lesser power of thinking. Given the materialistic tenor of Spinoza's metaphysics of the mind, we know that what this means is that the mind, as the idea of the body, thereby expresses the body's transition to a greater or lesser power of acting. "The idea of any thing that increases or diminishes, aids or restrains, our body's power of acting, increases or diminishes, aides or restrains, our mind's power of thinking" (IIIP11). Or, as he puts it more directly at the end of Part Three, "when I said above that the mind's power of thinking is increased or diminished, I meant nothing but that the mind has formed of its body (or of some part of it) an idea which expresses more or less reality than it had affirmed of the body" (G II.204/C I.543).

What does it mean to speak of the mind or the body experiencing an "increase [or decrease] in its power of acting"? Spinoza is referring simply to an improvement or deterioration in its condition, including the strength of its *conatus* or ability to preserve itself and resist outside forces. In the case of the body, this could be a weakening of its powers brought on by injury, sickness, ageing, or any of the myriad minor ways in which the body becomes less capable of doing things. Or it could be an improvement that comes about through training or nutrition, activities that make the body stronger, more flexible, more resistant to external powers seeking to weaken it – in general, more able to be "affected in a great many ways or . . . capable of affecting external bodies in a great many ways" (IVP38). Because the mind's capacities reflect those of the body, it too will experience correlative improvements or diminutions in its functioning as a thinking thing. These will include changes in its cognitive capacities, its activity or passivity, and its striving to pursue the knowledge that represents its highest good. "The human body is composed of a great many parts of different natures, which require continuous and varied food so that the whole body may be equally capable of doing everything which can follow from its nature, and consequently, so that the mind may also be equally capable of conceiving many things" (IV, Appendix, G II.274/C I.592–3).

Increases or decreases in an individual's powers can come about either through the action of external things or from within. A passive affect, or passion, is a change in the individual's power whose adequate cause lies not in the individual itself but partly in external things. Passions are modifications in power that an individual undergoes or suffers. An active affect, on the other hand, is a change in the individual's power whose adequate cause lies wholly in the individual itself (IIID3). If I am improved or harmed by my interaction with other people or objects, then the transition I suffer is a passion. If the improvement in my condition comes about wholly through my own resources and because of my knowledge of what is good for me, then the transition I experience is an action.

While passions or externally caused changes can be for the better or for the worse, actions are always improvements in an individual's power. This is because, as we know from the *conatus* doctrine itself, no individual will, through its own capacities, do anything except what it believes will preserve its being and increase its power. And when a rational being is truly active insofar as he is moved by adequate knowledge, the things he does are guided by a true understanding of what is in his own interest and thus bring about an improvement in his condition.

The following chart offers a general schema of the classification of the affects:

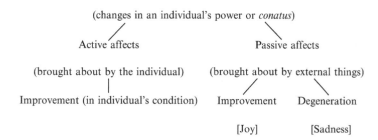

AFFECTS

(changes in an individual's power or *conatus*)

Active affects                                   Passive affects

(brought about by the individual)     (brought about by external things)

Improvement (in individual's condition)     Improvement     Degeneration

[Joy]          [Sadness]

### THE PASSIONS

Most of Spinoza's attention in Part Three is devoted to the passions and the ways in which a human being's condition – primarily mental but also, correlatively, physical – is affected by his causal interactions with the physical and social world he inhabits. The passions include all of our emotional, temperamental, and volitional responses to things. Our joys, loves, sympathies, feelings of hate, desires, inclinations, repulsions, and vacillations of the mind are all a function of the ways in which our power is improved or diminished by objects and people, as well as of the ways in which the mind associates ideas and moves from one thought to another.

Spinoza believes that there are three primary affects, and that all of the other affects are functions of or can be derived from the primary ones. The primary affects are joy, sadness, and desire. Joy (*laetitia*) is "that passion by which the mind passes to a greater perfection" (IIIP11s), or the passage to a greater power of acting caused by something outside the individual. It is the feeling of having one's condition improved by another thing. The corresponding affect in the mind/body composite is pleasure [*titillatio*]. Sadness (*tristitia*), on the other hand, is "that passion by which [the mind] passes to a lesser perfection." It is the feeling of having one's condition caused to deteriorate. The corresponding mind/body affect is, as one might expect, pain [*dolores*].

In the broader context of Spinoza's parallelism, according to which both joy and sadness (as well as pleasure and pain) represent the mental correlates of externally caused affects of the human body, much of this makes sense, especially when it is translated from Spinoza's technical language into the terms of everyday experience. When the body is injured – that is, when its power of acting is diminished by something other than the body (e.g., a knife) – the corresponding psychological and psycho-somatic events are, respectively, sadness and pain, which are an equal diminishing of the powers of the mind and the mind/body composite; the mind cannot do much when it is feeling pain. And when the body is improved, when something comes along that makes it better, then the corresponding event in the mind is joy and in the whole human being it is pleasure. Remember, though, that for Spinoza the bodily injury does not *cause* the pain experienced in the mind; rather, one and the same event that manifests itself in Extension as the body's decrease in power (injury) also manifests itself in Thought as the mind's decrease in power (sorrow and pain).

It is odd for Spinoza to speak of desire as a species of affect. This is because desire, at least as it is initially defined (IIIP9s), really just is the power or striving itself whose transitions constitute the affects. Perhaps what he means is that just as all the passive affects are (as he will show) species of either joy or sadness, so all affects generally are species of desire in so far as they are all increases or decreases in the power of acting. Thus, it seems that the primary affects, strictly speaking, are joy and sadness, each of which represents an externally caused increase or decrease, respectively, of the strength of desire. He says as much in the demonstration of IIIP57:

Joy and sadness are passions by which each one's power, or striving to persevere in his being, is increased or diminished, aided or restrained (by IIIP11 and IIIP11s). But by the striving to persevere in one's being, insofar as it is related to the mind and body together, we understand appetite and desire (see IIIP9s). So joy and sadness are the desire or appetite itself insofar as it is increased or diminished, aided or restrained by external causes.

All of the other passions either have joy or sadness at their core or are variations on joy or sadness. Love, for example, is nothing but joy accompanied by a conception of the object that is the cause of the joy. One loves the object that brings about an improvement in one's condition or the person who benefits one. Hate, similarly, is sadness accompanied by a conception of the object that is the cause of sadness. One hates the object that brings about a deterioration in one's condition or the person who causes one harm (IIIP13s). These passions bring about a corresponding modification of the individual's striving. Desire becomes focused on possessing (and, in some cases, possessing uniquely) the object or person that is loved or destroying the object or person that is hated.

From this point, Spinoza enters into a catalogue of the human passions, showing how each of them is related to the most basic passions and how it affects our behavior. There is no need here to enter into all the details of Spinoza's account. But a representative sampling drawn from some of the more important passive affects and the phenomena they generate will suffice to convey a good picture of what a life mired in the passions is like.

Thus, IIIP16 describes the sympathetic reaction we have to an object that resembles in even a non-essential way something that ordinarily brings about either an increase or a decrease in one's power (and that is the primary object of love or hate):

From the mere fact that we imagine a thing to have some likeness to an object that usually affects the mind with joy or sadness, we love it or hate it, even though that in which the thing is like the object is not the efficient cause of these effects.

On the other hand, if the object we are thinking about is one that usually brings about a decrease in our power, but nonetheless resembles an object that usually brings an equally great increase in our power, then we will, at the same time, both hate it and love it. Spinoza refers to this as "vacillation of the mind" (IIIP17s). Meanwhile, a person who thinks that an object that usually brings about an increase in his powers and thus that he loves has been destroyed, then this thought represents a decrease in his power of acting and he will feel sadness (IIIP19), but someone who believes that an object that he hates has been destroyed will feel joy (IIIP20). This is because, as a result of our basic *conatus* or striving to persevere, we tend to think about things that either improve our body's powers (that is, things that we love) or that destroy other things that harm the body (i.e., things that we hate). Thus, "the image of a thing that excludes the existence of what the mind hates aids this striving of the mind, i.e. (by IIIP11s), affects the mind with joy" (IIIP20).

Perhaps the most important of the secondary passions are hope and fear. Spinoza defines hope as "nothing but an inconstant joy which has arisen from the image of a future or past thing whose outcome we doubt," while fear is "an inconstant sadness, which has also arisen from the image of a doubtful thing" (IIIP18s2). We hope for a thing whose presence, as yet uncertain, will bring about joy. We fear, however, a thing whose presence, equally uncertain, will bring about sadness. When that the outcome of which was doubtful becomes certain, hope is changed into confidence, while fear is changed into despair. The importance of hope and fear derives from the fact that they are the foundation of the kind of life for which the *Ethics* is supposed to provide the antidote. To live a life according to hope and fear is to be governed by an anxious state of expectation or dread that has deleterious consequences for our well-being. Spinoza is in basic agreement with Seneca that both hope and fear

belong to a mind in suspense, to a mind in a state of anxiety through looking into the future. Both are mainly due to projecting our thoughts far ahead of us instead of adapting ourselves to the present. Thus it is that foresight, the greatest blessing humanity has been given, is transformed into a curse. Wild animals run from dangers they actually see, and once they have escaped them worry no more. We however are tormented alike by what is past and what is to come.[13]

These two emotions play a crucial role in our everyday lives and contribute to maintaining us in a perpetual state of "bondage." Hope and fear make us slaves to things outside us, objects and individuals that we value so highly but whose comings and goings are ultimately beyond our control. They also make possible a secondary, conventional kind of bondage that supplements this original, "natural" slavery. For hope and fear lie at the foundation of organized, sectarian religion. They keep us in a state of obedient expectation for what ecclesiastics, who know how to manipulate these emotions, hold out as the ultimate reward and punishment. We will return to these moral aspects of the passions in Parts Four and Five.

The structure of the passions gets denser when a richer social context is introduced. The passions represent not only an individual's responses to the singular things that affect him, but also features of his social relationships with other human beings. And the more people that are involved in the relationship, the more complex becomes the web of affect. What was originally a two-place relation between a person and a thing or another person now becomes a three-place (or four-place, etc.) relation between two people and a thing or three people. Thus, we come to love someone who affects with joy (i.e., who brings improvement to) a person whom we love, and hate someone who affects the beloved with sadness (IIIP22). This social dimension also opens the door to new passions, such as compassion, jealousy, envy, pride, pity, and self-esteem. Spinoza details how, in a very familiar way, a person's attitude toward a thing can be affected by the way that other people regard the thing.

IIIP31: If we imagine that someone loves, desires or hates something we ourselves love, desire, or hate, we shall therefore love, desire or hate it with greater constancy. But if we imagine that he is averse to what we love, or the opposite [NS: that he loves what we hate], then we shall undergo vacillation of mind.

He also shows how, "from the same property of human nature from which it follows that men are compassionate, it also follows that the

---

[13] Seneca, *Epistulae Morales ad Lucilium*, Letter V.

same men are envious and ambitious". For just as seeing someone else love a thing can make one love that same thing, so likewise "if we imagine that someone enjoys some thing that only one can possess, we shall strive to bring it about that he does not possess it" (IIIP32).

There are, Spinoza says, as many different kinds of passions as there are kinds of objects by which we are affected and ways by which they affect us.

There are as many species of joy, sadness and desire, and consequently of each affect composed of these (like vacillation of mind) or derived from them (like love, hate, hope, fear, etc.) as there are species of objects by which we are affected. (IIIP56)

Our emotional lives are immensely rich and diverse, and there seems to be no end to the variations to which the basic affects are subject. The relevant factors include not only the number of people or objects involved, but also the character of each element. Different people react to different things in different ways; even the same person may react to the same thing in different ways at different times. This does not mean that there is any kind of causal indeterminacy or choice or spontaneity in the passions. This is ruled out by Spinoza's determinism. But it does mean that when there are different causal ingredients involved, the effects will necessarily be different. The most important cause of the differences among the passions between people are the differences between their bodily constitutions, which will, of course, be paralleled by differences in the respective minds, whose modes mirror the affections of the body.

IIIP51: Different men can be affected differently by one and the same object; and one and the same man can be affected differently at different times by one and the same object.

DEM.: The human body (by IIPost. 3) is affected in a great many ways by external bodies. Therefore, two men can be differently affected at the same time, and so (by IIA1″) they can be affected differently by one and the same object.

Next (by the same Post.) The human body can be affected now in this way, now in another. Consequently (by the same axiom) it can be affected differently at different times by one and the same object, q.e.d.

The conclusion is that "what the one [person] loves, the other hates, what the one fears, the other does not, and that one and the same man may now love what before he hated, and now dare what before he was too timid for" (IIIP51s).

## EGOISM

The passions and the changes in power that they represent form the motivational basis for the things that human beings do. Our pursuits and avoidances of things, our choices of action and our judgments about what is good and bad are all moved by joy and sadness, love and hate, and pleasure and pain, by the modifications in our striving to persevere in existence. We pursue the things we do because we love them, and we love them because we are conscious of the way in which they bring about an increase in our capacities. Similarly, we avoid the things we do because we hate them, and we hate them because we are conscious of the way in which they bring about a diminution in our capacities. "We strive to further the occurrence of whatever we imagine will lead to joy, and to avert or destroy what we imagine is contrary to it, or will lead to sadness" (IIIP28).

In Spinoza's view, then, human beings are thoroughly egoistic agents. A person is moved to pursue or avoid this or that solely by the positive or negative effects that a thing has on his condition, on the contributions that it makes to his project of self-preservation. (This is true, as we shall see in the next chapter, even when a person is solicitous of the well-being of others.) The striving for perseverance is paramount. It constitutes "the very essence of man, from whose nature there necessarily follow those things that promote his preservation." Thus, "man is determined to do those things [that promote his preservation]" (IIIP9s). Spinoza's psychological egoism is similar to (and may have been influenced by) that of Thomas Hobbes, the English philosopher whose work Spinoza read in the 1660s while composing the *Ethics* and who claimed in his *Leviathan* that "of the voluntary acts of every man the object is some good to himself."[14]

---

[14] *Leviathan* XIV.8. For a comparison of Spinoza and Hobbes on this question, see Curley 1988, chapter 3. For Hobbes's discussion of the passions generally (which is strikingly similar in important respects to Spinoza's analysis), see *Leviathan* VI.

Spinoza's theory of the passions and their motivational role leads him to reverse what one might ordinarily think is the properly ordered relationship between value judgment and desire in a rational agent. Desire would, naively considered, seem to follow judgment. One desires and pursues those things that in one's opinion are worth pursuing. I want to do an action because I have judged it to be a good thing to do. And yet Spinoza insists, in a claim that he knows might strike the reader as counter-intuitive, that we do not strive for or desire things because we have judged them to be good; rather, we judge them to be good because we desire them, and we desire them because they affect us in the right way. "We neither strive for, nor will, neither want, nor desire anything because we judge it to be good; on the contrary, we judge something to be good because we strive for it, will it, want it, and desire it" (IIIP9s). Similarly, we do not shun something because we judge it to be bad; we judge it to be bad because we are naturally led away from it by desire, a desire grounded in the hatred that is only a reflection of the way in which the thing negatively affects us. Value judgments on this account necessarily become egoistic, since they follow from modifications in a striving for self-preservation. Something is "good" if it benefits *me*, and "bad" if it harms *me*.

Because passion-based value judgments cannot possibly be independent of those desires that derive from the way the body is affected by external things, there must be an individualistic relativism, even subjectivism in such judgments about what is good or bad. Given the differences among us in the ways in which we are affected by things, and thus the consequent differences in our passionate desires, judgments about what is good or bad that derive from the passions will differ from one person to the next.

By good here I understand every kind of joy, and whatever leads to it, and especially what satisfies any kind of longing, whatever that may be. And by evil [I understand here] every kind of sadness, and especially what frustrates longing . . . So each one, from his own affect, judges or evaluates, what is good and what is bad, what is better and what is worse, and finally, what is best and what is worst. (IIIP39s)

As long as our judgments of good and bad are limited to what each person desires on the basis of the passions, on how they are affected by things, there are no absolute standards of good and bad that will hold for all people.

> Because each one judges from his own affect what is good and what is bad, what is better and what is worse, it follows that men can vary as much in judgment as in affect. The result is that when we compare one with another, we distinguish them only by a difference of affects, and call some intrepid, others timid, and others, finally, by another name. (IIIP51s)

As we shall see in the next chapter, it will be a different matter entirely when it comes to value-judgments that are based not on the way we are affected by things in experience but on adequate knowledge.

### ACTIONS

Before leaving Part Three, something, however brief, needs to be said about actions (as opposed to passions). Spinoza himself seems to treat actions almost as an afterthought, in the final two propositions of the part, when he says that "this will be enough concerning the affects that are related to man insofar as he is acted on. It remains to add a few words about those that are related to him insofar as he acts" (IIIP57s). It is clear from Part Four, however, where it receives more considered treatment, that the activity of the mind is the cornerstone of his moral philosophy and the key to human freedom and happiness.

Something *acts* to the extent that its states follow from its innate power or *conatus* alone, its intrinsic striving to persevere in existence, rather than from the way that power is affected by external things.[15] This means that active affects must always be internally generated *increases* in one's power, since it is inconceivable that an individual's striving for preservation could, by itself, give rise to a decrease in itself. "No affects of sadness can be related to the mind insofar as it acts, but only affects of joy and desire" (IIIP59d).

In the mind, striving can be related to confused ideas or to clear and distinct ideas. In the case of the passions, as we have seen, the

---

[15] Rice (1999) argues that for Spinoza even actions involve an essential degree of passivity and being acted on by outside causes.

striving is related to confused or inadequate ideas. Because the passive affects of the body always involve the nature of an external thing in addition to the nature of our own body, the corresponding ideas in the mind are always inadequate ideas.

An affect that is called a passion of the mind is a confused idea, by which the mind affirms of its body, or of some part of it, a greater or lesser force of existing than before, which, when it is given, determines the mind to think of this rather than that . . . An affect or passion of the mind is a confused idea. For we have shown (IIIP3) that the mind is acted on only insofar as it has inadequate or confused ideas. (G II.203–4/C I.542)

In action, on the other hand, desire or appetite is related to adequate ideas. It is rational, not passionate, desire.

Our mind does certain things [acts] and undergoes other things, viz. insofar as it has adequate ideas, it necessarily does certain things, and insofar as it has inadequate ideas, it necessarily undergoes other things. (IIIP1)

In action, the mind's increase in its capacities derives from its own knowledge. That is, the mind is active when its striving for perseverence (desire) is guided not by the random ways in which external objects affect the body, but rather by understanding. The difference is like that between pursuing things because they make you feel good and pursuing things because you know that they are truly good for you. It is not that with the passions my desire is erroneously led, since it is directed at things that do indeed increase the powers of the body. But these goods that benefit the body are not, as we will see in Part Four, the highest goods. For one thing, they are unpredictable and beyond one's control. Moreover, the benefits they bring are short-lived. When desire is led by adequate ideas, on the other hand, the resulting desire and judgment is for what is truly in one's best interest as a rational being.

All of the human emotions, in so far as they are passions, are constantly directed outward, toward things and their tendencies to affect us one way or another. Aroused by our passions and the desires they generate, we seek or flee those things that we believe cause joy or sadness. Our hopes and fears fluctuate depending on whether we regard the objects of our desires or aversions as remote, near, necessary, possible, or unlikely.

What we so often fail to keep in mind, however, is the fact that the things that stir our emotions, being external to us, do not answer to our wills. I have no real power over whether what I hate is near me or distant, whether the person I love lives or dies. The objects of our passions are completely beyond our control. (This is, of course, all the more so in the absolutely deterministic universe that Spinoza describes.) Thus, the more we allow ourselves to be controlled by these objects – by their comings and goings – the more we are subject to fluctuating passions and the less active and free (that is, self-controlled) we are. The upshot is a fairly pathetic picture of a life mired in the passions and pursuing and fleeing the changeable and fleeting objects that occasion them. As Spinoza says in one of the more poetic moments of the work, summing up what he takes himself to have shown in Part Three: "We are driven about in many ways by external causes, and . . . like waves on the sea, driven by contrary winds, we toss about, not knowing our outcome and fate" (IIIP59s).

Everything that Spinoza says in Part Three about the passions is purely descriptive. He is merely showing what happens in the mind as a part of nature. He has made no normative claims about what is truly good or bad or right or wrong. And yet, the ultimate aim of the *Ethics* is to turn us from judging things according to the ways in which they affect us – that is, according to the passions – toward judging them on the basis of adequate knowledge. The passions, even those that represent increases in our powers of acting, are obstacles to true knowledge and, ultimately, well-being. The goal, then, is to be able to achieve some degree of control over the passions and become active, self-governing individuals, rather than individuals who are merely responding to the comings and goings of external things. We certainly cannot eliminate the passions altogether, nor even completely dominate them. We can, however, get to a point where we have "a power . . . to moderate and restrain" them (IIIP56s). In Part Four, Spinoza explains how this condition can be reached and the benefits it brings.

# CHAPTER 8

# Virtue and "the free man"

With Part Four, Spinoza's *Ethics* finally earns the right to its title and enters the domain of moral philosophy, understood in the classic sense as an investigation into human well-being and the good life.[1] Having laid the proper metaphysical, epistemological, and psychological foundations, and having established his essential claims about Nature and the place of the human being within it with geometric necessity, Spinoza can now begin his analysis and assessment of how human beings ordinarily pursue their lives, with a view ultimately toward discovering a remedy for the things that ail them and keep them from approaching human perfection.

The results of this analysis are not pretty, as the title of Part Four – "On Human Bondage, or the Powers of the Affects" – might suggest. For the most part, human beings live lives directed by the passions, not by reason. With our desires led about by pleasure and distracted by pain, we pursue transitory, false goods (such as material possessions, honor, and mundane power) and place our happiness in securing them, all the while ignoring the more permanent and valuable true good that, albeit with some effort, is within everyone's grasp, viz. knowledge and understanding. Spinoza is intimately acquainted with the life whereof he speaks, since he himself was once in its throes. It was only his disillusionment with the values embodied in such a life that made him turn to philosophy and the search for true happiness.

---

[1] There are not that many studies of Spinoza's moral philosophy. But see Curley 1973; Bennett 1984, chapter 12; and D. Garrett 1996, as well as some of the essays in Yovel and Segal 2004.

After experience had taught me that all the things which regularly occur in ordinary life are empty and futile, and I saw that all the things which were the cause or object of my fear had nothing of good or bad in themselves, except insofar as my mind was moved by them, I resolved at last to try to find out whether there was anything which would be the true good, capable of communicating itself, and which alone would affect the mind, all others being rejected – whether there was something which, once found and acquired, would continuously give me the greatest joy, to eternity.

(TIE, G II.5/C I.7)

The 'bondage' to which Spinoza refers in Part Four, then, is not a conventional servitude to other human beings, but rather the natural slavery to the passions that make up so much of our mental life, as well as to the external things that occasion them.

Man's lack of power to moderate and restrain the affects I call bondage [*servitutem*]. For the man who is subject to affects is under the control, not of himself, but of fortune, in whose power he so greatly is that often, though he sees the better for himself, he is still forced to follow the worse.

(IV, Preface, G II.205/C I.543)

In the *Short Treatise*, Spinoza had offered a rather harsh description of this everyday condition. It is, he insists, a life of "sadness, despair, envy, fright, and other evil passions," in short, "the real hell itself" (KV, II.18, G I.88/C I.128). It is only when one can transform oneself from this forlorn condition of passivity to something like an active and self-sufficient existence that one can claim to be free, happy, and, ultimately, blessed.

It is important to remember that the *servitus* to which Spinoza refers in Part Four is very different from the "enslavement" of the soul that is so often found in the thought of classical moral philosophers such as Plato and Augustine (not to mention St. Paul). It is not that Spinoza's mind is like a soul entrapped in body and all of its rational desires overcome by bodily appetites. The struggle to control the passions is not a struggle between soul and body and a striving to liberate the soul from the body's influence. As we know from Parts One through Three, for Spinoza such a desire for "liberation" must be based on a false conception of the soul's relationship to the body. Rather, it is a struggle on the part of the individual himself to become more active and less passive (in Spinoza's senses of these terms, as discussed in Part Three) and to acquire a certain kind of strength in both mind and body. It represents, above all, an attempt to achieve greater rationality and autonomy in one's life and a greater independence from the vicissitudes of fortune.

Spinoza begins Part Four with a preface in which he considers some basic ethical language: good and evil, perfect and imperfect. He insists that such terms do not refer to absolute and objective features of things, properties that they have independently of anything else (especially human perceivers). Nothing is, taken by itself, good or evil or perfect or imperfect, least of all when these words are understood in the normative sense. Whatever *is* just *is*, period. To put it another way, everything that exists is, if considered on its own, perfect to some degree, where 'perfection' is an ontological term to be understood simply as reality, or as the power to persevere in existence (i.e., *conatus*). But there is no evaluative element involved in saying that something has perfection in this descriptive sense. "[Things] are all equal in this regard," Spinoza says at the end of the Preface.

What 'good' and 'evil' (and 'perfect' and 'imperfect') in the normative sense do refer to, if not objective, mind-independent features of the world, is an evaluative measure of the degree to which a thing corresponds to some stipulated standard or model. The most obvious case in which this is so is the evaluation of an artifact. A building, for example, is deemed more or less perfect depending upon the extent to which it matches the architect's original conception, which serves as a standard to which the finished product is compared. "If someone has decided to make something, and has finished it, then he will call his thing perfect – and so will anyone who rightly knows, or thinks he knows, the mind and purpose of the author of the work." By contrast, if one has no idea of what the artificer intended to create, one will have no way of assessing how "perfect" the artifact is. Without such a model to compare the product to, the term is meaningless.

This evaluative practice gets extended to natural objects when human beings form universal ideas of kinds of things in nature. For example, from experience we conceive some ideal model – based, of course, on inadequate ideas, as all abstractions must be – of what a horse is, or a tree. We then call some particular horse or tree 'perfect' or 'imperfect' depending upon how well it matches with that randomly created and arbitrarily adopted model. "When they see something happen in nature which does not agree with the model they have conceived of this kind of thing, they believe that Nature itself has failed or sinned, and left the thing imperfect." What gives sustenance to this extension of normative terms from the world of artifacts to the world of nature is the human tendency to see teleology in nature, which in turn results from the traditional anthropo-morphic conception of a God who acts with purposes. Things thus become 'perfect' or 'imperfect' to the extent that they succeed or fail in achieving the end for which God supposedly created them. But Spinoza's God, of course, does not act to achieve any ends. "Nature does nothing on account of an end," Spinoza reminds the reader in the preface to Part Four. "That eternal and infinite being we call God, or Nature, acts from the same necessity from which he exists."

The problem is that we tend to ignore the real status of 'perfect' and 'imperfect' as only relative to selected and highly subjective standards and project our perceptions of things onto the things themselves. We think of things as perfect or imperfect in their own right, and overlook the fact that "perfection and imperfection . . . are only modes of thinking, i.e., notions we are accustomed to feign because we compare individuals of the same species or genus to one another." Thus, our ordinary approach to labeling natural things as 'perfect' or 'imperfect' derives "more from prejudice than from true knowledge of those things."

The same analysis applies to the terms 'good' and 'evil.' These evaluative labels are, likewise, always to be understood in the context of a thing's relationship to a standard or model. Something is 'good' if it is a means to a chosen end. More particularly, it is good if it promotes what appears, in the light of that standard, to be an individual's well-being and helps move it closer to a stipulated ideal condition; and it is 'evil' if it is detrimental to what is perceived to be an individual's well-being. The result is that 'good' and 'evil,' like 'perfect' and 'imperfect,' are totally relative terms (relative, that is, to the conception of some individual's interest), and what is good for one person may not be good for another person.

As far as good and evil are concerned, they also indicate nothing positive in things, considered in themselves, nor are they anything other than modes of thinking, or notions we form because we compare things to one another. For one and the same thing can, at the same time, be good and bad, and also indifferent. For example, music is good for one who is melancholy, bad for one who is mourning, and neither good nor bad to one who is deaf.

(IV, Preface, G II.208/C I.545)

It may seem as if Spinoza here goes beyond the analysis of 'good' and 'evil' that he offered earlier in the work. In Part Three, as we have seen, we are told that one judges that something is good because one desires it (and one desires it because it brings about an increase in one's power of acting). Thus, the claim that '*x* is good' must mean 'I desire *x*.' Such judgments would therefore seem to be not only relativized, but subjectivized. In the Preface to Part Four, however, while 'good' and 'evil' are still relativized, it now appears to be an objective matter of fact as to whether or not something matches up with a model or is conducive to what is taken to be some individual's interest. However, the standards themselves that are ordinarily used for determining whether something is 'good' or 'perfect' remain highly subjective. One person's conception of what constitutes an ideal tree or an ideal human being will differ from another person's conception, given the differences in their experiences and thus in the particulars from which they abstract their general notion, as well as in the features they focus on in creating that notion. Notice that I have been speaking only of what is "perceived to be" or "appears to be" in someone's interest. So it remains the case that something will be 'good' if, given what I believe about an ideal life and an individual's interests, I believe it to be good (as a means to that ideal). But there is no guarantee that my beliefs about these things are true, nor even that they will be shared by others. Indeed, the framing of standards and models is strongly dependent on an individual's very particular desires, and thus so will be judgments about what is good and perfect.[2]

---

[2] See Bennett 1984: "The thesis that our value judgments are based on models is not in conflict with the earlier thesis that they are guided by our feelings and desires. Rather, the two are aspects of a single unified account, the unifying factor being the view that our feelings and desires guide our value judgments *by* guiding our selection of models" (p. 292).

If this was all Spinoza had to say about 'good' and 'evil,' then he would indeed be left with a subjectivist analysis of those important moral terms. However, he notes that while 'good' and 'evil' do not refer to real features of the world, nevertheless "we must retain these words," but without giving up their relativist meaning. This is because Spinoza thinks they can, while remaining context-relative, also bear a more objectivist burden. Spinoza believes that there is, in fact, a specific ideal that can serve as an objective standard according to which things can be judged as truly "good" for a human being. There is a particular kind of person and life that represents a perfection of human nature.

Because we desire to form an idea of man, as a model of human nature which we may look to, it will be useful to us to retain these same words with the meaning I have indicated. In what follows, therefore, I shall understand by good what we know certainly is a means by which we may approach nearer and nearer to the model of human nature that we set before ourselves. By evil, what we certainly know prevents us from becoming like that model. Next, we shall say that men are more perfect or imperfect, insofar as they approach more or less near to this model.

This does not mean that 'good' and 'evil' are not relative terms. It is still the case that nothing, taken in and of itself and without comparison with or utility for some standard or model, is good or evil. However, the subjectivism that was introduced with the Part Three account of good and evil, and carried through in the preface to Part Four when 'good' and 'evil' are relativized to only haphazardly formed conceptions to serve as models for various kinds of things (including human beings), is now replaced by a more objective model. 'Good' no longer means simply what one desires. Nor does it mean only 'useful for making something approach what one may happen to believe to be a perfected specimen of its kind.' Rather, it now means 'useful for making a human being closer to what is truly a more perfected specimen of humanity.' What that more perfected specimen of humanity consists in, as we shall see, is an individual of maximal power of persevering, maximal activity.

This de-subjectivization of the model according to which we can judge what is good or evil for a human being is what allows Spinoza to define 'good' in Part Four as "what we certainly know to be useful to us" (IVD1), and 'evil' as "what we certainly know prevents us from being masters of some good" (IVD2). It is also what he has in mind when, as of IVP14, he begins speaking of "the true knowledge of good and evil," as opposed to merely "a knowledge of good and evil" (see, for example, IVP8). The latter refers to my perception of something as bringing about some increase in some aspect of my body's capacities (and thus as bringing about some increase in some aspect of my mind's capacities). Some things are judged 'good' because they are a source of joy and pleasure. This judgment is grounded only in the passions, however, and thus is based on inadequate knowledge of the thing and of oneself. But the "true knowledge of good and evil" is my rational perception – derived from adequate ideas and not just random experience, based on understanding and not simply on the positive way something affects my body – of what benefits me in a more complete and essential manner, truly bringing me as a whole individual to a more powerful condition. The difference is summed up by Spinoza in the demonstration of IVP35: "What we judge to be good or evil when we follow the dictate of reason must be good or evil."

Naturally, this objectivization of good and evil will work only if Spinoza can provide some objectivity for what he will claim is the ideal human being – what he will later in Part Four call 'the free man' or the person who lives according to the dictate of reason. Why should *this* conception of a human being, Spinoza's "model of human nature [*naturae humanae exemplar*]," be privileged? Why should it have an advantage over any other model of a human being that we might conceive? Unless he can provide a satisfactory answer to this question, he cannot escape the subjectivism that seems to be inherent in his relativization of 'good' and 'evil' to "modes of thinking." Spinoza, unfortunately, does not explicitly offer any response to this challenge. But one plausible way to answer the question on his behalf is to suggest that when an individual guided by reason and not the influence of the passions is put in front of a number of possible models of human nature, including Spinoza's *exemplar*, it is this latter model that that rational individual, acting from knowledge, will necessarily desire (from his striving to increase his power of acting) and endeavor to achieve.[3] This may seem to beg the question, since we can now ask why should the desires and choices of a rational individual (who, after all, represents the model itself that we are trying to justify) be privileged over the desires and choices of the individual acting out of passion. But remember that the individual acting out of passion is not really acting at all but rather *re*acting. Only the individual whose desires and choices are guided by adequate ideas is an individual whose actions are generated by his own nature and is thus doing what naturally and necessarily follows from his *conatus* alone. Thus, Spinoza can say that while good and evil will remain relative to some standard, the standard itself is not relative to just anyone's conception of what the good life is but is in conformity with human nature itself.

Spinoza's view of the human project as one of approximating, as much as one can, some specific ideal model (and, correlatively, his conception of 'good' and 'evil' as what will further or hinder that project) is present in his earliest extant works. Thus, in the *Treatise on the Emendation of the Intellect*, he says that "since . . . man conceives a human nature much stronger and more enduring than his own, and at the same time sees that nothing prevents his acquiring such a nature, he is spurred to seek means that will lead him to such perfection" (G II.8/C I.10). In the *Short Treatise*, we find him claiming that

We have already said before that all things are necessitated, and that in Nature there is no good and evil. So whatever we require of man, must relate only to his genus, and this is nothing but a being of reason. And when we have conceived an idea of a perfect man in our intellect, that [idea] could be a cause of our seeing (when we examine ourselves) whether we have any means of arriving at such perfection.

(KV II.4, G I.60/C I.103)[4]

---

[3] See Curley 1973 and Curley 1988, p. 123.

[4] Bennett (1984), in fact, suggests that the *naturae humanae exemplar* in the *Ethics*, which appears only in the preface, is "a relic of a time when Spinoza planned to make the concept of a favoured model of mankind do some work for him in the body of Part 4" (p. 296). I would say, however, that while the *exemplar* terminology does not reappear later in Part Four, nonetheless the concept of a "favoured model" that it represents does, in the form of the "free man."

While in the earlier works he may have believed this perfection to be something attainable, in the *Ethics* it is clearly an ideal to which we can draw near but never achieve.

## AFFECT VS. AFFECT

According to Spinoza, existence is a perpetual struggle. We see this clearly captured in the sole axiom at the beginning of Part Four: "There is no singular thing in nature than which there is not another more powerful and stronger. Whatever one is given, there is another more powerful by which the first can be destroyed" (IVA1). There are an infinite number of *conatus* in Nature, each striving for its own individual's perseverance. These come into conflict as they contend for existence and domination and causally impinge upon one another.

In the life of a human being, the struggle occurs both between the individual and forces outside him and among internal forces within him. His body with its own *conatus* strives against those things that would destroy or weaken it, while the mind works to increase its own power of acting. Success is always a more or less temporary affair, and no thing will survive forever – as the axiom says, there is always something stronger that will eventually come along and overcome it. There are no immortal or everlasting beings in the durational part of nature. "The force by which a man perseveres in existing is limited, and infinitely surpassed by the power of external causes" (IVP3). As parts of Nature, we are always being acted on (IVP2), even under the best of circumstances, and no person can completely liberate himself from the nexus of external causes. We cannot, that is, not be a part of Nature and not be involved in this constant struggle, what the ancient Greeks would have called an *agon*.

IVP4: It is impossible that a man should not be a part of Nature, and that he should be able to undergo no changes except those which can be understood through his own nature alone, and of which he is the adequate cause.

Were this not the case, if a person could truly become completely active (i.e., free of all passive affects) and resistant to the forces acting upon him, he would never die. "If it were possible that a man could undergo no changes except those which can be understood through the man's nature alone, it would follow (by IIIP4 and P6) that he could not perish, but that necessarily he would always exist" (IVP4d). But this is absurd, Spinoza insists, since it would mean either that the individual man could avoid every possible change for the worse that might arise from natural causes, or that Nature itself was directing things in such a way that he would undergo no changes except those which aid his preservation. Therefore, Spinoza concludes, "it is impossible that a man should undergo no other changes except those of which he himself is the adequate cause." This conclusion of IVP4 is simply an extension of the project of Part Three, whereby Spinoza intended to show that the human being is not some "dominion within a dominion" and outside the forces that govern the rest of Nature.

A human being, then, is "always subject to passions . . . follows and obeys the common order of Nature, and accommodates himself to it as much as the nature of things requires" (IVP4c). Sometimes those passions move him one way, at other times they move him in a different, even contrary way. What moves a person, we know from Part Three, are the affects – changes for better or for worse in the strength of his *conatus* or striving to persevere. We pursue the things that improve us and cause joy, and avoid the things that harm us and cause sadness. The affects and the modifications they make in desire are, as we have seen, the primary motivating factors in human behavior.

The force of any particular passion is a function of the ratio of the power of the external thing that causes the passion to the human being's own power of persevering in existence (IVP5). The latter's power of persevering can certainly be surpassed by the power of the external cause, in which case "the [passive] affect stubbornly clings to the man" and is hard to resist (IVP6). Moreover, the strength or weakness of an affect depends a good deal upon one's conception of the external thing to which it is directed. In IVP9–13, Spinoza surveys the relative intensities of the affects based on the temporal proximity and existential modality of their objects. An affect directed at a present object is stronger than one directed at an absent or non-existent object (IVP9), while an affect brought on by something regarded as necessary will be "more intense" than a passion for something that appears to be merely possible or contingent (IVP11). We are more moved by something right in front of us than by something out of sight (out of mind). And we are more affected by something we know for certain is going to happen than something whose presence is (from our point of view) uncertain.

Spinoza's view of life as a struggle between competing affects carries over into the cognitive realm as well. Even knowledge is incapable of moving a person unless it has an affective component. The presence of a true idea is not by itself – in its *truth* – sufficient to conquer false beliefs and the desires that arise from them. Just my knowing that something unpleasant is nonetheless good for me (taking bad-tasting medicine, for example) is not going to defeat my passionate resistance to doing it. It is only the strength of the affect accompanying a true belief that can overcome the affects of the inadequate ideas of the senses and the imagination. "No affect can be restrained by the true knowledge of good and evil insofar as it is true, but only insofar as it is considered an affect" (IVP14). To the extent that knowledge of what is true represents an increase in the mind's power of acting, it will be accompanied by an affective dimension that is opposed to the affect accompanying "the other imaginations by which the mind is deceived." In other words, only affects can oppose affects. "An affect cannot be restrained or taken away except by an affect opposite to, and stronger than, the affect to be restrained" (IVP7).

The clash between knowledge and the passions, then, is not a clash between the pure intellect and the emotions, as Plato portrays it; rather, it is an affective struggle, one characterized by competing desires each of which has a different source. "A desire which arises from a true knowledge of good and evil can be extinguished or restrained by many other desires which arise from affects by which we are tormented" (IVP15). And knowledge, despite its epistemic superiority, is often weaker in its affective component than the passionate affects that so often hold us in "bondage."

Spinoza uses this account of the affective struggle within a human being to explain how it is possible for a person to know very well what is good and right and yet fail to do it. This is a classic issue of moral psychology, one that was of great concern to Socrates, Plato, Aristotle, and many other philosophers and on which they very often strongly disagreed. Socrates, for one, believed that if a person truly knows what is good, he will pursue it. Aristotle's view is a bit more ambiguous, but essentially he argues that one can know what the right thing to do is but not do it.[5] The phenomenon is called (using the ancient Greek term) *akrasia*, and is usually translated as "weakness of the will" or "incontinence." It should be distinguished from another, somewhat similar issue, the motivational problem, wherein the question is whether it is possible for a person to know what is good or right and yet not be motivated to pursue it ("I know that *x* is the right thing to do, but why should *I* do it?"). With *akrasia*, one is motivated to pursue the good and do what is right but somehow fails to follow through on that motive.

Spinoza certainly believes that every individual is always *motivated* to do what is good – that is, what will best promote his own interest and aid his striving for perseverance. (One of the advantages of egoism is that it never has any trouble accounting for motivation.) But he is also struck by the fact that sometimes we fail to act appropriately. The explanation for this, he says, is "man's lack of power," in particular, his inability to control and moderate the affects.

Man's lack of power to moderate and restrain the affects I call bondage. For the man who is subject to affects is under the control, not of himself, but of fortune, in whose power he so greatly is that often, though he sees the better for himself, he is still forced to follow the worse.

(IV, Preface, G II.205/C I.543)

Reason, even with the help of its affective forces, is often no match for the affects caused by external things, especially those that represent an immediate increase in some aspect of one's power of acting and thus are strong pleasures. "A desire which arises from a true knowledge of good and evil, insofar as this knowledge concerns the future, can be quite easily restrained or extinguished by a desire for the pleasures of the moment" (IVP16). Similarly, a rational desire

---

[5] And yet, Aristotle's explanation for such behavior usually involves showing how such a person lacks some important piece of knowledge; see *Nicomachean Ethics* VII.3.

(based on "a true knowledge of good and evil") for something that may or may not exist is easily overcome by a desire for something that is present (IVP17). It is an unhappy condition, Spinoza says, one fraught with regret and longing.

With this I believe I have shown the cause why men are moved more by opinion than by true reason, and why the true knowledge of good and evil arouses disturbances of the mind, and often yields to lusts of every kind. Hence that verse of the poet [Ovid],

> . . . video meliora, proboque,
> deteriora sequor . . .
> [I see and approve the better,
> but follow the worse]

Ecclesiastes also seems to have had the same thing in mind when he said: "He who increases knowledge increases sorrow."

What can such a person do to free himself from this affective bondage, one that forces him often to act against his own best interests, and ameliorate the unreasonable demands of the passions?

### VIRTUE

We now come, at last, to the ethics of the *Ethics*. Things begin to brighten considerably with IVP18. In this and the following propositions, Spinoza moves beyond the pathetic picture of life enslaved to the passions and begins drawing the model human life, the *exemplar*, that represents the perfection of human nature and the maximization of its power of persevering. It is a life guided by reason and based in knowledge and understanding, where an individual does only what is truly useful for himself but also aids others in their own pursuit of perfection. The resulting moral philosophy is virtue-oriented. What matters most is not the actions that one performs, or even the intentions that one has, but above all the kind of person one is and the character one possesses. Like Socrates, Plato, Aristotle, and the Stoics before him, Spinoza's model human being is one endowed with virtue and a settled disposition to do certain things and behave in determinate ways.

'Virtue' for Spinoza is not exactly the same thing that *areté* was for the ancient Greek philosophers – that is, a trait that causes a thing to perform its characteristic function with excellence. Rather, Spinoza defines virtue, in IVD8, as power. "By virtue and power I understand the same thing, i.e. (by IIIP7), virtue, insofar as it is related to man, is the very essence, or nature, of man, insofar as he has the power of bringing about certain things, which can be understood through the laws of his nature alone." There is a lot packed into this definition, and it is important to separate the various elements that for Spinoza constitute living according to virtue.

In IVP18s, Spinoza – in a statement that strongly recalls the ancient Stoic doctrine of virtue as "acting in accordance with nature" – offers a more condensed version of the definition: "virtue . . . is nothing but acting from the laws of one's own nature." But the nature of any thing is just its *conatus*, or striving to persevere in existence. Thus, the laws of any thing's nature prescribe that the thing strive to preserve its being. Therefore, as Spinoza concludes, "the foundation of virtue is this very striving to preserve one's own being." The virtuous person is the person who successfully follows the laws of his own nature and acts so as to preserve his own being. Virtue, in other words, is successful striving for preservation. "The more each one strives, and is able, to preserve his being, the more he is endowed with virtue" (IVP20d). The opposite of virtue, on the other hand – and this presumably would be vice, although Spinoza does not use this term but rather the phrase 'lack of power' – is acting not according to one's own nature but according to the nature of things outside oneself. The person lacking virtue or power "allows himself to be guided by things outside him, and to be determined by them to do what the common constitution of external things demands, not what his own nature, considered in itself, demands" (IVP37s1). This should sound familiar, since it just is the person who is enslaved to the passions and to the external things that cause them.

Spinoza has so far provided a rather formalistic account of virtue, one that does not yet have any real content. No substantive information on what kind of person best strives for self-preservation or on *how* to act in such a way that one is following the laws of one's own nature is contained in the claim that "the more each one strives, and is able, to seek his own advantage, i.e., to preserve his own being, the more he is endowed with virtue" (IVP20). We need to be told just what the vague notions of 'following the laws of one's own nature' and striving 'to seek one's own advantage' imply and how a person can put them to work in his life.

This is where Spinoza's rationalism comes back into play, this time not just as a metaphysical or epistemological principle, but as a moral one. Spinoza identifies 'living according to one's own nature' with 'living according to the guidance of reason.' This is because a human being lives according to his own nature when the things he does have their adequate cause in that nature alone and not in the ways external things affect him; that is, he lives according to his own nature when he is active, not passive. And, as we have seen, a human being is active when what he does follows from his own adequate ideas, from his rational knowledge of things, and not from inadequate ideas or the passions.

Reason's guidance comes embodied in what Spinoza calls (in IVP18) the "dictates of reason [*dictamina rationis*]." These rational dictates are grounded in the individual's *conatus* and represent a kind of enlightened propositional expression of that natural striving. They demand

> that everyone love himself, seek his own advantage, what is really useful to him, want what will really lead man to a greater perfection, and absolutely, that everyone should strive to preserve his own being as far as he can.
> (IVP18s)

More important, reason also provides guidance on how to achieve these ends. It does so universally and objectively, without regard to a person's particularities. Like Kant's categorical (moral) imperatives, the dictates of reason transcend personal differences and make universal demands on human behavior. This is clear from Spinoza's claim in IVP72, where he considers whether the person guided by reason would ever act deceptively, that "if reason should recommend that, it would recommend it to all men."

Among the first things that reason demands is that "we ought to want virtue for its own sake, and that there is not anything preferable to it, or more useful to us." But because we are necessarily always a part of Nature and unable ever to bring it about "that we require nothing outside ourselves to preserve our being, nor that we live without having dealings with things outside us," reason also prescribes that we should strive to possess the "many things outside us which are useful to us" (IVP18s). Spinoza's virtue, in other words, does not lead to an ascetic withdrawal from the world, but rather a more knowledgeable and successful navigation within the world and a more efficient use of things in it. The virtuous person is able to determine what is *truly* conducive to his well-being and what is not. "Acting absolutely from virtue is nothing else in us but acting, living, and preserving our being (these three signify the same thing) by the guidance of reason, from the foundation of seeking one's own advantage" (IVP24).

The reason why this is so is because the virtuous person acts from knowledge. He is endowed with adequate ideas, and these guide him in his endeavors. His desires and choices are determined by understanding, not by the passions. Everybody, of course, by the laws of his own nature, wants what he judges to be good and is repelled by what he judges to be evil (IVP19). The virtuous person guided by reason has the advantage that what he judges to be good or evil – in Spinoza's definition of those terms, as what will aid or diminish one's power – really is so. His judgments are based not on the pleasures or pains he undergoes because some aspect of his bodily being is experiencing a temporary increase or decrease in its striving to persevere, but on a more secure and active foundation. (As Spinoza says at one point, "we call a desire blind which arises from an affect which is a passion" [IVP59s].) What he desires is not merely what relates to one or even several parts of his being, but what serves "for the advantage of the whole" (IVP60). Immediate gratification does not mislead him into pursuing false or transitory or partial goods. Thus, he is virtuous just because, given his cognitive advantage, he does truly succeed in his striving.

IVP23: A man cannot absolutely be said to act from virtue insofar as he is determined to do something because he has inadequate ideas, but only insofar as he is determined because he understands.

To the extent that a person has inadequate ideas, he is acted upon; what he does, therefore, follows not from his own nature alone but from his own nature combined with the nature of the external cause. But a person whose behavior is determined solely by his adequate ideas, and not by the way external things affect him, is truly active; what he does, therefore, follows from his nature alone and is certain to be in accordance with that nature's striving to persevere.

It is a consequence of this that what is truly in a person's interest, what best aids his striving to persevere, what maximizes his power is nothing other than knowledge or understanding itself. "What we strive for from reason is nothing but understanding; nor does the mind, insofar as it uses reason, judge anything else useful to itself except what leads to understanding" (IVP26). The rational person, the virtuous person, sees that nothing benefits him more than knowledge. Knowledge is thus the supreme good, since it is what moves one closer to the state of human perfection, which is itself a state of understanding. Thus, he also judges that nothing else is good except what leads to understanding, while nothing is evil except what prevents one from achieving understanding (IVP27).

One might ask, understanding of what? Understanding of nature, of course, particularly as this is embodied in knowledge of the second and third kinds. These species of knowledge, as we have seen, relate things to their eternal and universal causes, the attributes and their infinite modes. They show, that is, how things are related to God or Nature itself *sub specie aeternitatis*. But this means that, ultimately, the knowledge sought by the virtuous person just is knowledge of God (in Spinoza's sense of the term).

IVP28: Knowledge of God is the mind's greatest good; its greatest virtue is to know God.

DEM.: The greatest thing the mind can understand is God, i.e. (by ID6), a being absolutely infinite, without which (by IP15) it can neither be nor be conceived. And so (by IVP26 and IVP27), the mind's greatest advantage, or (by IVD1) good, is knowledge of God.

Next, only insofar as the mind understands (by IIIP1 and IIIP3) does it act, and can it be said absolutely to act from virtue (by IVP23). The absolute virtue of the mind, then, is understanding. But the greatest thing the mind can understand is God (as we have already demonstrated). Therefore, the greatest virtue of the mind is to understand, or know, God, q.e.d.

All of this comes together nicely when, at the end of Part Four, Spinoza concludes in the Appendix that what the virtuous person wants for himself is

to perfect, as far as [he] can, [his] intellect, or reason . . . Perfecting the intellect is nothing but understanding God, his attributes, and his actions, which follow from the necessity of his nature. So the ultimate end of the man who is led by reason, i.e., his highest desire, by which he strives to moderate all the others, is that by which he is led to conceive adequately both himself and all things which can fall under his understanding. (G II.267/C I.588)

With knowledge of God (or Nature) – essentially, the deepest kind of scientific knowledge of nature, in all its various phenomena, human and non-human – the virtuous person has found a good that is permanent and not subject to the vagaries of fortune, something that he can achieve through his own devices. It is also a good that an infinite number of individuals can equally possess without discord or competition, since it is not a finite and nonrenewable resource. Indeed, the virtuous person sees that knowledge of God is a good in the pursuit of which others are to be encouraged. Virtue therefore provides a solid foundation for peaceful and cooperative social relations, as well as for supportive ethical behavior toward others (see below).

### "THE FREE MAN"

So far, we can see that Spinoza basically identifies power, virtue, rationality, and activity. To be virtuous is to be successful in the endeavor to increase one's power or striving to persevere. To be powerful is to act, to be the adequate cause of one's own states of being. But one is an adequate cause of one's own states of being (including what one does) when those states follow from one's adequate ideas alone; and when one's activities follow from one's adequate ideas alone, one is guided by reason. The virtuous person thus lives what might be called the life of reason, a life of increased power and activity.

The virtuous person is also an individual that has acquired a greater degree of freedom. This is to be understood not as a lack of determination or freedom of the will – both of which are fictions for Spinoza – but as a degree of autonomy and causal independence relative to external things. What happens to the virtuous person follows from his own nature. The virtuous person, the person who has perfected his intellect and lives according to the dictate of reason, is thus what Spinoza labels "the free man [*homo liber*]." Like the "wise man [*sophos* or *sapiens*]" of ancient Stoicism – and Spinoza occasionally uses that phrase itself (e.g., IVP45s) – the free person represents a kind of human ideal.[6] It is, I believe, the *naturae humanae exemplar* itself with which Spinoza begins Part Four, the model according to which things in the human domain are to be judged good (or bad) and perfect (or imperfect), insofar as they allow us (or prevent us) to come closer to that ideal condition.

Spinoza devotes a good deal of the second half of Part Four to describing the life of the free person (thereby adding some detail to our understanding of the life of virtue). The free person is a person in whom belief and desire are led by knowledge, not the passions and random experience. Thus, he (and not external things) is in control of himself.

The desires which follow from our nature in such a way that they can be understood through it alone are those that related to the mind insofar as it is conceived to consist of adequate ideas. The remaining desires are not related to the mind except insofar as it conceives things inadequately, and their force and growth must be defined not by human power, but by the power of things that are outside us. (IV, Appendix, G II.266/C I.588)

The life of reason is a life in which the passions are well in check. The free person does not feel excessive love and desire for external goods and the pleasures they cause, nor hate for the evil things that may come his way. And because it is these emotions that lead to greed, ambition, lust, envy, jealousy, and the like, the free person does not experience such "troublesome" attitudes, which he will regard "as a species of madness" (IVP44s). He knows neither sadness nor melancholy, and his cheerfulness is not inordinate but solidly grounded in the general well-being of his condition (IVP42). It is, in short, a life of moderation. He does not pursue sensory pleasures indiscriminately and to excess, but neither is he immune to them, as

[6] See Wolfson 1934, II.255–9.

the ascetic might be. Indeed, he recognizes their necessity for the good life.

It is the part of a wise man, I say, to refresh and restore himself in moderation with pleasant food and drink, with scents, with the beauty of green plants, with decoration, music, sports, the theater, and other things of this kind, which anyone can use without injury to another.

He can distinguish what is good for the whole person, body and mind, from what is only temporarily pleasant for one part of himself.

For the human body is composed of a great many parts of different natures, which constantly require new and varied nourishment, so that the whole body may be equally capable of all the things which can follow from its nature, and hence, so that the mind also may be equally capable of understanding many things. (IVP45s)

The free person is moved by reason, not passion, even when it involves performing the same action ("To every action to which we are determined from an affect which is a passion, we can be determined by reason, without that affect" (IVP59)). He will pursue things from a true knowledge of what is good, and his rational desires for those things he recognizes as good are "never excessive" (IVP61). He does what is right and good not out of hope or fear (for example, of the pleasant or unpleasant consequences), but out of understanding that this is what is truly in his own best interest.

Because his knowledge of things is a knowledge of the second and third kinds, the free person can regard them *sub specie aeternitatis* and with the appropriate appreciation for their necessity. Thus, the de facto temporal ordering of things in his sense experience is irrelevant to his evaluation of and desire for them, and he is not so easily moved by the call of the moment that he will sacrifice his long-term interest for it. The free person keeps his eye equally on the future as well as on the present – since from the eternal perspective they appear the same – and will not allow the enticement of immediate pleasure to overcome his rational commitment to some not yet existing good.

IVP62: Insofar as the mind conceives things from the dictate of reason, it is affected equally, whether the idea is of a future or past thing, or of a present one.

DEM.: Whatever the mind conceives under the guidance of reason, it conceives under the same species of eternity, or necessity (by IIP44c2) and is affected with the same certainty (by IIP43 and IIP43s). So whether the idea is of a future or a past thing, or of a present one, the mind conceives the thing with the same necessity and is affected with the same certainty. And whether the idea is of a future or a past thing or of a present one, it will nevertheless be equally true (by IIP41), i.e. (by IID4), it will nevertheless always have the same properties of an adequate idea. And so, insofar as the mind conceives things from the dictate of reason, it is affected in the same way, whether the idea is of a future or a past thing, or of a present one, q.e.d.

The free person, in other words, will never experience *akrasia* or weakness of the will.

If we could have adequate knowledge of the duration of things, and determine by reason their times of existing, we would regard future things with the same affect as present ones, and the mind would want the good it conceived as future just as it wants the good it conceives as present. Hence, it would necessarily neglect a lesser present good for a greater future one ...
(IVP62s)

Because of his perception of the necessity of things, the free person is less susceptible to the affects of hope and fear, both of which depend upon a sense of contingency and uncertainty in what will come to pass (IVP47). Nor, for the same reason, will he exhibit some common modes of behavior toward others – mockery, disdain, blame, praise, anger, and vengeance.

He who rightly knows that all things follow from the necessity of the divine nature, and happen according to the eternal laws and rules of nature, will surely find nothing worthy of hate, mockery, or disdain, nor anyone whom he will pity. Instead, he will strive, as far as human virtue allows, to act well, as they say, and rejoice. (IVP50s)

The free person will also have strong self-esteem (*acquiescentia in se ipso*), one that derives from reflection upon his power of acting and his own honest and adequate appraisal of himself (IVP52). It is a rational self-esteem "born" of virtue, and involves the joy (an increase in one's power of persevering) that comes with the idea of one's own heightened capacities. It needs to be distinguished from the "empty" self-esteem that derives from one's sense of how one is regarded by others. The "opinion of the multitude" is a temporary and unpredictable thing, and when it ceases, so does the self-esteem which depends upon it. "That is why he who exults at being esteemed by the multitude is made anxious daily, strives, sacrifices, and schemes, in order to preserve his reputation. For the multitude is fickle and inconstant; unless one's reputation is guarded, it is quickly destroyed" (IVP58s). The free person will not care at all for a self-esteem – or indeed any good – that is so far beyond his control.

In short, the free person "leads himself . . . by the free judgment of reason, and . . . [does] only those things that he himself knows to be most excellent" (IVP70). He will avoid the praise and favors of the ignorant as far as he can (IVP70), always act honestly and never deceptively (IVP72), be thankful for the goods that he obtains (IVP71), and always follow the greater of two goods or the lesser of two evils (IVP65). Spinoza also suggests that a *perfectly* free person – that is, someone who is only active and never passive – will have no conception of evil. This is because knowledge of evil is nothing but a consciousness of sadness (i.e., consciousness of a decrease in one's power of acting), and sadness is brought about only by external things. A perfectly free person, who has only adequate ideas and thus is the cause of all of his own states of being, will never suffer a decrease in his power of acting, since no thing will ever bring about a decrease in its perfection through its own activity. "If the human mind had only adequate ideas, it would form no notion of evil" (IVP64). Above all, Spinoza says, in one of the more memorable phrases of the work, that the free person thinks least of all of death. "A free man thinks of nothing less than of death, and his wisdom is a meditation on life, not on death" (IVP67). Like Socrates on the eve of his execution, the free person is not afraid of dying. He will not dwell on the end of his durational existence or worry about what it may or may not bring. On the contrary, the free person is focused on preserving his being and seeking his own advantage. He is consumed with the joys that a powerful, active, and self-sufficient life bring.[7]

---

[7] For a discussion of Spinoza on the joys of living, see Smith 2003.

Now when Spinoza talks about the free person, it is natural to wonder what kind of freedom he has in mind, especially since the tenor of what has gone before has led the reader to believe that human beings are not, in fact, free at all. What does freedom mean for human beings within Spinoza's deterministic universe?

There is one relatively easy answer to this question, an answer that again hearkens back to the Stoic conception of the wise person. Spinoza's free person, like Cicero's *sapiens*, is "free" in so far as many of the disturbances that contribute to unhappiness, anxiety, and despair are absent from his life.[8] According to this sense, 'free' means "free of . . .", or unencumbered by certain things. The knowledge that leads the free person, Spinoza insists in the *Short Treatise*, "frees us from sadness, despair, envy, fright, and other evil passions, which . . . are the real hell itself" (G I.88/C I.128).

We know, however, that that is not all there is to the freedom of Spinoza's free person. On the other hand, we also know that the free person cannot be free in the robust sense in which those with libertarian inclinations tend to think of human freedom, namely, that which requires a lack of determination, an uncaused will. No one is free in that sense, according to Spinoza, not even God.

Is the free person "free" in the same sense in which we saw that God is free? More generally, is there a univocal and consistent conception of 'freedom' in the *Ethics*? God or Nature is free because it is completely self-determining substance; there is nothing outside of it that can causally determine it to bring about one effect rather than another. "That thing is free which exists from the necessity of its own nature alone, and is determined to act by itself alone" (ID7). But how can the free person be free in *this* sense? After all, the free person is a finite mode; thus, like every finite mode, as we have been told, it "can neither exist nor be determined to produce an effect unless it is determined to exist and produce an effect by another cause, which is also finite and has a determinate existence" (IP28). Does this not rule out *self*-determination on the part of the free person? I do not think so. What it does rule out is freedom/self-determination of the will – or, more precisely, freedom/self-determination in one's volitions. Every volition (like any mental

---

[8] *Tusculan Disputations* IV.27, section 58.

state) is caused by another mental state and thus is (relative to the volitional state itself) externally determined – the mental cause of a volition is distinct from and external to the volition, even when both occur within the same mind. But while any particular state of the free person is causally (externally) determined by some other state of that person, this does not mean that the free person himself is not self-determining. We need to distinguish, in other words, freedom of the will from freedom of the person. Spinoza's free person may not have freedom of the will, but he can still be free in the ID7 sense of freedom.[9] His freedom consists precisely in the fact that the adequate cause of what he thinks, what he desires, and what he does lies within him, namely, his adequate ideas and his power of persevering.

I call him free who is led by reason alone. Therefore, he who is born free, and remains free, has only adequate ideas . . . (IVP68d)

We shall easily see what the difference is between a man who is led only by an affect, or by opinion, and one who is led by reason. For the former, whether he will or no, does those things he is most ignorant of, whereas the latter complies with no one's wishes but his own, and does only those things he knows to be the most important in life, and therefore desires very greatly. Hence, I call the former a slave, but the latter, a free man. (IVP66s)

To be free is to be active. To be active is to be autonomous, relative to external things. It is to live according to reason. This does not mean that what one wills or does is undetermined. Rather, it means that what one wills and does follows from one's own nature – one's own internal striving to persevere – and reason. The freedom of the free person is no different from the freedom of God (or Nature).

There is and can be, of course, no such thing as a perfectly free person. As Spinoza reminds us a number of times, a human being can never not be a part of nature and "undergo no changes except those which can be understood through his own nature, and of which he is the adequate cause" (IVP4). The free person is, rather, an ideal model which reason approves and thus toward which the *conatus* of a person who is beginning to be guided by reason will necessarily strive. An individual who is acting rationally will

---

[9] See the discussion of this in Bennett 1984, pp. 315–17.

endeavor to emulate the free person. It is, as one scholar puts it, a limiting case.[10] We can approximate the nature of the free person to a greater or lesser degree. A person is thus more or less free depending upon the extent to which he approaches or falls short of the ideal free condition.

Is it the case that one *ought* to try to be like the free person? *Should* we strive to live the life of reason? This is one of the most vexed questions raised by the *Ethics*. It might seem hard for Spinoza to offer the reader any kind of 'ought' or 'should.' After all, without freedom of the will in the indeterminist sense, it might seem impossible for someone who is in bondage to the passions to make a deliberate choice to change his or her life. How can it be that a person "ought" to do something when his doing so or not doing so is not under his control? One will just necessarily be or do whatever one is determined to be or do, and this would appear to leave little room for normativity.

But this response presumes that moral prescriptions are incompatible with determinism. And while that may seem right to the libertarian, it will not seem right to the compatibilist, who believes that freedom and responsibility can coexist with determinism. Some scholars argue that, at least to a certain degree, Spinoza's determinism is consistent with his offering a "hortatory ethic."[11] *Ought* I to strive to be like the free man and live a life according to reason, as well as to do those things that are conducive to that end? Absolutely, since doing so is in my own self-interest, and nature tells me to pursue my self-interest. If 'ought' implies 'can,' and 'can' means only 'not impossible,' then even though given my current condition I will not do *x*, it might still be the case that I ought to do *x*. Other scholars insist that Spinoza can do nothing more than provide for the reader a naturalistic and descriptive account of what is "good" for a human being and what is "bad," all in the expectation that anyone who truly perceives the truth about these things – that is,

---

[10]  Bennett 1984, p. 317.

[11]  Curley (1973), for example, insists that as long as what is urged is not absolutely impossible, then "it makes perfectly good sense to issue a general prescription to people to avoid acts of a certain kind, even if you know that some of them, in some circumstances, will be unable to comply" (p. 372).

anyone who reads and understands the *Ethics* – will thereby necessarily be determined to pursue virtue and strive for knowledge.[12] Moral philosophy offers us truths that are just as "natural" as the truths presented by natural science. In fact, since the human being is a part of nature, moral philosophy is a sub-discipline of the study of nature. This sub-discipline is concerned with a certain sub-domain of cause–effect relationships within nature, namely, those that are of particular importance for human well-being.

## ETHICS

Of course, ethics, ordinarily understood, is not just about one's own self-development. It must also have something to say about how one is to treat other human beings, even if it turns out that this is itself to be motivated by the pursuit of self-interest. Spinoza is aware of this, and offers in Part Four a brief discussion of the ways in which an individual guided by reason will act toward others. While it is certainly possible to adopt an ethics that permits one to run roughshod over the well-being of others in the unrestricted pursuit of self-interest, Spinoza wisely argues that the egoism at the heart of his system in fact supports those benevolent and considerate ways of treating other human beings that we intuitively recognize as "ethical."

Spinoza begins his discussion of human sociability with a claim that properly belongs to his metaphysics of the individual and to the egoistic striving that characterizes it. He says that "insofar as a thing agrees with our nature, it is necessarily good," since it will aid the preservation of that nature. This is because a thing that shares my nature must, like anything, strive to preserve its own nature; and to the extent that its own nature is like my nature, it is therefore necessarily striving to preserve *my* nature. On the other hand, to the extent that a thing is of a nature different or contrary to my own, it is either indifferent for me (neither good nor bad) or evil (since, as contrary to my nature and to what agrees with my nature, it necessarily works against its preservation (IVP31)).[13] Thus, Spinoza

---

[12] For an example of the non-normative or naturalistic reading, see D. Garrett 1996, p. 286.
[13] For a harsh but, I think, justified assessment of IVP30–1, see Bennett 1984, pp. 299–302.

concludes (although the claim actually appears in an earlier proposition), there is "[nothing] more excellent than those [things] that agree entirely with our nature," and nothing is better for preserving one's own being than uniting oneself with something that shares one's nature – that is, another human being who is very much like oneself.

> For if, for example, two individuals of entirely the same nature unite with one another, they compose an individual twice as powerful as each one. To man, then, there is nothing more useful than man. Man, I say, can wish for nothing more helpful to the preservation of his being than that all should so agree in all things that the minds and bodies of all would compose, as it were, one mind and one body; that all should strive together, as far as they can, to preserve their being; and that all, together, should seek for themselves the common advantage of all. (IVP18s)

Although much is left unsaid by Spinoza in this passage, he seems to be arguing that two human beings represent a strengthening (by doubling) of one and the same power – just as two energy drinks provide twice as many carbohydrates and thus twice as much fuel to the body, or just as two people pushing a car provide more power than one person. This seems to be suggested by his claim that "our power of acting . . . can be determined, and hence aided or restrained, by the power of another singular thing which has something in common with us" (IVP29d). Two things of the same nature, thus two things striving on behalf of the same goal (i.e., the preservation of that nature), will increase the power working on behalf of that goal and thus the likelihood of its successful achievement.

Of course, human beings are also useful to each other insofar as they are *not* like each other. A community made up only of carpenters will function much less efficiently than a community made up of people with a variety of talents and skills who complement each other. But Spinoza's deeper point here is that human beings are good for and useful to each other only to the extent that they agree with one another in nature and thus share a common project and a common vision of things. It is our differences and particularities, not our commonalities, that divide us and set us against each other. And nothing contributes more to our mutual differences – not to mention differences and changes within the same person over time – than the passions. Our biggest differences and disagreements are in the ways in which we perceive and feel about things. "Insofar as men are subject to passions, they cannot be said to agree in nature" (IVP32). "Men can disagree in nature insofar as they are torn by affects which are passions; and to that extent also one and the same man is changeable and inconstant" (IVP33). Our bodily differences and differences in the objects with which we come into contact and in the ways in which they affect us – and these can include changes that a single individual undergoes over his lifetime – give rise to different ways of perceiving the world and reacting to it. Human discord is based on our passionate desires for things, along with a basic fact about the things that, through our inadequate ideas, we value: namely, not everyone can equally share in their possession. Passionate desires tend to be directed at finite, mutable goods that, very often, only one or a few people can obtain. Thus, they (and, consequently, their subjects) frequently come into conflict.

A man – Peter, say – can be a cause of Paul's being saddened, because he has something like a thing Paul hates (by IIIP16), or because Peter alone possesses something which Paul also loves (see IIIP32 and P32s), or on account of other causes . . . And so it will happen, as a result (by Def. Aff. VII), that Paul hates Peter. Hence it will easily happen (by IIIP40 and P40s) that Peter hates Paul in return, and so (by IIIP39) that they strive to harm one another; i.e. (by IVP30), that they are contrary to one another. But an affect of sadness is always a passion (by IIIP59). Therefore, men, insofar as they are torn by affects which are passions, can be contrary to one another. (IVP34d)

On the other hand, virtuous human beings who live according to reason "agree in nature" (IVP35). This should be understood both in a negative sense and a positive sense. In the negative sense, they agree in nature because those factors that, above and beyond what is common in human beings, lead to differences – i.e., the passions – are diminished. In a positive sense, individuals who live according to reason value the same things and pursue the same goods. Unlike the case of the rivals Peter and Paul, however, the good that virtuous rational people value and pursue is not a finite commodity but something that is eternal, imperishable, and capable of being shared equally by all: knowledge.

IVP36: The greatest good of those who seek virtue is common to all, and can be enjoyed by all equally.

DEM.: To act from virtue is to act according to the guidance of reason (by IVP24), and whatever we strive for from reason is understanding (by IVP26). Hence (by IVP28), the greatest good of those who seek virtue is to know God, i.e. (by IIP47 and IIP47s), a good that is common to all men, and can be possessed equally by all men insofar as they are of the same nature, q.e.d.

To the extent that a person is guided by reason, he does only what is good for his nature, that is, for human nature. But this is exactly what he has in common with all other human beings. Thus, what the virtuous person strives for is what is good not only for himself but for all human beings. "Insofar as men live according to the guidance of reason, they must do only those things that are good for human nature, and hence, for each man, i.e. (by IVP31c), those things that agree with the nature of each man" (IVP35d). The virtuous person pursues rational goods that are good for everyone and acts in such a way that he aids the human striving for perseverence. This is why Spinoza concludes that "there is no singular thing in nature that is more useful to man than a man who lives according to the guidance of reason" (IVP35c1) and "men will be most useful to one another when each one most seeks his own advantage [according to the guidance of reason]" (IVP35c2).

However, the utility to me of the virtuous person goes beyond the general and rather vague fact that the things he pursues are what are good for everyone, hence good for me. There is in Spinoza's account an even more direct relationship between the virtue of others and my own well-being. First, a person guided by reason will be useful to me in my own rational striving for perseverance because he will be free of such divisive and even harmful passions as jealousy, envy, and hate – just those affects that would make him oppose me in my endeavors. Indeed, because a person guided by reason is striving for the same goods as myself (knowledge), he is likely to be of positive assistance to me in this project, especially since he will clearly see that the more rational *I* become, the more free I will be of the divisive passions and thus the more useful I will be to *him*. Second, Spinoza also seems to believe that surrounding myself with rational and virtuous individuals will do much positively to reinforce my own desire to live according to reason and thus my own pursuit of perfection, and this is a good thing. He says that "if we imagine that someone loves, desires, or hates something we ourselves love, desire or hate, we shall thereby love, desire or hate it with greater constancy" (IIIP31). Seeing someone else who loves virtue and desires knowledge will make me love and desire them all the more. Thus, it is useful to me and in my interest to have others love virtue and desire knowledge.[14]

The good which man wants for himself and loves, he will love more constantly if he sees that others love it (by IIIP31). So (by IIIP31c), he will strive to have the others love the same thing. And because this good is common to all (by IVP36), and all can enjoy it, he will therefore (by the same reason) strive that all may enjoy it. (IVP37d2)

Finally, seeing an improvement in a being similar to oneself – that is, seeing another human being experience the true joy (or increase in the power of acting) that comes through virtue – causes one to feel a sympathetic joy and undergo a similar increase in one's power. "If we imagine a thing like us, toward which we have had no affect, be affected with some affect, we are thereby affected with a like affect" (IIIP27). Thus, again, it is to my own good that there are other virtuous people.

Spinoza's claims are, of course, highly paradoxical. For they mean that a person is most useful to other people when he is rationally pursuing his own self-interest. "When each man most seeks his own advantage for himself, then men are most useful to one another" (IVP35c2). Enlightened egoism, in other words, leads to maximal mutual utility. Spinoza insists, however, that this conclusion is not only deductively certain, but is also in fact "confirmed by daily experience" and obvious to everyone. We all know, he suggests, that "man is a god to man" (IVP35s).

The upshot of all this is that a person guided by reason, who sees what is truly in his own interest, will strive to bring other people to the same level of rational perfection as himself. He will act to insure that other people are also guided by reason and pursue the good, knowledge. For this is what will maximize their utility to him as he

---

[14] For an analysis of this argument, see Della Rocca 2004.

strives for his own perfection. "The good which everyone who seeks virtue wants for himself, he also desires for other men" (IVP37). In other words, a virtuous person will act so that other people also become virtuous. He will behave toward them in such ways as will help them achieve the life of reason themselves. But because it is also in *their* best interest to be rational and virtuous, all this is just to say that the person guided by reason will strive to further the interests of others, to act in ways that truly benefit them, albeit from selfish and not altruistic motives.

This is how Spinoza's egoism leads to what we would ordinarily consider ethical behavior. A desire to do good for others and help them in their striving is generated by one's own living according to reason. "The desire to do good generated in us by our living according to the guidance of reason, I call morality" (IVP37s1). The person who is virtuous in Spinoza's sense will also exhibit those traits of character and modes of behavior that are traditionally regarded as "virtues" – ethical and social virtues – all of which follow naturally from his rational pursuit of self-interest. "A man who is guided by reason" will have "strength of character." He "hates no one, is angry with no one, envies no one, is indignant with no one, scorns no one, and is not at all proud"; he will avoid "whatever he thinks is troublesome and evil, and moreover, whatever seems immoral, dreadful, unjust and dishonorable" (IVP73s).

Spinoza's view, then, is that rational egoism leads in fact not to the rampant disregard of the well-being of others but to the highest ethical behavior. "I have done this to win, if possible, the attention of those who believe that this principle – that everyone is bound to seek his own advantage – is the foundation, not of virtue and morality, but of immorality" (IVP18s).[15]

Unfortunately, as Spinoza concedes, we ordinarily do not live according to reason. And this becomes especially problematic in so far as we do live, and need to live, in a social context.

It rarely happens that men live according to the guidance of reason. Instead, their lives are so constituted that they are usually envious and

---

[15] Bennett (1984), for one, is not impressed with these propositions of the *Ethics.* "Spinoza fails at every step in his journey toward his collaborative morality" (p. 306).

burdensome to one another. They can hardly, however, live a solitary life; hence, that definition which makes man a social animal has been quite pleasing to most. And surely we do derive, from the society of our fellow men, many more advantages than disadvantages. (IVP35s)

Human beings recognize that it is to their own advantage to unite with others. They can more easily acquire the things they need and more securely protect themselves from "the dangers that threaten on all sides" – both from the forces of nature and from other human beings. For this reason, the striving for perseverance naturally leads individuals to organize themselves into states.

SOCIETY AND THE STATE

Spinoza's main contributions to social and political philosophy are found in his *Theological- Political Treatise* and the unfinished *Political Treatise*. But sometime between putting the *Ethics* aside in 1665 to work on the *Theological-Political Treatise* and the early 1670s, when he returned to complete it, he had the opportunity to read some of Hobbes's political writings, especially the Dutch (1667) or Latin (1668) translation of *Leviathan.* He was obviously struck by the way in which Hobbes was able to show how purely egoistic individuals in a pre-political "state of nature" can be moved voluntarily to give up some of their natural rights to self-preservation and combine to form a polity. The brief discussion of political organization in the *Ethics* takes its lead from Hobbes's account, although there are significant differences between the two, both in terms of starting point and in the nature of the commonwealth that results from the social contract.

Hobbes had famously claimed that life in the state of nature, a theoretical lawless situation in which everyone lives according to the unrestrained pursuit of self-interest and is entitled to do whatever he can for self-preservation, is "solitary, poor, nasty, brutish and short."[16] It is a dangerous condition of constant threat, "a war of every man against every man," full of "fear and danger of violent death," with each person entitled to anything he can procure by

---

[16] *Leviathan* I.13.ix.

force. A reasonable individual motivated solely by self-interest will soon see that it is in fact in his best interest, for the sake of greater security, to give up some of those natural rights and transfer them to a sovereign, on the condition that everyone else does so as well. The sovereign will thenceforth be authorized by the group to create and enforce civil law and establish peace through guaranteeing protection against the encroachment of others. This transfer of authority from individuals to a sovereign occurs through a kind of agreement that modern political thinkers call (after Rousseau) a "social contract," and represents the origin of and justification for a political state.

Spinoza likewise offers what is essentially a social contract theory of the state. He, too, takes as his starting point a state of nature, wherein

everyone exists by the highest right of nature, and consequently everyone, by the highest right of nature, does those things that follow from the necessity of his own nature. So everyone, by the highest right of nature, judges what is good and what is evil, considers his own advantage according to his own temperament (see IVP19 and P20), avenges himself (see IIIP40c2), and strives to preserve what he loves and destroy what he hates. (IVP37s2)

Like Hobbes's state of nature, Spinoza's pre-political condition is one of unrestrained pursuit of self-interest. If all individuals were virtuous and living according to the guidance of reason, this would not be a problem. Each would recognize their mutual utility and would act to maximize the virtue or well-being of others. There would, then, be no need or desire for a coercive state. As Spinoza says in the *Theological-Political Treatise,*

If men were so constituted by nature as to desire nothing but what is prescribed by true reason, society would stand in no need of any laws. Nothing would be required but to teach men true moral doctrine, and they would then act to their true advantage of their own accord, wholeheartedly and freely.[17]

The point is made more succinctly in the *Ethics*: "If men lived according to the guidance of reason, everyone would possess this

---

[17] TTP, Chapter 5, G III.73/S 63.

right of his [for self-preservation] (by IVP35c1) without any injury to anyone else" (IVP37s2).

It is important to note, though, that if all people were rational and virtuous, while they would not submit themselves to the commands of a higher political authority, they would nonetheless still form a society. They would recognize that there is nothing more useful to a human being than other human beings, and especially other virtuous human beings. So even in a "state of nature" – that is, a condition without an authorized political sovereign – entirely rational, free individuals would enter into organized social relations with each other. Without a state, virtuous individuals would not be hermits, but form a naturally cooperative association.

"But," Spinoza continues, "because [men] are subject to the affects (by IVP4c), which far surpass man's power or virtue (by IVP6), they are often drawn in different directions (by IVP33) and are contrary to one another (by IVP34), while they require one another's aid (by IVP35s)" (IVP37s2). People are, in other words, usually governed not by reason but by their passions. As he puts the point in the continuation of the passage above from the *Theological-Political Treatise*, "human nature is not so constituted [to desire nothing but what is prescribed by true reason]. All men do, indeed, seek their own advantage, but by no means from the dictates of sound reason." Thus, the state is needed to guarantee harmony and mutual assistance. Individuals, therefore, motivated once again solely by self-interest, and especially by the fear of being harmed that is a naturally preponderant affect in the state of nature, voluntarily give up the right to unrestrained pursuit of self-interest and form an agreement with others.

In order, therefore, that men may be able to live harmoniously and be of assistance to one another, it is necessary for them to give up their natural right and to make one another confident that they will do nothing which could harm others . . . By this law, therefore, society can be maintained, provided it appropriates to itself the right everyone has of avenging himself, and of judging concerning good and evil. In this way, society has the power to prescribe a common rule of life, to make laws, and to maintain them – not by reason, which cannot restrain the affects (by IVP17s), but by threats. This society, maintained by laws and the power it has of preserving itself, is called a state, and those who are defended by its law, citizens. (IVP37s2)

The ideal state for Spinoza, as becomes clear in the *Theological-Political Treatise* and the *Political Treatise*, is a democracy, where power and prerogative is transferred to all citizens, not (as Hobbes believes) a monarchy. Moreover, the move from the state of nature into the political state for Spinoza, unlike the transition that Hobbes describes, seems to be motivated as much by the quest for rational perfection as for basic safety. And the state is to provide the actualizing conditions for such a project. While it is certainly about freeing its citizens from fear and securing their material possessions, it is also about allowing, even encouraging the pursuit of virtue. For Spinoza, one enters into the state not just to escape war, but to benefit from the advantages it provides, including the opportunity to live the life of reason.

# CHAPTER 9

# Eternity and blessedness

The deeper one goes into the *Ethics*, and the further one proceeds from the metaphysics and epistemology of the early propositions into the domains of psychology, social and political philosophy, and moral philosophy, the wider is the range of intellectual contexts within which Spinoza's ideas can be situated. While Parts One and Two should be understood primarily in a Cartesian framework, with Spinoza offering a kind of critical commentary on Descartes's conception of substance and the human being, Parts Three and Four clearly owe a debt to Spinoza's study of Hobbes and of ancient Stoic thinkers. The Stoic element is, as we shall see, in even greater evidence in Part Five, wherein Spinoza finally provides some instruction as to how to move toward the life of reason. But Part Five also represents Spinoza's dialogue with another important tradition, medieval Jewish rationalism. This relationship is only rarely studied in connection with the *Ethics* – a fact that is quite surprising, given Spinoza's personal background and education. In fact, much of the scholarly frustration directed at some central features of Part Five is, I believe, due to the failure to appreciate the degree to which Spinoza is engaged with his Jewish philosophical ancestors.

By the end of Part Four, we know a good deal about the free person, including many things about what he believes and how he acts. His desires are directed by reason and his deeds informed by virtue. But Spinoza has not really told us how one becomes (or, at least, comes to approximate) a free person. We know *what* freedom is, but precious little about how to go about achieving freedom. This is the subject of Part Five. Spinoza's goal is, if not to provide a thoroughly detailed account, at least to point us in the direction of how generally to enter upon the path of freedom. The key, as we now know, is to learn how to use reason to bring about a diminishing of the passions and an increase in one's own activity.

There is one *caveat* that is essential to understanding what is distinctive about Spinoza's views here, and especially how they differ from those of Descartes and the ancient Stoics. The Preface to Part Five serves as a warning to the reader about what can and cannot be achieved through the life of reason. Throughout the work, Spinoza insists quite forcefully that no human being can thoroughly eliminate the passive affects from his life. As he has reminded us several times,

it is impossible that a man should not be a part of Nature, and that he should undergo no changes except those which can be understood through his own nature alone, and of which he is the adequate cause . . . From this it follows that man is necessarily always subject to passions, that he follows and obeys the common order of Nature, and accommodates himself to it as much as the nature of things requires. (IVP4, P4c)

As the Part Five preface now makes clear, neither does Spinoza believe that a human being can ever exercise complete control over the passions. Not only will the passions always be there, but they will also always be to some degree efficacious. Contrary to Descartes[1] (as well as the ancient Stoics), Spinoza insists that, speaking realistically and not in terms of some unrealizable ideal, even the most rational human mind "does not have absolute dominion over [the affects]" (V, Preface). The most we can achieve in this life is to "restrain and moderate" them. The subject of much of Part Five is the therapy through reason and virtue that will help us to achieve this end.[2]

### MODERATING THE PASSIONS

Spinoza begins Part Five by reminding the reader of a central tenet of his metaphysics of mind and body: because the mind is the idea of the body, and because the order and connection of the modes of

---

[1] See *Passions of the Soul*, articles 44–50.
[2] This notion of Spinoza's *Ethics* as offering a kind of "therapy" is well investigated in A. Garrett 2003.

Thought is the same as the order and connection of the modes of Extension (IIP7), the order and connection of ideas in the human mind is naturally and necessarily correlated with the order and connection of affections (or images of things) in the body, and vice versa (VP1). It follows from this that if one can effect a change in the order and connection of one's ideas, there will necessarily be a concomitant change in the order and connection of affections of the body. Remember that it is not that the one change *causes* the other; rather, reconfiguring one's ideas just *is* to have one's body undergo a certain change in its condition. Spinoza will show us how we can use this basic metaphysical fact to our own advantage and achieve a higher degree of self-control and resistance to external forces.

The initial therapeutic step in moving toward a more rational existence, one less troubled by the passions, is to diminish the strength of those passions by changing one's beliefs about their causes.[3] Ordinarily, a person's love (or hatred) is directed at a single object, because of his belief that it is that object that has brought about some improvement (or change for the worse) in his condition. But to focus all of one's attention on just that one object is to be guided by inadequate knowledge, since that object is just one finite link in an infinitely extended chain of causes. It is thus, at best, only a partial factor. Spinoza says that

> if we separate emotions, or affects, from the thought of an external cause, and join them to other thoughts, then the love, or hate, toward the external cause is destroyed, as are the vacillations of mind arising from these affects. (VP2)

It may appear that Spinoza is here recommending that one completely separate the idea of the affect from *any* external cause whatsoever and think of it only in connection with other ideas in the mind. This would seem to have the result that thoughts and desires so transformed cease altogether to be outwardly directed; and since love (and hate) are always directed at external things – the presumed causes of joy (and sadness) – they would consequently

---

[3] The idea that this first strategy is a matter of belief-modification is suggested by Curley (1988, pp. 128–31).

disappear. Passions would thereby be replaced by knowledge. This transformative reading is often suggested by Spinoza's language: he speaks on occasion of the "removal" of a passion (VP20s), or of an affect "ceasing to be a passion" (VP3). However, it sometimes seems that what Spinoza is saying is that one should separate the affect from the idea of any *single* external cause and look at it in the grander causal scheme of things. In this way, the intense love or hatred that is directed at one thing becomes more diffuse and weaker as it is spread out over many things. "If an affect is related to more and different causes which the mind considers together with the affect itself, it is less harmful, we are less acted on by it, and we are affected less toward each cause, than is the case with another, equally great affect, which is related only to one cause, or to fewer causes" (VP9). In this case, the affect remains a passion but has been dissipated or weakened.

More generally, the remedy against strong passions that Spinoza is proposing is the pursuit of an adequate knowledge of those affects. He argues, in VP3, that "an affect which is a passion ceases to be a passion as soon as we form a clear and distinct idea of it." When one perceives adequately and truly what the causes of an affect are and why one is experiencing it, a partial, accidental, and passive cognizance of one's own condition is replaced by fuller insight, and a feeling is replaced by understanding. Where one once was undergoing a passion, one is now active, since knowledge (adequate ideas) represents a condition of activity. "The more an affect is known to us, then, the more it is in our power, and the less the mind is acted on by it" (VP3c). This transformation in our condition is something we can do with any passion. "There is no affection of the body of which we cannot form a clear and distinct concept" (VP4). What Spinoza is recommending here is that instead of allowing ourselves to be passively affected by things, we should take the initiative and transform ourselves into active beings by striving for a knowledge of ourselves, especially of the ways in which our bodies (and, correlatively, our minds) respond to and are affected by things.

The result of such a process is a re-ordering of our ideas. They are no longer connected according to the order of random experience, but instead reflect the true causal order of things.

We must, therefore, take special care to know each affect clearly and distinctly (as far as this is possible), so that in this way the mind may be determined from an affect to thinking those things which it perceives clearly and distinctly, and with which it is fully satisfied, and so that the affect itself may be separated from the thought of an external cause and joined to true thoughts. The result will be not only that love, hate, etc., are destroyed (by VP2), but also that the appetites, or desires, which usually arise from such an affect cannot be excessive (by IVP61). (VP4s)

Instead of a mind filled with ideas set by the "common order of nature," there is a mind in which ideas have a rational ordering, what (as we have seen) Spinoza calls "the order of the intellect."

Now because the order and connection of affections of the body must be a reflection of the order and connection of ideas in the mind, this transformation of the mind from passivity to activity, from emotional responses to understanding, is paralleled by a correlative transformation of our physical condition. "So long as we are not torn by affects contrary to our nature, we have the power of ordering and connecting the affections of the body according to the order of the intellect" (VP10). The body thereby becomes more resistant to the influences of external things – and especially more resistant to sadness, a decrease in its powers – and more governed by the mind itself, since its affects are now set systematically (according to the order of reason) and not just haphazardly. "By this power of rightly ordering and connecting the affections of the body, we can bring it about that we are not easily affected with evil affects. For (by VP7) a greater force is required for restraining affects ordered and connected according to the order of the intellect than for restraining those which are uncertain and random" (VP10s). Spinoza's point is that the more one knows about oneself and about one's reactions to things (the affects), the more control one can exercise over those reactions – which, in effect, cease to be reactions and become actions, anchored as they now are in adequate ideas.

But VP1–P4 leave the reader wanting to know more about how this reordering of ideas and affects and setting them in connection with their adequate causes is supposed to lead to a weakening of the passions and the strengthening of resistance. Spinoza says that "we can devise no other remedy for the affects which depends on our power and is more excellent than this, which consists in a true knowledge of them. For the mind has no other power than that of thinking and forming adequate ideas" (VP4s). It is fine to talk in general terms of knowledge, virtue, power, and activity replacing the passivity and "bondage" that characterizes a life guided by the senses and imagination. Somehow the clear and distinct knowledge of things is supposed to give us a greater control over our emotions. But what exactly does the person with adequate ideas of the affects see that the uninformed person does not? And what does it do for him? VP10 provides only some clarification about the power of knowledge versus the passions. What we really need now is one of those useful scholia in which Spinoza leaves his technical language behind and appeals to something familiar from experience to explain more clearly *what* it is we know and *how* it effects the desired transformation.

Fortunately, he does not disappoint. He reminds us in VP6 that what adequate knowledge provides is an understanding of the necessity of things, of the fact that any bodily or mental event is "determined by an infinite connection of causes to exist and produce effects." He then claims that "insofar as the mind understands all things as necessary, it has a greater power over the affects, or is less acted upon by them." This is because when a person sees the necessity of something, he is less moved or troubled by it. His desire or anxiety, his hope or fear, are diminished by the perception that the attainment or loss of that thing is not subject to his will but necessitated by an infinite number of causal factors.

Spinoza has shown that all of the human emotions, in so far as they are passions, are constantly directed outward, toward things and their tendencies to affect us one way or another. And aroused by our passions and desires, we seek or flee those things that we believe cause joy or sadness. Such is the life of bondage. It is, as we know, a troubled existence. He says that it is a kind of disease to suffer too much love for a thing that is mutable and never fully under our power, even when we do, for a time, have it within our possession.

Sickness of the mind and misfortunes take their origin especially from too much love toward a thing which is liable to many variations and which we can never fully possess. For no one is disturbed or anxious concerning anything unless he loves it, nor do wrongs, suspicions and enmities arise except from love for a thing which no one can really fully possess. (VP20s)

When a person sees the necessity of all things, however, and especially the fact that the objects that he values are, in their comings and goings, not under his control, that person is less likely to be overwhelmed with emotions at their arrival and passing away. We see that all bodies and their states and relationships – including the condition of our own body – follow necessarily from the essence of matter and the universal laws of physics; and we see that all ideas, including all the properties of minds, follow necessarily from the essence of thought and its universal laws. When we come to this level of understanding, we realize that we cannot control what nature brings our way or takes from us, and consequently we are no longer anxious over what may come to pass and are no longer obsessed with or despondent over the loss of our possessions. Here is the scholium we have been waiting for:

The more this knowledge that things are necessary is concerned with singular things, which we imagine more distinctly and vividly, the greater is this power of the Mind over the affects, as experience itself also testifies. For we see that Sadness over some good which has perished is lessened as soon as the man who has lost it realizes that this good could not, in any way, have been kept. Similarly, we see that [because we regard infancy as a natural and necessary thing], no one pities infants because of their inability to speak, to walk, or to reason, or because they live so many years, as it were, unconscious of themselves. (VP6s)

A person who sees the necessity of things regards them with equanimity, and is not inordinately and irrationally affected in different ways by past, present, or future events. He will bear the slings and arrows of outrageous fortune with self-control and a calm mind. The resulting life is more tranquil, and not given to sudden disturbances of the passions. With this scholium, Spinoza makes good on a promissory note that he had introduced at the end of Part Two, where he insists that his doctrine

teaches us how we must bear ourselves concerning matters of fortune, or things which are not in our power, i.e., concerning things which do not follow from our nature – that we must expect and bear calmly both good fortune and bad. For all things follow from God's eternal decree with the same necessity as from the essence of a triangle it follows that its three angles are equal to two right angles. (G II.136/C I.490)

Spinoza's proposed solution to the power of the emotions and the predicament to which they give rise is an ancient one: focus on what is within. Since we cannot control the external objects that we tend to value and that we allow to influence our well-being, we ought instead to try to control our evaluations and responses themselves and thereby minimize the sway that objects and the passions have over us. We do this, as we have just seen, by re-ordering our ideas. We can never eliminate the passive affects entirely. But we can, ultimately, counteract them, understand and control them, and thereby achieve a certain degree of relief from their turmoil. Despite Spinoza's critique of the Stoics for their belief that the wise person can completely master the passions, his own account recalls the doctrines of thinkers such as Seneca and Epictetus:

Human power is very limited and infinitely surpassed by the power of external causes. So we do not have an absolute power to adapt things outside us to our use. Nevertheless, we shall bear calmly those things which happen to us contrary to what the principle of our advantage demands, if we are conscious that we have done our duty, that the power we have could not have extended itself to the point where we could have avoided those things, and that we are a part of the whole of nature, whose order we follow. If we understand this clearly and distinctly, that part of us which is defined by understanding, i.e. the better part of us, will be entirely satisfied with this, and will strive to persevere in that satisfaction.

(IV, Appendix, G II.276/C I.593–4)

Spinoza adopts a common Stoic notion – that the wise person lives "according to nature" – when he insists that for the person who has achieved the proper level of understanding, recognizes the necessity of things, and accordingly modifies his desires, "the striving of [his] better part agrees with the order of the whole of nature."

A clear and distinct perception of my own place in nature and of the determinism that governs all natural things will lead not to some kind of fatalistic resignation, but to a satisfaction with my cognitive achievement as being what is truly in my best interest. It will also lead to an ability to bear things with equanimity, as I experience a release from the anxieties to which outwardly directed desires that are based on a false belief in the freedom and contingency of things give rise. In other words, knowledge and understanding, which, as we have seen, Spinoza identifies with virtue, lead to tranquility and self-control. The virtuous person, the individual who follows "the order of nature," will experience "true peace of mind" (VP42s); by contrast, the ignorant person is "troubled in many ways by external causes."

Incidentally, through this discussion of knowledge as the remedy for the passions, it should now be clear that a number of terms in Spinoza are co-extensive and refer to the same ideal human condition. We can set up the following equation for Spinoza:

virtue=knowledge=activity=freedom=power=perfection

Necessarily, the more virtuous a person is, the more knowledge he has, the more free, active and powerful he is, and the more he has achieved of human perfection.

### LOVE OF GOD

The path to "restraining and moderating" the passions, then, is through virtue. Controlling the emotions is not a step on the way to becoming virtuous; rather, it is one of the effects of *being* virtuous. But for Spinoza there is more to the value of virtue than its beneficial consequences, as a "remedy for the affects" and the cause of happiness. He does not merely offer a utilitarian defense of the life of virtue and reason. (In fact, at the beginning of the scholium to VP20, Spinoza says that "with this I have covered all the remedies for the affects," suggesting that what is to follow goes beyond this merely instrumental value of knowledge and virtue.) He believes that virtue is its own reward, that it is "blessedness itself" and to be pursued for its own sake. Virtue and knowledge not only bring relief from the turmoil of the passions, but constitute an absolute good in their own right.

We know from the earlier parts of the *Ethics* that the kind of knowledge at the heart of virtue, and thus which Spinoza has in mind as a remedy for the passions, is the deep understanding of nature that he identifies with the second and, especially, the third kinds of knowledge. He reiterates this point at VP25: "The greatest striving of the mind, and its greatest virtue is understanding things by the third kind of knowledge." He also reminds the reader (at VP24) that "the more we understand singular things, the more we understand God." Adequate knowledge ultimately relates things to their highest causes, the attributes of God or Nature, and situates them *sub specie aeternitatis*, in an eternal or timeless perspective, unrelated to the durational ordering they occupy in random experience. Thus, the more one understands oneself, the more one knows the body and its affects, as Spinoza's therapy for the passions demands, the more one relates these modes to God. "The mind can bring it about that all the body's affections, or images of things, are related to the idea of God" (VP14). The result is a body of ideas in the mind whose logical ordering mirrors the causal ordering of things in the world, with (the idea of) God anchoring the order.

Moreover, this perception of things in relationship to God generates in a person a love of God (*amor Dei*). When ideas in the intellect are properly ordered, the idea of God is the ultimate ground of all the other ideas, that is, the cause of our knowledge itself. And this knowledge represents an increase in one's powers, as all true knowledge does. It is, thus, a joy. One therefore apprehends God as the cause of one's joy. But joy together with an awareness of the object that is the cause of the joy is a love of that object. Thus, knowledge of oneself leading toward knowledge of God brings about a love of God.

vp15: He who understands himself and his affects clearly and distinctly loves God, and does so the more, the more he understands himself and his affects.

dem.: He who understands himself and his affects clearly and distinctly rejoices (by IIIP53), and this joy is accompanied by the idea of God (by VP14). Hence (by Def. Aff. VI), he loves God, and (by the same reasoning) does so the more, the more he understands himself and his affects, q.e.d.

More generally – since this is the case whether what one knows is one's own body or some other particular thing – the third kind of knowledge, whatever its object, terminating as it does in a perception of God (or Nature), the highest possible object of knowledge, results in the love of God.

Spinoza returns to this theme later in Part Five, when he is discussing his doctrine of the mind's eternity (see pp. 259–72 below), and in this case it is worth breaking with the formal order of propositions in order to add more content to this all-important notion of the love of God. "Insofar as our mind knows itself and the body under a species of eternity," he says at VP30, "it necessarily has knowledge of God, and knows that it is in God and is conceived through God." The third kind of knowledge represents "the greatest human perfection," Spinoza insists (in VP27), and thus the person who achieves it experiences "the greatest joy." He is also necessarily conscious of God as the cause of this joy: "Whatever we understand by the third kind of knowledge we take pleasure in, and our pleasure is accompanied by the idea of God as a cause" (VP32).

But if God is the cause of this joy, then why is the love of God not just another passion? Granted, it would not be subject to the disadvantages that plague most passive affects. In the *Short Treatise*, Spinoza eloquently describes "the poison and the evil that lie hidden in the love of [corruptible] things" (G I.63/C I.106). But because God is an eternal and unchanging being, this passion would not fluctuate in the way that so many emotions, directed as they are to ephemeral things, do. The love of God, Spinoza insists, like the knowledge that generates it, is something completely under one's control. It will therefore be a stable and constant love, just because its (eternal) object is itself stable and constant. "This love is the most constant of all the affects . . . [it is] a love toward a thing immutable and eternal (see VP15), which we really fully possess (see IIP45), and which therefore cannot be tainted by any of the vices which are in ordinary love . . ." (VP20s). But hasn't Spinoza just substituted one (albeit more controllable and reliable) passion for the others?

In fact, Spinoza insists that the love of God is not a passion at all – it is not like what he calls "ordinary love." It is indeed affective, since it is tied to an increase in one's power. But because it is associated with knowledge it constitutes an active, not a passive, affect. To be sure, God is the cause of the joy accompanying the third kind of knowledge. But remember that, with respect to the human mind, God is not an external object. The human mind *is* God, conceived not absolutely but through one of its finite modes (of the attribute Thought). Thus, an individual endowed with the third kind of knowledge will indeed perceive God as the cause of that knowledge, but will thereby perceive God not as outside the mind but as that of which the mind is a finite expression. "Insofar as our mind knows itself and the body under a species of eternity, it necessarily has knowledge of God, and knows that it is in God and is conceived through God" (VP30). The increase in one's power of acting (or *conatus*) represented by the third kind of knowledge has its adequate cause in the mind itself.

The love of God, then, is not a passionate love. And it is certainly not the kind of religious love encouraged by sectarian faiths, mixed with fear and awe. It is, Spinoza says, employing an important medieval notion, an intellectual love (*amor dei intellectualis*). While there is indeed a pleasure involved in this love (VP32), it is grounded in knowledge and the intellect, not the senses.[4] It involves not passivity but activity and an appreciation of one's own powers, and is the proper accompaniment of virtue. Above all, the intellectual love of God – unlike the mutable love that unites us to material things and other people – is eternal, just because it derives from knowledge that is itself eternal and directed at an eternal object. "The intellectual love of God, which arises from the third kind of knowledge, is eternal" (VP33). This is why such a love is dealt with most fully only after Spinoza has addressed the question of the eternity of the mind itself.

And this brings us to some of the most enigmatic and troubling passages of the *Ethics*.

## THE ETERNITY OF THE MIND

Spinoza closes the long scholium of VP20 with a curious statement, one that has caused many readers a good deal of bewilderment.

With this I have completed everything which concerns this present life. Anyone who attends to what we have said in this scholium, and at the same time, to the definitions of the mind and its affects, and finally to IIIP1 and P3, will easily be able to see what I said at the beginning of this scholium, viz. that in these few words I have covered all the remedies for the affects. *So it is time now to pass to those things which pertain to the mind's duration without relation to the body* [my italics].

---

[4] See especially Maimonides, *Guide of the Perplexed* III.51. For Spinoza's relationship to the medieval tradition of the intellectual love of God, see Wolfson 1934, II.20.

A natural way to read these remarks is that Spinoza, having demonstrated what he hoped to about achieving well-being in this life, is now going to enter into a discussion of immortality and the world-to-come, understood in its traditional Judeo-Christian sense as the postmortem survival of the soul and, more importantly, of the self. But the notion that Spinoza is about to discuss the afterlife and the immortality of the soul immediately gives rise to some pressing questions about consistency. First, one must wonder how the human mind *can* be immortal in the sense of surviving the death of the body if the mind just is, as Spinoza has demonstrated in Part Two, the idea of an actually existing body? One would think that the metaphysical parallelism should in principle rule out "the mind's duration without relation to the body"; as the body goes, so goes the mind, or so it would seem. Second, and more generally, would not such a religiously charged doctrine as the immortality of the soul, with its hints of divine reward and punishment, go against everything Spinoza has been saying about the dangers of anthropomorphizing God into a moral and provi-dential being? So what, then, can Spinoza be talking about in the final twenty propositions of the work when he speaks of the "eternity of the mind"?

Spinoza's views on immortality – like his views on so many issues – are notoriously difficult to fathom. One prominent scholar, in what seems to be a cry of frustration after wrestling with the relevant propositions in Part Five, claims that this part of the work is "an unmitigated and seemingly unmotivated disaster . . . rubbish that causes others to write rubbish."[5] Another, more equanimous scholar insists that "in spite of many years of study, I still do not feel that I understand this part of the *Ethics* at all." He adds, "I feel the freedom to confess that, of course, because I also believe that no one else understands it adequately either."[6] Because of the complexity and opacity of his account of the eternity of the mind, which

---

[5] Bennett 1984, pp. 357, 372. He adds that "I don't think that the final three doctrines [of Part Five] can be rescued. The only attempts at complete salvage that I have encountered have been unintelligible to me and poorly related to what Spinoza actually wrote . . . After three centuries of failure to profit from it, the time has come to admit that this part of the *Ethics* has nothing to teach us and is pretty certainly worthless . . . this material is valueless."

[6] Curley 1988, p. 84.

involves some of the most difficult and puzzling propositions of the *Ethics*, there has been, since the posthumous publication of his writings, a great deal of debate over whether Spinoza believes in personal immortality or rejects it; even today no consensus has emerged.[7]

In contrast with Descartes, who, as we saw (pp. 152–3), took pride in the fact that his metaphysical dualism of mind and body lent support to a robust doctrine of immortality, Spinoza nowhere in the *Ethics* explicitly says that he will establish that the soul is immortal.[8] Indeed, the word "immortality [*immortalitas*]" occurs in the work once and only once. It appears in a context in which Spinoza is describing the foolish beliefs of the multitude, who are often motivated to act virtuously only by their hope for an eternal reward and their fear of an eternal punishment. If they were not convinced that the soul lived on after the body, then morality – difficult as it is – would, in their eyes, not be a burden worth bearing. Such an opinion, he notes,

seems no less absurd to me than if someone, because he does not believe he can nourish his body with good food to eternity, should prefer to fill himself with poisons and other deadly things, or because he sees that the mind is not eternal, *or* immortal, should prefer to be mindless, and to live without reason. (VP41s)

The main point of his discussion here is the importance and value of virtue in *this* life; that virtue is, in essence, its own reward. But the passage might also seem important with respect to the question of Spinoza's views on immortality since it makes it look as though he is willing to equate the thesis of the eternity of the mind (something for which he does argue) with the thesis of the immortality of the soul. However, he is here only describing, in a rather derisive way, the naïve and potentially self-destructive opinions of the vulgar who

---

[7] A number of scholars have thought that what Spinoza is up to, at least in the *Ethics*, is a denial of personal immortality, although there is very little agreement on just how he accomplishes this; see Hampshire 1951, Curley 1988, Morrison 1994, and Yovel 1989. On the other hand, many scholars insist that Spinoza is affirming personal immortality; see, for example, Donagan 1979 and Wolfson 1934.

[8] But see KV II.23, which bears the title *Van des Ziels Onsterfelijkheid* – "On the Immortality of the Soul." Spinoza seems perfectly comfortable with using the term "immortal [*onsterfelijk*]" to describe the soul in this work.

feel that a life of virtue is worth living only if it leads to the alleged eternal rewards in the fictitious afterlife described by manipulative preachers. It is clearly a view that he holds in great contempt.

When the *Ethics* does get around to discussing the fate of the mind or soul after a person's death, Spinoza is obviously very careful to avoid any talk of *immortalitas*, lest his reader – on the lookout for individual immortality – mistake the whole moral of his story. There are parts of the mind that will persist after the demise of the body, Spinoza allows, but this should definitely not be mistaken for any kind of real immortality.

Spinoza defines 'eternity' as that which stands outside of all duration or time. "Eternity can neither be defined by time nor have any relation to time" (VP23s). Something is not eternal merely if its duration is without beginning or end; this is nothing but sempiternity, or everlastingness in time. True eternity, which Spinoza explicitly contrasts with sempiternity (in ID8), stands outside of all temporal categories whatsoever. 'Before,' 'after,' 'now,' 'later' and all such ascriptions are completely inapplicable to what is eternal.[9] God, or substance, is eternal; so are the attributes Thought and Extension. In a certain respect, particular finite things are also eternal – when they are considered not in their temporally and (in the case of bodies) spatially bound relationships to other finite things, that is, when what is in question is their actual, durational existence, but rather when they are considered from a more abstract perspective as atemporal essences, that is, *sub specie aeternitatis*.

Now the human mind itself partakes of eternity in two distinct but related ways. As we shall see, neither way amounts to anything more than the fact that when a person dies, the knowledge in his mind – as a set of eternally true and adequate ideas – will persist.

First, there is the eternity that belongs to the mind because it is the idea (or the expression in the attribute of Thought) of the material essence (in the attribute of Extension) of the human body.

---

[9] Some commentators have argued that the eternity at stake here *is* just a sempiternity, or what Donagan calls "omnitemporality"; see Kneale 1973 and Donagan 1979. Most, however, have – correctly, I believe – seen that what Spinoza is talking about is a complete atemporality, or timelessness; see Harris 1975, Hampshire 1951, Steinberg 1981, and Joachim 1901.

vP22: Nevertheless, in God there is necessarily an idea that expresses the essence of this or that human body, under a species of eternity.

DEM.: God is the cause, not only of the existence of this or that human body, but also of its essence, which therefore must be conceived through the very essence of God, by a certain eternal necessity, and this concept must be in God.

Any actually existing human body persists durationally, in time and within the causal nexus of other finite things that affect it and determine it. Toes stub against tables; arms throw balls; snow forts come crashing down on us. This sequence of affairs begins in time, pursues its course in time, and comes to an end in time. The duration of the body as actually existing is limited; so are all the numerous modifications of the body that come about through its interactions with other extended finite modes. But every human body – in fact, every existing body of any type – also has an aspect *sub specie aeternitatis,* "under a form of eternity." Within the domain of Extension, there is an essence of that body in its extensional being, an extended nature abstracted from its temporal duration. Whether it is a case of a table, a baseball, a snow fort, or a human body, its essence would be a type of formulaic mathematical or dimensional mapping of that body that identifies it as the particular parcel of extension that it is, as the particular possible way of being extended that that body represents. Any body is nothing but a specific ratio of motion and rest among a collection of material parts. Its unity and individuality consist only in a relative and structured stability of minute bodies. And this is what is reflected in its essence, its eternal being. At this level, no question whatsoever is raised about whether the body actually exists in nature or not. Because it is outside all duration, making no reference to time, this essence of the body is eternal.

Now the essence of a body as an extended mode is in God (or Substance) under the attribute of Extension. It is "eminently" contained within Extension as one of its infinite potentialities or possible generations. It is, in other words, just one out of infinitely many ways of being extended, and thus belongs as an eternal finite mode within Extension's immediate infinite mode. Given Spinoza's general parallelism between the attributes of Extension and Thought, and given the resulting and more particular parallelism in a human being between what is true of the body and what is true of the mind, there are, then, likewise – and necessarily – two aspects of the human mind, which is nothing other than the idea *of* the body. First, there is the aspect of the mind that corresponds to the durational existence of the body. This is the part of the mind that reflects the body's determinate relationships in space and time with the other bodies surrounding it. Sensations and feelings – pain, pleasure, desire, revulsion, sadness, fear, and a host of other mental states – are all expressions in the mind of what is concurrently taking place in the body in its temporal interactions with the world. I feel pain when I stub my toe. These passions belong to the mind to the extent that the human being is a part of "the order of nature" and, through his body, subject to being affected by the world around him.

The parallelism also requires, however, that this part of the mind comes to an end when the duration of the body comes to an end, that is, at a person's death. When the body goes, there are no more pleasures and pains, no more sensory states. All of the affections of the body of which these sensations, images, and qualia are mental expressions cease at death – the body is no longer "in the world" responding to its determinations. Thus, their correlative expressions in the mind cease as well. But there is another part of the mind – namely, that aspect of it that corresponds to the eternal aspect of the body. This is the idea or expression in the attribute of Thought of the body's extended essence; and just as the body's essence is an eternal finite mode in the immediate infinite mode of Extension, so the idea of the body's essence is an eternal finite mode in the immediate infinite mode of Thought, that is, in the infinite intellect. If the essence of the body, once its durational existence is over, is simply a possible but non-existing material thing in Extension, so the eternal part of the mind just is the idea of such a non-existing material thing. Like its correlate in Extension, this aspect of the mind is eternal. It is, therefore, a part of the mind that remains after a person's death.

VP23: The human mind cannot be absolutely destroyed with the body, but something of it remains which is eternal.

DEM.: In God there is necessarily a concept, or idea, which expresses the essence of the human body (by VP22), an idea, therefore, which is necessarily something that pertains to the essence of the human mind.

But we do not attribute to the human mind any duration that can be defined by time, except in so far as it expresses the actual existence of the body, which is explained by duration and can be defined by time, i.e., we do not attribute duration to it except while the body endures. However, since what is conceived, with a certain eternal necessity, through God's essence itself is nevertheless something, this something that pertains to the essence of the mind will necessarily be eternal. There is, then, this idea which expresses the essence of the body under a species of eternity, a certain mode of thinking, which pertains to the essence of the mind, and which is necessarily eternal.

The mind thus includes, as an essential component of its nature, an idea-correlate in Thought of the essence of the body in Extension. This idea-correlate is eternal because it, like the essence of the body that corresponds to it, is situated non-durationally within one of God's/Nature's eternal attributes. The mind as the idea of (the eternal essence of) the body is itself eternal. Put another way, an essential constituent of the human mind is a knowledge of the essence of the body; and this knowledge, like the essence that is its object, is eternal and survives a person's death.

Notice, however, that this is a rather unimpressive kind of eternity. It is not something in which human beings can take any pride or comfort, for it is an eternity that belongs to *all* things, human and otherwise. Given Spinoza's metaphysics, and especially the universal scope of the parallelism between Extension and Thought, or bodies and ideas, there is nothing about this eternity of the mind that distinguishes the human being from any other finite being – or, more properly, there is nothing that distinguishes this eternity belonging to the human mind from the eternity belonging to the idea of any other finite body. When a tree dies, its extended essence also remains eternally in Extension, and its "mind" (the idea of that essence) also remains eternally in Thought. What Spinoza claims with respect to the general parallelism between modes of extension and modes of thought applies necessarily in this particular case as well: "The things we have shown . . . are completely general and do not pertain more to man than to other individuals . . . and so whatever we have said of the idea of the human body must also be said of the idea of anything" (IIIP13s). Human minds are, of course, significantly different from the Thought-modes or ideas corresponding to other, non-human bodies – they have more functions and greater capacities (including memory and consciousness), because the actually existing bodies of which they are the ideas are themselves more complex and well-endowed than other bodies (such as trees). But this means only that what remains in Thought after a person's death is, like the essence of the body it expresses, more internally complex, so to speak, than the ideas and essences that remain after the dissolution of some other kind of body. It is not, however, more eternal.

Nor is it more "personal." It is only the correlate in Thought (the idea) of a specific ratio of motion and rest in Extension. It expresses a particularly complex ratio, to be sure, but it is generically no different from the idea of the essence of any other body. And there is nothing distinctly personal about this eternal idea of the body – nothing that would lead me to regard it as my "self," identical to the self I currently am in this life.

There is more to Spinoza's doctrine of the eternity of the mind, however, than just this persistence of the (eternal) idea of the (eternal) essence of the body. This brings us to the second way in which the mind partakes of eternity.[10] A good way to approach this is by considering something that Spinoza says that would be hard to understand were the eternity of the mind limited only to its being the idea of the essence of the body. In VP38 and VP39, Spinoza implies that one can *increase* the extent to which the mind is eternal, that one can take steps to insure that more of the mind partakes of eternity.[11] But how can this be if the eternity of the mind is just the eternity of the idea of the eternal essence of the body, something that would seem to be rather static and not capable of degrees?

Like the first element of the eternity of the mind, the second element also involves the kind of atemporal being characteristic of

---

[10] For a good discussion of the distinction between the two ways in which the mind is eternal, see Garber 2005.

[11] Bennett, for example, is troubled by the fact that Spinoza believes both that the eternal mind is nothing but the (unchanging) idea of the eternal essence of the body *and* that "how much of my mind is eternal depends upon some facts about my conduct and my condition"; in other words, that we can *increase* our share of eternity (1984, pp. 361–2). Curley (1969, p. 143), too, claims that he finds this dimension of the doctrine of the eternity of the mind "completely unintelligible".

ideas of essences. However, this second element represents an aspect of eternity that is available *only* to human minds, since it is acquired only by rational agents exercising their intellects. Moreover, with this second element, the mind's eternity becomes closely related to a person's activity in this lifetime. One might even say that there is at least one point of resemblance here between Spinoza's doctrine and the traditional doctrine of immortality insofar as this aspect of the mind's eternity is determined by a person's virtue.

We have seen that the pursuit of the second and, especially, the third kinds of knowledge constitute human virtue and the project that represents our greatest self-interest as rational beings. "The greatest striving of the mind, and its greatest virtue, is understanding things by the third kind of knowledge" (VP25). And when we perceive things through the third kind of knowledge, we see them *sub specie aeternitatis*, from the infinite and eternal perspective of God, without any relation to or indication of time and place.

We conceive things as actual in two ways: either insofar as we conceive them to exist in relation to a certain time and place, or insofar as we conceive them to be contained in God and to follow from the necessity of the divine nature. But the things we conceive in this second way as true, or real, we conceive under a species of eternity, and to that extent they involve the eternal and infinite essence of God. (VP29s)

When we perceive things in time, according to "random experience," they appear in a continuous state of change and becoming; when we re-order our ideas according to the intellect and perceive things "under a form of eternity," what we apprehend abides permanently. This kind of knowledge, because it is atemporal and because it is basically God's knowledge (as this is represented by ideas in the infinite intellect), is eternal. It is, above all, not connected to the actual existence of any finite, particular thing, least of all the existence in time of the human body.

Now as we have seen, Spinoza insists, first of all, that the acquisition of true and adequate ideas – that is, the understanding of the necessity of all things – is beneficial to a person in this lifetime, as the source of an abiding happiness and true peace of mind. But with the doctrine of the eternity of the mind, Spinoza introduces an additional reason why we should strive to acquire and maintain our store of adequate ideas. Because adequate ideas are nothing but an eternal knowledge of things, a body of eternal truths in the infinite intellect that a finite rational being can possess or tap into in this lifetime, it follows that the more adequate ideas one acquires as a part of his mental makeup in this life – the more he "participates" in eternity now – the more of him remains after the death of the body and the end of his durational aspect. Since the adequate ideas that one comes to possess are eternal, they are not affected by the demise of the body and the end of our (or any) temporal and durational existence. In other words, the more adequate knowledge we have, the greater is the degree of the eternity of the mind.

vp38: The more the mind understands things by the second and third kind of knowledge, the less it is acted on by affects which are evil, and the less it fears death.

DEM.: The mind's essence consists in knowledge; therefore, the more the mind knows things by the second and third kind of knowledge, the greater the part of it that remains, and consequently the greater the part of it that is not touched by affects which are contrary to our nature, i.e., which are evil.

As we shall see, it is a bit misleading to say, as I have above, that this eternal knowledge is a part of *me* that remains after death. Rather, what remains is something that, while I lived and used my reason, belonged to me and made up a part – the eternal part – of the contents of my mind. The striving to increase my store of adequate ideas is, in this way, a striving to increase my share of eternity. Thus, Spinoza claims, the greater the mind's intellectual achievement in terms of the acquisition of adequate ideas, "the less is death harmful to us." Indeed, he insists, "the human mind can be of such a nature that the part of the mind which we have shown perishes with the body is of no moment in relation to what remains" (VP38s).

Spinoza concludes (in VP40c) that "the part of the mind that remains . . . is more perfect than the rest." This is because "the eternal part of the mind . . . is the intellect" (with "intellect" understood not as a faculty but only as one's set of adequate ideas). With this statement, Spinoza reveals the extent to which his account of the eternity of the mind represents a fascinating dialogue – so often ignored in scholarly discussions of the *Ethics* – with some of his Jewish rationalist forebears.[12] In fact, we can regard Spinoza's doctrine as a kind of natural and logical culmination of earlier Jewish philosophical approaches to immortality. Spinoza's third kind of knowledge, the body of adequate ideas that persist after one's death, is, for all intents and purposes, the "acquired intellect" posited by Maimonides and others and which they use to explain what they call "immortality." For Spinoza, as well as for those medieval thinkers, the eternal (or "immortal") element of the mind consists only in the sum of a person's intellectual achievements in this life. And because the pursuit of such knowledge is, for these philosophers, the life of virtue, the eternity that ensues after death as a result of such cognitive pursuit is, in a sense, the reward for virtue. "But," Spinoza seems to be saying, "if that is all you mean by immortality, a persisting body of intellectual knowledge, then here is what you must ultimately conclude – namely, that the traditional and highly personal doctrine of the immortality of the soul is a myth grounded in superstition."

If what one is looking for after this temporal existence is a personal immortality in the world-to-come – a conscious, full-blooded (but body-less) life after death in heaven – then the eternity of the mind held out by Spinoza will seem a very thin and disappointing recompense for having lived a life of good. The eternal part of the mind is simply an objective body of truths. Spinoza will absolutely *not* allow it to be said that a *person* is immortal or eternal. For Spinoza, my person or self is an actually existing body together with the mind that is its expression. Or, more precisely, a person is the mode that expresses itself in time as an actually existing body in Extension and as a corresponding mind (or idea) in Thought. A person is not a soul or mind that just happens to be embodied, as many philosophers from Plato onwards have pictured it; nor is it the body alone – it is, instead, the unity of the two. "A man consists of a Mind and a Body" (IIP13c).[13] Because, as Spinoza makes clear,

---

[12] This has been remarked upon in a fairly cursory – and, I would argue, misleading – way by Wolfson (1934, II.20). For a study of Spinoza's account of the eternity of the mind and its relationship to medieval Jewish rationalist thought, see Nadler 2002.

[13] Morrison (1994) offers a good defense of this point.

the bodily component of a person must be an actually existing human body (IIP13), there can be no persistence of a *person* after his death. The end of durational existence is the end of the person.

Moreover, it appears that Spinoza has rendered it impossible to establish a postmortem connection *within consciousness* between the eternal part of the mind and what was a particular durational consciousness in this lifetime and thus confer upon the former a truly *personal* dimension. As long as a person lives, the eternal elements of his mind – his knowledge or adequate ideas – are a part of that person's consciousness. But it would seem that at the moment of death, the link between that body of knowledge and the consciousness to which it belonged is necessarily broken. For Spinoza, consciousness and memory (the latter being that which gives unity to consciousness) seem to be intimately tied to the (full) person. At one point in the *Ethics*, Spinoza suggests that someone who has undergone a radical change in consciousness has, *ipso facto*, undergone a radical change in personhood.

Sometimes a man undergoes such changes that I should hardly have said he was the same man. I have heard stories, for example, of a Spanish Poet who suffered an illness; though he recovered, he was left so oblivious to his past life that he did not believe the tales and tragedies he had written were his own. (IVP39s)

It would seem to be the case, as well, that a radical change in personhood through extreme alteration or destruction of the body would, through the parallelism of mind and body, entail a radical change in, or even loss of consciousness.

Now Spinoza explicitly links self-consciousness to the actual existence of the body, and particularly to its interaction with other existing bodies. "The mind does not know itself, except insofar as it perceives the ideas of the affections of the body" (IIP23). This alone is enough to suggest that after death a person's particular and personal consciousness comes to an end. But if, in addition, consciousness and personhood are so closely connected, then it would seem that as personhood is terminated (with the body's demise) so is consciousness. A postmortem mind, then, would no longer be endowed with its living consciousness. Even if it did have *a* consciousness – and I see no reason for thinking that it could – it would

certainly have no memory of the conscious life it led in its durational term, for memory itself also depends upon the actually
existing body: "The mind can neither imagine anything, nor
recollect past things, except while the body endures" (VP21).
Spinoza suggests, in fact, that to believe in a conscious immortal
soul that is linked via memory to its durational (lived) consciousness is simply to fall prey to a popular misconception of what
persists after a person's death, a misconception that involves projecting onto the eternal mind features that properly characterize
only a living, embodied consciousness.

If we attend to the common opinion of men, we shall see that they are
indeed conscious of the eternity of their mind, but that they confuse it with
duration, and attribute it to the imagination, or memory, which they
believe remains after death. (VP34s)

An eternal mind looks like nothing but a body of knowledge that,
after death, is permanently cut off from any kind of consciousness
(including access to an earlier consciousness). There will thus be no
connection *within* consciousness between the mind in duration and
the postmortem mind *sub specie aeternitatis*, and consequently no
abiding sense of personhood. For Spinoza, what survives death is
not a self.

   Eliminating the belief in the immortality of the soul is an important part of Spinoza's project of showing how one can govern the
passions and move to the life of reason and freedom. For what
greater and more compelling emotions can be imagined than the
hope of eternal reward and the fear of eternal punishment that
characterize someone who believes in an immortal soul? These two
passions are responsible for a good deal of our submissiveness to
sectarian ecclesiastic authority, the secondary bondage into which
we commit ourselves as a result of our primary bondage to the
passions. The consequence of understanding the truth about the
mind's eternity is supposed to be a direct diminution of the strength
of these two particular and very influential affects, just because
Spinoza's propositions undermine a foundational belief – in personal
immortality – from which those affects draw so much of their power.

   This does not mean that achieving eternity through the mind is of
no real practical value to a person. On the contrary, Spinoza's goal is

to show us just how important it is – not in some afterlife, but in the durational world in which we live. As he insists, one can experience eternity in this life: "We feel and know by experience that we are eternal" (VP23s). To put the same point in other terms, virtue is to be pursued not out of hope for otherworldly rewards or fear of otherworldly punishments, since there are no such things; rather, it is to be pursued for the benefits it brings us in the here and now. Indeed, it is to be pursued for its own sake.

### BLESSEDNESS

Spinoza, as we have seen, has nothing but scorn for those who regard virtue as a burden to be borne for the sake of some supernatural goal. And while he certainly recognizes the advantages that virtue naturally brings to a person in this world, he does not want to leave the impression that all that he is offering is a kind of consequentialist defense of the life of virtue. Virtue, the acquisition of the highest knowledge, *is* power, activity, freedom, and human perfection.

We clearly understand how far they stray from the true valuation of virtue, who expect to be honored by God with the greatest rewards for their virtue and best actions . . . as if virtue itself, and the service of God, were not happiness [*felicitas*] itself, and the greatest freedom.
(IIP49s4, G II.136/C I.490)

Virtue is itself, as he says in the final proposition of the *Ethics*, the true good, our greatest joy and blessedness.

vp42: Blessedness [*beatitudo*] is not the reward of virtue, but virtue itself; nor do we enjoy it because we restrain our lusts; on the contrary, because we enjoy it, we are able to restrain them.

dem.: Blessedness consists in love of God (by VP36 and P36s), a love which arises from the third kind of knowledge (by VP32c). So this love (by IIIP59 and VP3) must be related to the mind in so far as it acts. Therefore (by IVD8), it is virtue itself.

The person who is virtuous has achieved the supreme natural condition of well-being and happiness. He experiences what the ancient Greeks called *eudaimonia*, happiness or flourishing as a human being. Spinoza also says (in VP36s) that the virtuous person or "wise man" enjoys "salvation [*salus*]."

It may seem odd to see Spinoza turning to such traditional religious language at this point. After all, blessedness and salvation would seem to be possible only if there is some being – presumably a divine and providential being – doing the blessing and the saving. Has Spinoza decided at the last moment to cover himself and tack on a few pious sentiments at the end of the work? Or can he provide a naturalistic meaning to these notions, just as he has already provided naturalistic meanings to such concepts as 'God' and 'miracle'?

In a related vein, it is clear from Spinoza's description of the love of God that is engendered in the wise person by his knowledge of things that it must remain an unrequited love. God, on Spinoza's understanding, is not capable of any kind of affect. "God is without passions, and is not affected with any affect of joy or sadness" (VP17). This is because God cannot pass to a greater or lesser state of power or perfection. Thus, Spinoza insists, "strictly speaking, God loves no one" (VP17s). However, in VP35s, when discussing "our salvation or blessedness," Spinoza speaks of "God's love for men" as the source of this salvation and blessedness. Is there an inconsistency here?

Not necessarily. For Spinoza says, in yet another one of those extremely difficult propositions, that God's love of a person is identical with the person's intellectual love of God.

VP36: The mind's intellectual love of God is the very love of God by which God loves himself, not in so far as he is infinite, but in so far as he can be explained by the human mind's essence, considered under a species of eternity; i.e., the mind's intellectual love of God is part of the infinite love by which God loves himself.

Because the human mind just *is* God – albeit not God in its absolute essence but God as modified by a particular finite mode in Thought – it follows that the human mind's love of God just *is*, ultimately, God's love of itself. Thus, "God's love of men and the mind's intellectual love of God are one and the same" (VP36c). Blessedness and salvation, therefore, insofar as they are a function of God's love of a human being, are reducible to the human being's intellectual love of God. There is nothing here that requires attributing to God any kind of psychological or moral characteristics. Spinoza's naturalistic reduction of all things religious seems, at this point, to be complete.

It is, of course, one thing to make virtue, happiness, and blessedness a function of our natural cognitive powers; it is another thing entirely to say that they come easily. There is no better way to close a book on Spinoza's *Ethics* than simply to offer his own remarks at the end of the work's final scholium:

If the way I have shown to lead to these things now seems very hard, still, it can be found. And of course, what is found so rarely must be hard. For if salvation were at hand, and could be found without great effort, how could nearly everyone neglect it? But all things excellent are as difficult as they are rare [*omnia praeclara tam difficilia quam rara sunt*].

# References

There is an enormous body of literature on Spinoza in English, French, Dutch, German, Italian, Spanish, and other languages. For the most part, I have in this book confined my references to the secondary literature to works in English, since those will be the most accessible to the person approaching Spinoza for the first time with little scholarly background. The only exception is (because of its importance and influence) Gueroult's magisterial and unavoidable two-part work.

In the notes, the reader will find a number of monographs cited more frequently than others, especially Allison 1987, Bennett 1984, Curley 1969 and 1988, and Wolfson 1934. These are, in my opinion, excellent general studies of Spinoza's philosophy that are either particularly useful for trying to understand the *Ethics* or have had a substantial impact on recent scholarship; thus I thought it worthwhile often to direct the reader to the discussions in them of the relevant topics.

Allison, Henry. 1987. *Benedict de Spinoza: An Introduction.* Revised edition. New Haven: Yale University Press.

Aubrey, John. 1898. *Brief Lives.* Ed. Andrew Clark. Oxford: Clarendon Press.

Bayle, Pierre. 1965. *Historical and Critical Dictionary.* Trans. Richard Popkin. Indianapolis: Bobbs-Merrill.

Bennett, Jonathan. 1984. *A Study of Spinoza's Ethics.* Indianapolis: Hackett Publishing.

    1991. "Spinoza's Monism: A Reply to Curley." In Y. Yovel, ed., *God and Nature: Spinoza's Metaphysics.* Leiden: E. J. Brill, pp. 53–60.

    1996. "Spinoza's Metaphysics." In D. Garrett, ed., *The Cambridge Companion to Spinoza.* Cambridge: Cambridge University Press, pp. 61–88.

Bergson, Henri. 1934. *La Pensée et le mouvant: essais et conférences,* 5th edn. Paris: Alcan.

Carraud, Vincent. 2002. *Causa sive Ratio: La raison de la cause, de Suarez à Leibniz.* Paris: Presses Universitaires de France.

Chappell, Vere. 1994. "Descartes's Compatibilism." In J. Cottingham, ed., *Reason, Will and Sensation: Studies in Descartes's Metaphysics.* Oxford: Clarendon Press, pp. 177–90.

Curley, Edwin. 1969. *Spinoza's Metaphysics.* Cambridge, MA: Harvard University Press.

1973. "Spinoza's Moral Philosophy." In M. Grene, ed., *Spinoza: A Collection of Critical Essays.* Notre Dame, IN: University of Notre Dame Press, pp. 354–76.

1988. *Behind the Geometric Method.* Princeton: Princeton University Press.

1990. "On Bennett's Spinoza: The Issue of Teleology." In E. Curley, ed., *Spinoza: Issues and Directions.* Leiden: E. J. Brill, pp. 39–52.

1991. "On Bennett's Interpretation of Spinoza's Monism." In Y. Yovel, ed., *God and Nature: Spinoza's Metaphysics.* Leiden: E. J. Brill, pp. 35–51.

Curley, Edwin and Gregory Walski. 1999. "Spinoza's Necessitarianism Reconsidered." In R. Gennaro and C. Huenemann, eds., *New Essays on the Rationalists.* Oxford: Oxford University Press, pp. 224–40.

Damasio, Antonio. 2003. *Looking for Spinoza: Joy, Sorrow, and the Feeling Brain.* New York: Harcourt.

Della Rocca, Michael. 1996a. "Spinoza's Metaphysical Psychology." In D. Garrett, ed., *The Cambridge Companion to Spinoza.* Cambridge: Cambridge University Press, pp. 192–266.

1996b. *Representation and the Mind-Body Problem in Spinoza.* Oxford: Oxford University Press.

2004. "Egoism and the Imitation of Affects in Spinoza." In Y. Yovel and G. Segal, eds., *Spinoza on Reason and the Free Man.* New York: Little Room Press, pp. 123–48.

Donagan, Alan. 1979. "Spinoza's Proof of Immortality." In M. Grene, ed., *Spinoza: A Collection of Critical Essays.* Notre Dame, IN: University of Notre Dame Press, pp. 241–58.

1988. *Spinoza.* Chicago: University of Chicago Press.

Freudenthal, J. 1899. *Die Lebensgeschichte Spinoza's in Quellenschriften, Urkunden und Nichtamtlichen Nachrichten.* Leipzig: Verlag Von Veit.

Garber, Daniel. 2004. "Dr. Fischelson's Dilemma: Spinoza on Freedom and Sociability." In Y. Yovel and G. Segal, eds., *Spinoza on Reason and the Free Man.* New York: Little Room Press, pp. 183–208.

2005. "A Free Man Thinks of Nothing Less Than of Death." In C. Mercer and E. O'Neill, eds., *Early Modern Philosophy: Mind, Matter, and Metaphysics.* Oxford: Oxford University Press, pp. 103–18.

Garrett, Aaron. 2003. *Meaning in Spinoza's Method.* Cambridge: Cambridge University Press.

Garrett, Don. 1991. "Spinoza's Necessitarianism." In Y. Yovel, ed., *God and Nature: Spinoza's Metaphysics.* Leiden: E. J. Brill, pp. 79–96.

1996. "Spinoza's Ethical Theory." In D. Garrett, ed., *The Cambridge Companion to Spinoza*. Cambridge: Cambridge University Press, pp. 267–314.

1999. "Teleology in Spinoza and Early Modern Rationalism." In R. Gennaro and C. Huenemann, eds., *New Essays on the Rationalists*. Oxford: Oxford University Press, pp. 310–35.

2002. "Spinoza's *Conatus* Argument." In O. Koistinen and J. Biro, eds., *Spinoza: Metaphysical Themes*. Oxford: Oxford University Press, pp. 127–58.

Giancotti, Emilia. 1991. "On the Problem of Infinite Modes." In Y. Yovel, ed., *God and Nature: Spinoza's Metaphysics*. Leiden: E. J. Brill, pp. 97–118.

Gueroult, Martial. 1968. *Spinoza*. 2 vols. Hildesheim: Georg Olms Verlag (reprint 1975).

Hampshire, Stuart. 1951. *Spinoza*. Harmondsworth: Penguin.

Harris, Errol. 1975. "Spinoza's Theory of Human Immortality." In M. Mandelbaum and E. Freeman, eds., *Spinoza: Essays in Interpretation*. La Salle: Open Court.

Huygens, Christiaan. 1893. *Oeuvres complètes*. 22 vols. The Hague: Martinus Nijhoff.

Joachim, H. H. 1901. *A Study of Spinoza's Ethics*. Oxford: Clarendon Press.

Kneale, Martha. 1973. "Eternity and Sempiternity." In M. Grene, ed., *Spinoza: A Collection of Critical Essays*. Notre Dame, IN: University of Notre Dame Press.

Kolakowski, Leszek. 1969. *Chrétiens sans église*. Paris: NRF/Editions Gallimard.

Leibniz, Gottfried Wilhelm. 1999. *Sämtliche Schriften und Briefe*. Berlin: Akademie-Verlag.

Lloyd, Genevieve. 1986. "Spinoza's Version of the Eternity of the Mind." In M. Grene and D. Nails, eds., *Spinoza and the Sciences*. Dordrecht: D. Reidel, pp. 216–30.

McRae, Robert. 1965. "'Idea' as a Philosophical Term in the Seventeenth Century." *Journal of the History of Ideas* 26: 175–84.

Manning, Richard N. 2002. "Spinoza, Thoughtful Teleology, and the Causal Significance of Content." In O. Koistinen and J. Biro, eds., *Spinoza: Metaphysical Themes*. Oxford: Oxford University Press, pp. 182–209.

Mason, Richard. 1997. *The God of Spinoza*. Cambridge: Cambridge University Press.

Mendes, David Franco. 1975. *Memorias do estabelecimento e progresso dos Judeos Portuguezes e Espanhoes nesta famosa citade de Amsterdam*. Studia Rosenthaliana 9.

Morrison, James. 1994. "Spinoza on the Self, Personal Identity and Immortality". In G. Hunter, ed., *Spinoza: The Enduring Questions*. Toronto: University of Toronto Press.

Nadler, Steven. 1989. *Arnauld and the Cartesian Philosophy of Ideas*. Princeton: Princeton University Press.

    1999. *Spinoza: A Life*. Cambridge: Cambridge University Press.

    2002. *Spinoza's Heresy: Immortality and the Jewish Mind*. Oxford: Oxford University Press.

Radner, Daisie. 1971. "Spinoza's Theory of Ideas." *The Philosophical Review* 80: 338–59.

Revah, I. S. 1959. *Spinoza et Juan de Prado*. Paris: Mouton & Co.

Rice, Lee. 1999. "Action in Spinoza's Account of Affectivity." In Y. Yovel, ed., and G. Segal, eds., *Spinoza on Reason and the Free Man*. New York: Little Room Press, pp. 155–68.

Smith, Steven B. 2003. *Spinoza's Book of Life: Freedom and Redemption in the Ethics*. New Haven: Yale University Press.

Steinberg, Diane. 1981. "Spinoza's Theory of the Eternity of the Human Mind." *Canadian Journal of Philosophy* 11: 35–68.

Vlessing, Odette. 1996. "The Jewish Community in Transition: From Acceptance to Emancipation." *Studia Rosenthaliana* 30: 195–211.

Watson, Richard A. 1987. *The Breakdown of Cartesian Metaphysics*. Highlands, NJ: Humanities Press.

Wilson, Margaret. 1999a. "Infinite Understanding, *Scientia Intuitiva*, and *Ethics* I.16." In M. Wilson, *Ideas and Mechanism*. Princeton: Princeton University Press, pp. 166–77.

    1999b. "Objects, Ideas, and 'Minds': Comments on Spinoza's Theory of Mind," in *Ideas and Mechanism*, pp. 126–40.

Wolfson, Harry. 1934. *The Philosophy of Spinoza*. 2 vols. Cambridge, MA: Harvard University Press.

Yolton, John. 1975. "Ideas and Knowledge in Seventeenth-Century Philosophy." *Journal of the History of Philosophy* 13: 145–66.

Yovel, Yirmiyahu. 1989. *Spinoza and Other Heretics*, vol. I: *The Marrano of Reason*. Princeton: Princeton University Press.

    1991. "The Infinite Mode and Natural Laws in Spinoza." In Y. Yovel, ed., *God and Nature: Spinoza's Metaphysics*. Leiden: E. J. Brill, pp. 79–96.

    (ed.). 1994. *Spinoza on Knowledge and the Human Mind*. Leiden: E. J. Brill.

    (ed.). 1999. *Desire and Affect: Spinoza as Psychologist*. New York: Little Room Press.

Yovel, Yirmiyahu and Gideon Segal, eds., 2004. *Spinoza on Reason and the Free Man*. New York: Little Room Press.

Zac, Sylvain. 1991. "On the Idea of Creation in Spinoza's Philosophy." In Y. Yovel, ed., *God and Nature: Spinoza's Metaphysics*. Leiden: E. J. Brill, pp. 231–42.

# Index